Movements in
European History

Movements in European History

D. H. LAWRENCE

Oxford New York Toronto Melbourne

OXFORD UNIVERSITY PRESS

1981

Oxford University Press, Walton Street, Oxford OX2 6DP

London Glasgow New York Toronto
Delhi Bombay Calcutta Madras Karachi
Kuala Lumpur Singapore Hong Kong Tokyo
Nairobi Dar es Salaam Cape Town
Melbourne Auckland
and associate companies in
Beirut Berlin Ibadan Mexico City

Epilogue © the Estate of Frieda Lawrence Ravagli 1971
Introduction © Oxford University Press 1971

Original edition first published by Oxford University Press 1921.
Illustrated edition published 1925. The present edition was first
published in 1971 and reissued as an Oxford Paperback 1981.

All rights reserved. No part of this publication may be reproduced,
stored in a retrieval system, or transmitted, in any form or by any means,
electronic, mechanical, photocopying, recording, or otherwise, without
the prior permission of Oxford University Press

This book is sold subject to the condition that it shall not, by way
of trade or otherwise, be lent, re-sold, hired out, or otherwise circulated
without the publisher's prior consent in any form of binding or cover
other than that in which it is published and without a similar condition
including this condition being imposed on the subsequent purchaser

British Library Cataloguing in Publication Data
Lawrence, D. H.
Movements in European History
1. Europe—History
I. Title
940   D102
ISBN 0–19–285113–6

Printed in Great Britain by
Richard Clay (The Chaucer Press) Ltd.
Bungay, Suffolk

Contents

Introduction to the New Edition

'There are only two great dynamic urges in *life*: love and power.' Rawdon Lilly's remark in the final chapter of *Aaron's Rod* (1922) may fairly be regarded as Lawrence's own. We are very much aware of the author's voice in that novel; the work was clearly seen as an opportunity to explore issues with which Lawrence was currently preoccupied; it lacks the obliqueness of the earlier novels and, especially in the last chapter, manifests a surface dialectic. Lawrence had been through the period of the *Rainbow* and *Women in Love*, novels—to put it simply—about the 'love urge'; in *Aaron's Rod*, and later in *Kangaroo* and the *Plumed Serpent*, his primary concern was with the morality of political power and the future of social institutions. 'It is now daytime, and time to forget sex, time to be busy making a new world.'[1] The same concern is variously reflected in *Ladybird* and essays such as *Democracy* and *Education of the People*. For whatever reason the focus had shifted. No single explanation for it is fully satisfying: the impact of the war and humiliations to which wartime experiences had subjected Lawrence; his bitterness over the suppression of the *Rainbow* and his failure before 1920 to place *Women in Love* (completed in 1916) with a publisher; his sensitivity to the appearance of the new political force symbolized by the Russian revolution; or difficulties in his

[1] *Fantasia of the Unconscious* (New York, 1922), p. 151.

relations with Frieda. Each perhaps made its contribution. But the shift of interest is plain. Basil, in *Ladybird*, sums up the ethic of Lawrence's earlier works when he remarks that there is 'only one supreme contact, the contact of love'. Lawrence's new preoccupations are signalled in Count Dionys's answer to Basil: 'You must use another word than love. . . . Obedience, submission, faith, belief, responsibility, power.'[2] These were the concepts—set in the context of history—which Lawrence explored in *Movements in European History*.

The intimate relationship in which this book stands to his fiction of the same period is clarified by juxtaposing Rawdon's final statement in *Aaron's Rod* (begun late in autumn 1917 though not completed till 1921), and a quotation from the first letter (on 3 July 1918) in which Lawrence referred to the proposal by the Oxford University Press that he should 'do a school book, of European History'. Rawdon pronounces:

All men say, they want a leader. Then let them in their souls *submit* to some greater soul than theirs. At present, when they say they want a leader, they mean they want an instrument, like Lloyd George. A mere instrument for their use. But it's more than that. It's the reverse. It's the deep, fathomless submission to the heroic soul in a greater man.

In his letter to the musician, Cecil Gray, Lawrence remarked:

The chief feeling is, that men were always alike, and always will be, and one must view the species with contempt first and foremost, and find a few individuals, if possible—which seems at this juncture not to be possible—and ultimately, if the impossible were possible, to *rule* the species. It is a proper ruling they need, and have always needed.[3]

To these quotations can be added a third, from the Epilogue (written in 1924) which was intended for the second edition

[2] *Ladybird* (1923), p. 59.
[3] *Collected Letters*, ed. Harry T. Moore (1962), i. 561.

of Lawrence's history book. Having stated as axiomatic that in society 'we *must* have authority, and there *must* be power', and distinguished between 'power' and 'force', Lawrence wrote:

Now we begin to understand the old motto, *Noblesse Oblige*. *Noblesse* means, having the gift of power, the natural or sacred power. And having such power obliges a man to act with fearlessness and generosity, responsible for his acts to God. A noble is one who may be known before all men . . . .

This is our job, then . . .: to recognise the spark of nobleness inside us, and let it make us. To recognise the spark of *noblesse* in one another, and add our sparks together, to a flame. And to recognise the men who have stars, not mere sparks of nobility in their souls, and to choose these for leaders.[4]

Such words might well be an extract from a conversation between Ramón and Cipriano in the *Plumed Serpent*. Though, then, Lawrence's penury—of which he often tells his correspondents in the years after 1915—may have induced him to accept the Oxford Press's invitation, the opportunity offered him was fully consistent with his current interests. Whether his mode was historical or fictional, Lawrence's personal engagement was equally intense.

The invitation resulted from the initiative of Lawrence's friend, Vere H. G. Collins, who was employed by the Press (in its London office). Collins persuaded Humphrey Milford, then Publisher to the University, to agree that Lawrence should prepare a book 'for junior forms in grammar, or upper forms in primary schools'.[5] The 1914–18 war had prompted a widening of the scope of history taught in schools and the Ministry of Education was encouraging

---

[4] See below, pp. 319, 321. Cf. 'The next relation has got to be a relationship of men towards men in a spirit of unfathomable trust and responsibility, service and leadership, obedience and pure authority. Men have got to choose their leaders, and obey them to the death. And it must be a system of culminating aristocracy, society tapering like a pyramid to the supreme leader.' *Fantasia of the Unconscious*, p. 270.

[5] E. Nehls, *D. H. Lawrence: A Composite Biography* (Madison, Wisconsin, 1957–9), i. 471.

greater attention to European history. 'Several books had
been recently published for upper forms of grammar schools,
but none for junior pupils.'[6] The commercial and educational interests of the Press (seconded by the desire of
Milford and Collins to help Lawrence) happily coincided
with Lawrence's 'historical mood'.[7]

Lawrence worked swiftly. On 26 July 1918, from the
Derbyshire village of Middleton-by-Wirksworth, he sent the
first three chapters to Mrs. Nancy Henry with the comment:
'I wanted to make a serious reader that would convey the
true historic impression to children who are beginning to
grasp realities. We should introduce the deep, philosophic
note into education: deep, philosophic reverence.'[8] He
suspected that his style might not commend itself—'I
shan't mind if they don't want me to go on'—but there is
no evidence that the Press felt his manner was inappropriate
to his brief: 'not . . . to write a formal, connected, text book,
but a series of vivid sketches of movements and people'.[9]
In December he requested the loan of *Legends of Charlemagne* from his dramatist friend, Henry Farjeon, explaining
that he was 'struggling with a European History for
Schools, and cursing [himself] black in the face'.[10] This
last remark is perhaps clarified in a further letter to Mrs.
Henry on 23 January 1919: 'Every chapter, I suffer before
I can begin, because I do loathe the broken part of historical
facts. But once I can get hold of the thread of the developing significance, then I am happy, and get ahead.[11] 'I am

[6] Ibid.

[7] *Collected Letters*, i. 561.

[8] *Letters of D. H. Lawrence*, ed. Aldous Huxley (1932), p. 450. (Mrs.
Henry was presumably a free-lance employee of the Press.)

[9] Nehls, op. cit. i. 471.

[10] *Collected Letters*, i. 567. On 1 January 1919 he requested from his
friend Samuel S. Koteliansky a copy of Scheffel's *Ekkehard: A Tale of the
10th Century* (in Everyman's Library). See *The Quest for Rananim:
Lawrence's Letters to Koteliansky*, ed. George J. Zytaruk (Montreal, 1970),
p. 154.

[11] *Letters*, ed. Huxley, p. 466.

rather pleased with it,' Lawrence added; 'there is a clue of developing meaning running through it: that makes it real to me.' Like Gibbon, whom he had been reading and from whom he borrowed,[12] Lawrence perhaps found difficulty in hitting 'the middle tone between a dull Chronicle and a Rhetorical declamation'; once he achieved it, then he advanced 'with a more equal and easy pace'.[13] Certainly the manuscript of the first eight chapters[14] gives evidence of heavy revision, innumerable deletions, and much over-writing, characteristic of the laborious care with which Lawrence prepared his early drafts. However, the last four chapters were sent to Mrs. Henry on 3 February 1919; the title eventually adopted for the book was proposed at the same time.[15] Revision was completed in April.[16] The final draft was read for the Press by the historian C. R. L. Fletcher, a Fellow of All Souls and a Delegate of the Press. With only minor reservations about 'dates and names' he approved it.[17] No further work on the manuscript is recorded except for the addition of a chapter on the reunification of Italy; this was written in November 1920, at the request of the Press, when Lawrence had finished reading proof on the rest of the book.[18]

One problem remained: under what authorial name should the book be published? Humphrey Milford was adamant: Lawrence could not be identified on the title-page.[19] Lawrence was himself acutely aware of the dubious reputation attaching to his name following the suppression of the *Rainbow* in November 1915. In April 1919, he used the pseudonym 'Grantorto' for his essay 'Whistling of

[12] See *Collected Letters*, i. 550, 551, 561.
[13] Edward Gibbon, *Memoirs of My Life*, ed. G. A. Bonnard (1966), pp. 155–6.
[14] In the possession of Mr. George Lazarus.
[15] *Letters*, ed. Huxley, p. 467.
[16] See *The Quest for Rananim*, ed. G. J. Zytaruk, pp. 173, 176.
[17] Nehls, op. cit. i. 471.
[18] *Collected Letters*, i. 636.
[19] Nehls, op. cit. i. 471.

Birds' published by Middleton Murry in the *Athenaeum*.[20]
Two months earlier he had commented to Mrs. Henry that
the Oxford Press would probably not wish to attach his
name to his history book: 'I don't want it on the book,
either.'[21] Thus when the contract with the Press was
signed by Lawrence (and witnessed by his friend, the
painter and writer Alan Insole), in Taormina, Sicily, on 4
April 1920, the pseudonym 'Lawrence H. Davison' was
agreed.[22] Precisely one year later he sent the agreement to
his agent, Curtis Brown, with the news that the book had
appeared.[23]

Movements in European History was published in
February 1921 at 4s. 6d.; 2,000 copies were printed. On 28
April Lawrence told Curtis Brown that 'one edition is sold
out', but that Oxford had failed to place the book with their
American branch.[24] (In fact it was unsuitable for teaching
use in America and no edition was ever published there.)
The sale of the first edition was not so brisk as Lawrence
believed. Oxford University Press records show that a
second printing was not required until the year ending
March 1923 when a further 2,000 copies were produced.
By August 1924 the total stock (in Oxford and in London)
had been reduced to 366.

At this point the Clarendon Press (the Oxford headquarters of the University Press) gradually assumed responsibility for the book and—probably on the initiative of
John Johnson, then Assistant Secretary—negotiated with
Lawrence the production of a second, illustrated, edition.
Lawrence was given the opportunity to revise his text; advice was also sought in September from the author and

[20] Warren Roberts, *A Bibliography of D. H. Lawrence* (1963), p. 257.

[21] *Letters*, ed. Huxley, p. 467.

[22] A review in the *Adelphi*, April 1924, signed 'L. H. Davidson', is thought
to be by Lawrence. There is no evidence that this pseudonym (in any
spelling) was adopted by him on other occasions (see Roberts, *Bibliography*,
p. 267).

[23] *Collected Letters*, i. 648.

[24] Ibid. i. 650.

editor, Miss V. F. Boyson; she reported favourably—'it is an attractive book, vividly written'—and corrected a few small inaccuracies.[25]   In the same month Lawrence was invited to write an Epilogue to bring his narrative more up to date, and to suggest illustrations.   Writing from New Mexico on 13 September he passed the news of these requests in characteristic style to the American bibliographer, Edward D. McDonald:

The Oxford Press are doing a new edition of *Movements in European History* & want illustrations and an epilogue.   The epilogue, all right.   But they are pestering me here to suggest what illustrations they shall use—they want about a dozen. And do old woodcuts & such grow like leaves on Rocky Mountain pine trees!—I suppose you don't know off-hand where one could find a few suitable things that the Oxford Press might reproduce?—They're an incompetent show, if ever there was one. But pleasant with it.[26]

McDonald obliged with some pictures and was asked for more (all of which were subsequently rejected by the Press), and Lawrence also sought the assistance of an acquaintance, H. Milne, in the Manuscript department of the British Museum.   The Epilogue he composed at high speed, sending it to Curtis Brown on 30 September for transmission to Oxford.[27]   On the same day he wrote to Vere Collins: 'I sent an epilogue for *Movements* to Curtis Brown. If you don't like it, don't use it.   Or if you want to omit any part of it, do so.'   His misgivings proved fully justified.

The Epilogue did not reach the publisher until about mid-October (on 15 October Lawrence told McDonald that he had received a cable from Oxford asking him 'to hurry the Epilogue').[28]   The Clarendon Press at once invited comments on it from two 'readers': the poet Charles Williams

[25] This and other information for which no printed source is given comes from the Clarendon Press file on Lawrence's *History.* Permission to quote from it was kindly given by the Secretary to the Delegates.

[26] *The Centaur Letters* (University of Texas, Austin, 1970), p. 14.

[27] *Collected Letters,* i. 810.

[28] *Centaur Letters,* p. 16.

(then employed by the London Office of the O.U.P.) and probably C. R. L. Fletcher, who had advised on the original book.[29]   Williams proposed (on 13 November) that, with slight modifications, the Epilogue should be printed:

Since DHL 'got religion' I have rather lost interest in him; and all this *Epilogue* only comes back to general advice to 'be good' (or indeed to Tennyson: 'we needs must love the highest'). But he has even in his hectic emphasis, his feverish shouts of piety, a curious fascination. I *do* like it, though I mourn for the dead DHL.

I don't see that there's anything hurtful about it; indeed I wonder whether some of Mr. Sisam's[30] cuts aren't perhaps un-necessary: e.g.—p. 4: why should 'now we are directionless' come out? I should leave in the paragraph about the 'two selves' on p. 7; and something equivalent to the top par. on p. 15. But it makes me feel like the 18th century contemplating the 'enthusiasts'.

Fletcher was much more censorious. He reported on 18 November:

I read this last night with considerable impatience (and failed to read the last four pages, but it seems to go on much as it had begun). If it were my responsibility I think I should refuse to print most of the passages marked by Sisam; the remarks for example about Lloyd George and Horatio Bottomley, not so much because they are grossly unjust to the former—and it is surely indecent to bracket a former Prime Minister with a convict?—as because the passage is in my opinion a libel upon the British people, and indeed upon humanity. The whole story seems to me to be radically false and self-contradictory. If we are all, or nearly all, the cowardly hounds D. H. L. thinks us, what is the good of looking to our 'Natural Noblesse' for future salvation?

But if Sisam's passages, or most of them, are removed, I don't think what is left is any worse nonsense than one may read every day; though the style is epileptic (at the twenty-seventh iteration of *growing tip* I almost screamed aloud) and even

[29] The slight uncertainty arises from the anonymity of his report in the Clarendon file.

[30] Kenneth Sisam, Secretary to the Delegates.

ungrammatical; 'Like a tree' is not a sentence (page 3). The doctrine that the war was either the cause or the effect of the sudden death of humanity appears to me such vicious and cowardly nonsense that I am always tempted to suppose it an outbreak of injured vanity. But a great many people seem to hold this doctrine.

This aggressive reaction (with which Sisam sympathized) carried the day; the Epilogue was not added to the second edition; it was first published in 1971 (when the Oxford Press reprinted the book).[31]

The contract for the illustrated edition was signed between Lawrence and the Press on 3 April 1925. Humphrey Milford was expressing doubts as late as February on the wisdom of using Lawrence's name on the title-page. Finally he agreed. The book was published on 21 May: 2,000 copies in a 'Prize' edition (at 8*s*. 6*d*.); 6,000 copies of the ordinary edition (at 4*s*. 6*d*.). Only one day later a letter from the American historian Samuel E. Morison drew John Johnson's attention to an error in the caption for an illustration of the Old South Church in Boston.[32] The illustration was cancelled and replaced by one of Boston harbour; but the original caption remained unchanged in the list of illustrations. Knowing that the blunder over the picture of Boston would be of interest to a bibliographer, Lawrence told McDonald of it in a letter of 29 June 1925; he conveyed his irritation about the rejected Epilogue at the same time:

I'll send you a copy of the new *Movements*, with the pictures. They are nice pictures. The Oxford Press people were too conceited to use yours: chosen in America. I did them an Epilogue which they were frightened to use. It was for the

[31] The text is that of a typescript copy in the Lawrence Clark Powell Library of the University of California, Los Angeles. I am grateful to the Librarian for making it available.

[32] While apologizing for the error, Johnson told Morison by letter that the caption describing the Old South Church as the location for Patrick Henry's 'Liberty or Death' speech (actually delivered in Richmond, Virginia) was formulated by an (unidentified) American Professor.

future rather than the past. But why shouldn't a history book
reach both ways!—Apparently they're cancelling that picture
of Boston—Milk St.—& putting in a view of Boston from the
sea.   So this may make another bibliographical item.[33]

One further edition was published: for use in Irish schools.
Lawrence's *History*—written by a man with a Protestant
nonconformist background for a largely Protestant England—was quite unsuited to Irish Roman Catholic Schools.
(The opening paragraphs of Chapter XII will illustrate the
point.)   Lawrence told his sister Ada by letter on 26 October 1925 that, for the Irish edition, he had to remove every
word in praise of Luther and any suggestion that the Pope
had erred.   In fact the censoring of the text was under-
taken in Ireland by Patrick O'Daly, a Director of the Irish
publishing house; it was rigorously, even ruthlessly done
and resulted in scores of textual changes; and Lawrence's
anger (expressed to Vere Collins on 17 November 1925) can
readily be understood:

I'm sending the mauled History by this mail.   When I went
through it, I was half infuriated, and half amused.   But if I'd
had to go through it, personally, and make the decision merely
from myself, I'd have sent those Irish b—s seven times to hell,
before I'd have moved a single iota at their pencil stroke.—But
do me a favour.   Please keep this particular marked copy for
me, will you, when you are through with it.   Send it me back
here, if you can.   It will always serve to stimulate my bile, and
to remind me of the glory of the human race.[34]

Another letter to Collins, on 16 July 1926, makes clear
Lawrence's relief at being able to leave to him the proof-
correction of this edition.   The book was published in September 1926 by the Educational Company of Ireland; ap-
proximately 3,000 copies were printed of which the Clarendon Press bought 500 in anticipation of sales to Roman
Catholic schools in England.   This hope proved vain.   In

---

[33] *Centaur Letters*, p. 20.
[34] *Collected Letters*, i. 865.

September 1929 Collins tried to return unsold copies to the Irish publishers; they refused his offer and reported:

It is a very fine book and we are more than disappointed that the sale has been so discouraging. In this country the Christian Brothers took exception to many of the statements, but it is doubtful if these exceptions were based on strict historical accuracy. History is the most difficult subject we have to deal with in Ireland, and it is obvious that Mr. Lawrence is not the man to write a History for Catholic Schools.

Collins commented ruefully to Sisam: 'I fear that Lady Chatterley and the Pictures and the Pansies have ruined this book (now with his name on it) for R.C.'s.' His lament was understandable. *Lady Chatterley's Lover* was suppressed in London in 1928; the police raided the London exhibition of Lawrence's paintings on 5 July 1929; and shortly after Collins's memorandum the postal authorities seized the typescript of *Pansies* on instructions from the Home Office. The circumstances could scarcely have been less propitious.[35]

Nevertheless the Clarendon Press edition sold steadily in the cheaper version; for example 630 copies were sold in the nine months up to January 1931. Stocks were then down to 380 copies and it was decided to print a further 3,000 copies for 1 May. The prize edition was disposed of at the lower price. But sales even of the cheap reprint gradually fell off; 179 copies were still unsold in 1943. These were almost certainly pulped because of the desperate wartime paper shortage. In 1944 Clarendon declared the book out-of-print.

Neither in 1921 nor in 1925 did the *History* attract much attention from reviewers. A solitary review of the first edition appeared in the *New Statesman* on 26 November 1921. The reviewer complimented 'Mr. Davison' on 'a good example of the latest method of writing history for

[35] For a full account of recently discovered information about the production and publication of the Irish edition see Philip Crumpton, 'D. H. Lawrence's "mauled History": the Irish edition of *Movements in European History*', in *D. H. Lawrence Review*, xiii, 2 (September 1980), 105–18.

schools'. The book had 'one of the liveliest and best introductions ever written for a class-book', and though the author was moderately censured for some lack of proportion, the reviewer considered his methods 'so refreshing, and his book, generally, shows such an extraordinary advance on anything that was available for school use ten or fifteen years ago, that one hesitates to pick holes'. Reviewers of the 1925 edition could not be so objective. Thus the *Sunday Times* reviewer amused himself with the difference between 'Mr. Lawrence and Mr. Davison', complimenting the latter on his 'direct, lucid account, suitable for fourth forms at school'. Kenneth Pickthorn in the *London Mercury* objected to 'the traditional schoolboy view' in the *History*, but acknowledged the originality of Lawrence's manner as well as his 'clear, personal, and vigorous English'.

Noticeably the *History* was not reviewed in the educational journals. It did not, apparently, satisfy the market for which it was intended. Though the sale (excluding the Irish edition) of 15,000 copies in, say, twenty-five years does not constitute a failure, a successful school textbook would achieve a markedly better performance.[36] The most damaging blow to the *History's* commercial prospects was its failure to attract the attention of examining boards or a sufficient number of influential teachers. Not a single board either specified it as an examination text or recommended it for study; nor was it listed in the *Handbook for History Teachers* (1929) which suggests that it was little known in elementary schools. That it was used in some schools is beyond question; that it was not regarded as a significant

[36] Cf. E. H. Spalding and P. Wragge, *The Nation and its Government from 1485 to the Present Day*, first published 1914 and reprinted twenty-four times by 1932. *Life in Past Ages*, ed. J. M. Wood: Books I and II of the series were reprinted nine times between 1932 and 1946, Books III and IV seven times. For this, and other information in the next paragraph, I am indebted to the unpublished M.Ed. dissertation, 'A consideration of history textbooks published between 1750 and 1939' by D. J. Wilkins (University of Nottingham, 1969).

contribution to history-teaching is equally certain.

Yet the Oxford University Press, in its instructions to Lawrence, had showed itself sensitive to the new trends in the teaching of history. He was asked to write not 'a formal, connected, text book, but a series of vivid sketches'. This is what educationalists and historians were themselves proposing. James Welton urged teachers not to be 'trammelled by chronology' but to concern themselves with important historical movements; divisions into periods should be made 'at turning-points in history, and not at mere artificial points, such as the reigns of monarchs'.[37] As early as 1905 the Board of Education expressed support for the new approach, and an official report in 1926 stated that 'the general principles governing the teaching of history can no longer be summed up in terms of the information supplied'. The era of rote learning in history was officially pronounced closed; the long reign—effectively over a century—of Richmal Mangnall's *Historical and Miscellaneous Questions* was at an end. Moreover the study of international history was increasingly supplementing the virtually exclusive concentration on British affairs. Indeed 'history at last came into its own, in the Fisher era of multiplied secondary schools and Advanced courses after 1918'.[38]

'The old bad history is abolished.' So Lawrence announced in his Introduction. 'The old bad history consisted of a register of facts. . . . No more of this.' He rejected, too, both 'graphic' and 'scientific' history, the former as 'all heart', the latter 'all head'. Instead he proposed to chart 'the great, surging movements which rose in the hearts of men in Europe'. Lawrence had, it seemed, responded to the new mood.

This was the promise; the achievement was otherwise. Undoubtedly Lawrence often writes with a vividness which

---

[37] *Principles and Methods of Teaching* (2nd edn., 1909), pp. 242–3.
[38] A. C. F. Beales in *The Historical Association: Jubilee Addresses, 1956* (1956), p. 51.

would be refreshing to pupils accustomed to traditional
textbooks; yet despite this and in spite of his introduction
the framework for his historical vision was conventional.
The list of chapter-headings proves that. Furthermore his
book is a strange amalgam: judgements of unusual perci-
pience jostle with bizarre statements; a Carlylean approach
to the European past at times conflicts oddly with a
simplistic approach which partly validates Pickthorn's
charge about a 'school-boy view'. 'Thus the Feudal System
begins'; 'And so the Holy Roman Empire was really established'; 'After the Age of Faith dawned the Age of Reason:'[39]
this simple-minded shorthand almost inevitably imposed
itself on a writer attempting to survey two and a half
thousand years of history for school-children. Occasionally,
too, Lawrence is misleading (though rarely factually wrong).
For example, the significance of the murder of Gothic
hostages by the Romans was far less dramatic than he
suggests; to place the chapter on the Huns after rather
than before that on the Goths and Vandals is misleading
since it was the western advance of the Huns that prompted
the major Germanic migrations; and (like other historians)
Lawrence makes the Crusades, especially the First, bulk
much larger in European history than the facts allow. Indeed he was not capable of the finer discriminations required of a distinguished historian.

Yet a cursory dismissal of the book as bad history is
inadequate. It may not be a repository of historical truth;
it remains of interest and significance in the Lawrentian
canon. Lawrence may be accused of creating historical
personages rather than complimented on depicting persons
of history, but there is no denying his success in vivifying
men such as Clovis, Peter the Hermit, or Savonarola. His
descriptive power, so clearly a feature of the novels and
essays, is here too. The account of Constantine's vision as
he gazed from the hills near Byzantium is instinct with the

[39] See pp. 112, 118, 170.

vivid response to colour, movement, shapes, and natural beauty found in such an essay as 'Flowering Tuscany'. Lawrence is equally capable of creating the grotesque (as in his account of the Huns); informing with imaginative life the diurnal activities of Germanic tribes or Celtic families; and impressionistically suggesting (here through biblical metaphor) the movement of vast numbers of men: 'More than the stars in heaven or the sands of the shore these people came, and they passed like devouring locusts.'[40] As in his other writings he brings into sharp contrast emblems of life and death: 'then the holiday-makers looked at the corpses [of Frenchmen slaughtered during the "Sicilian Vespers"] lying among the sunny flowers'; or two men symbolic of the cultures with which they are identified: Dante and dying medievalism juxtaposed against Petrarch who is associated with 'gardens, sunny and still and rich with foliage and flowers'.[41] Above all there is Lawrence's delight in the achievement of men of imagination and creative vision. It is present in his description of the splendour of Italian cities in the late thirteenth century; in his evocation of Boccaccio with his associates 'all rich and rare and bright women and men, delighting in life'; or in his celebration of the Renaissance: 'The human spirit was then like a butterfly which bursts from the chrysalis into the air. A whole new world lies about it. The narrow, devouring little world of the caterpillar has disappeared, all heaven and all earth flash around.'[42] Such memorable features were the products of a poetic imagination brought into vital activity by contemplating historical fact but liberated from the constricting demands of chronology. It may not be convincing history; it is often a vivid literary experience.

And there is, as Lawrence assured Nancy Henry, 'a clue of developing meaning running through it'. He believed

[40] p. 145.
[41] pp. 159, 192-4.
[42] pp. 195, 197.

nb. distinction btwn instinct and artifice; cf. Twil. in Italy
nb. also, DH choosing the Renn. as the crucial pt. of change.

xxii   INTRODUCTION TO THE NEW EDITION

that the grand process which operated through history had
its roots in the supersession of martial violence and conquest by commercial enterprise. Up to the Renaissance,
according to Lawrence, man was 'alive but blind and
voracious'; from the Renaissance onwards 'men do not live
just to fight and conquer and capture possessions. They
live now in the joy of producing, the joy of making things'.
Thus, since commerce requires stability and tranquillity if
it is to thrive, 'peace begins to win her great victories over
war'. By the early eighteenth century a nation's life no
longer consisted of 'war and power. Its real purpose is in
its productive work'. Money then begins to 'arrogate the
privileges of birth'.[43]   With the destruction of aristocratic
privileges at the French Revolution money firmly assumed
pre-eminence. Thus, through the movements of history,
Lawrence detected the working of two 'great passions': 'the
passion of pride and power and conquest, and the passion
of peace and production'. Nations in the modern sense
emerge when societies succumb to the second rather than
the first. 'The time comes when the leaders of industry, the
rich men of the middle class really rule, as they do in
Britain today [1921], and in the great republics.'[44]   The
individual talents of Gerald Crich and Clifford Chatterley,
as it were, had been stimulated and allowed to become
dominant through the working of inscrutable historical
forces. Such men and the ethos they symbolize would
eventually give way to 'the last reign of wisdom, of pure
understanding, the reign which we have never seen in the
world, but which we must see'.[45]

Another aspect of the 'developing meaning' running
through Lawrence's interpretation of history is his implied
argument that to achieve political, social, even moral
greatness human societies have always selected as their
leaders powerful individuals in whom they see their

[43] pp. 197, 231.
[44] p. 293.
[45] p. 198.

distinctive qualities best embodied. From the days of Constantine the Greek Church taught 'that strange passionate humility' which encouraged millions to 'leave their lives in the hands of one man'. Later the Gauls humbled themselves before the 'arrogance and bravery' of their chieftain and willingly found 'their glorification in one man'. Innocent III failed to rule Europe because he lacked the necessary power of the sword; Napoleon succeeded because he held absolute power. Moreover 'he was supreme because the people willed it'.[46] These two conditions are essential: there must be absolute power; but it must be accompanied by the conviction on the part of the governed that the leader rules by their wish and with their consent. Consequently when Lawrence turned his attention to the contemporary world, certain that the 'law of life' which he had discovered operating in the past was permanently valid, he felt able to predict the course of affairs in Germany and Russia, the scenes of the most revolutionary political changes. Absolutism of one kind had been replaced by 'government by the masses of the proletariat'; this he believed would not flourish securely, satisfying the alternate human desire for 'martial adventure' and for peace, unless the unity of the working-classes was focused in 'one great chosen figure'. The leader must be capable of leading 'a great war' as well as administering 'a wide peace'. And, importantly, while he would be absolute, 'he must be chosen'.[47]

Neither Italian Fascism nor Soviet Communism—he added in the Epilogue—would produce such a leader. These systems, relying on bullying and brutality, gave temporary satisfaction by ministering solely to material needs. But the 'true natural power' essential to a leader is not derived from a voting majority who merely ascribe greatness to a person promising higher wages and lower taxation. A nation must first reject the *bassesse* symbol-

[46] pp. 18, 86–7, 251.
[47] pp. 305–6.

ized for Lawrence by Horatio Bottomley (the wartime demagogue and post-war swindler); it will then be capable of selecting as its leader an individual who pre-eminently embodies the 'true or natural nobility' that exists in all men. The majority will—as Rawdon Lilly remarks in *Aaron's Rod*—'in their souls *submit* to some greater soul than theirs'.

JAMES T. BOULTON

ACKNOWLEDGEMENTS

Thanks are due to the following for their kind assistance with the writing of the Introduction: Professor Donald Bullough, Mr. Philip Crumpton, Professor R. Draper, Mr. George Lazarus, Dr. Warren Roberts, Dr. K. M. Sagar, and Mr. D. J. Wilkins.

Introduction

AT the present moment, history must either be graphic or scientific. The old bad history is abolished. The old bad history consisted of a register of facts. It drew up a chart of human events, as one might draw up a chart of the currants in a plum-pudding, merely because they happen promiscuously to be there. No more of this.

The new history is different. It is, we repeat, either graphic or scientific. Graphic history consists of stories about men and women who appear in the old records, stories as vivid and as personal as may be. And this is very nice for little children : the only trouble being that with so much *personal* element there can be very little historic. No doubt the great people of the past were personages, and quite as personal as we are. Unfortunately, nothing is more difficult than to re-create the *personal* reality of a bygone age. Personality is local and temporal. Each age has its own. And each age proceeds to interpret every other age in terms of the current personality. So that Shakespeare's Caesar is an Elizabethan, and Bernard Shaw's is a Victorian, and neither of them is Caesar. The *personal* Caesar we shall never know. But there is some eternal, impersonal Caesar whom we *can* know, historically. And for this reason, let us beware of too much of the personal element, even for little children. It tends to *shut out* the strange, vast, terrifying reality of the past, even as the charming cosiness of a garden shuts out the great terror and wonder of the world. And even for tiny children, if we proceed to speak at all of the past, we must not shut out the space and fear and greatness. We must not make it too personal and familiar. We must leave in the impersonal, terrific element, the sense of the unknown, even as it is left in Red Riding Hood or any *true* nursery tale. It is wrong to envelop our children in so much cosiness and familiar circumstance. It is wrong to feed their souls on so many personal tit-bits. It is an insult to the past, which was not personal as we are personal, and it is a ridiculous exaggeration of the present. We are not the consummation of all life and time. Yet we put our sentiments and our personal feelings upon Caesar, as if Caesar were no more than a dummy figure whom we have to dress up to our own personal mode. Then we call it history—graphic history.

No wonder the scientific school protests. But if graphic history is all heart, scientific history is all head. Having picked out all the currants and raisins of events for our little children, we go to the university and proceed to masticate the dough. We must analyse the mixture and determine the ingredients. Each fact must be established, and put into relation with every other fact. This is the business of scientific history : the forging of a great chain of logically sequential events, cause and effect demonstrated down the whole range of time. Now this is all very well, if we will remember that we are not *discovering* any sequence of events, we are only abstracting. The logical sequence does not exist until we have made it, and then it exists as a new piece of furniture of the human mind.

The present small book is intended for adolescents, for those who have had almost enough of stories and anecdotes and personalities, and who have not yet reached the stage of intellectual pride in abstraction.

It is an attempt to give some impression of the great, surging movements which rose in the hearts of men in Europe, sweeping human beings together into one great concerted action, or sweeping them apart for ever on the tides of opposition. These are movements which have no deducible origin. They have no reasonable cause, though they are so great that we must call them impersonal.

There is no earthly reason for such a vast madness as that of the Crusades. Given every circumstance of the year 800 A.D. in Europe, could the First and Second Crusades be deduced? Logical sequence does not exist until it is abstracted by the human mind. In the same way, there is no more *reason* for the Renaissance than there is reason for the singing of a blackbird. A rook is a black bird which makes a nest in spring. And yet it does *not* sing.

And so, we must not be so assured when we regard the historic faculty as a faculty for the ascertaining and verifying of facts, and the ascribing of certain sequence and order to such facts. This is only the hack-work of history —science, it may be. But history proper is a true art, not fictional, but nakedly veracious.

Inside the hearts, or souls, of men in Europe there has happened at times some strange surging, some welling-up of unknown powers. These powers that well up inside the hearts of men, these are the fountains and origins of human history. And the welling-up has no ascribable cause. It is naked cause itself.

Thus the Crusades, or the Renaissance, these are great motions from within the soul of mankind. They are the sheer utterance of life itself, the logic only appearing afterwards. Logic *cannot* hold good beforehand, even in the inorganic world. Earthquakes are disasters from without. They should be predictable. Yet no one can predict them, because the mysterious and untellable motion within the hearts of men is in some way related to the motion within the earth, so that even earthquakes are unaccountably related to man's psychic being, and dependent upon it.

Therefore this little history is an attempt to count some of the great pulsations that have shaken the hearts of men in Europe, and made their history. Events are details swirling in the strange stream. Great motions surge up, men sweep away upon a tide. Some are flung back. The same passional motive that carried the north of Europe into Protestantism caused the Spaniards to flood to America and to react in the Inquisition. It is all beyond reasonable cause and effect, though these may be deduced later. It is all outside personality, though it makes personality. It is greater than any one man, though in individual men the power is at its greatest.

We cannot say, for example, that the Reformation arose because the Pope sold Indulgences. It arose because a new craving awoke in the hearts of men, a craving which expressed itself later as a passion for immediate, individual relationship of a man with God. There is no *reason* why such a passion, such a craving should arise. All that the reason can do, in discovering the logical consequence of such passion and its effects, afterwards, is to realise that life *was* so, mysteriously, creatively, and beyond cavil.

All that real history can do is to note with wonder and reverence the tides which have surged out from the innermost heart of man, watch the incalculable flood and ebb of such tides. Afterwards, there is a deducible sequence. Beforehand there is none.

Life makes its own great gestures, of which men are the substance. History repeats the gesture, so we live it once more, and are fulfilled in the past. Whoever misses his education in history misses his fulfilment in the past.

I. Rome

THE date of the founding of the city of Rome is given as 753 B.C. But at that time Rome could scarcely have been more than a savage little village of shepherds or herdsmen. None the less, it was a village of brave, active men, and it grew gradually into a town, fortified in the seven hills by the bank of the Tiber. Surrounding it were hostile races, hostile cities bigger than itself. But the Romans knew how to stick to one another, and they made headway. Gradually Rome became the leader of the towns and peoples in the wide plain of Latium, which surrounded her. She was head of the Latin League.

After the year 500 B.C. we can be fairly certain of Roman history. At that time Rome was a republic. It had now no king, and no nobles, dukes or counts or lords, as we know them. Yet it was divided into two classes, the upper and lower—patrician who were rich and proud, and plebeian who were poor. These two classes held great meetings, to decide what was to be done, and to choose leaders. The chief men in Rome were the two consuls, who were elected in the council of the people, to hold office for one year only.

So we see in the beginning the difference between the Romans and the people of Britain and Gaul. The Britons and the Gauls were subject to chieftains, who said ' Come,' and the people came ; ' Go,' and they went. But in Rome each citizen was free to come and go as he pleased. Only he must abide by the laws that he himself had helped to make. To be a Roman citizen, in the days of the real greatness of Rome, was to be a proud, free man, subject to no master, a fearless supporter of the laws of freedom.

By the year 275 B.C. Rome was mistress of Italy, south of the Po. The peninsula of Italy lies in the centre of the Mediterranean; the city of Rome lies in the centre of the peninsula; and the Mediterranean, as its very name says, was the centre of the world at that time. So that Rome held a great position of advantage: she was the very centre and hub of the world of that day. And soon the whole world turned upon that hub.

Gradually Rome extended her dominion. In 242 B.C. she took Sicily, her first overseas possession. Then she defeated Carthage in North Africa; then Macedonia, in the Balkan Peninsula; then Greece, then Spain, and so on, till all the lands of the Mediterranean were under her power. In the year 61 B.C. Pompey the Great returned from the East. He had been as far as the Euphrates, had defeated the Persian Mithridates, who fled to the Crimea, and Syria was added to Rome. In the year 58 B.C. Julius Caesar marched north to Gaul, and across from Gaul he came to Britain. By Gaul we mean the land now occupied by France, stretching from the Mediterranean to the Rhine.

We see the empire spreading west, south, east, and north, under the Roman armies. The empire was won by the armies, and it must be kept by the armies. The wonderful thing is that it *was* kept, and governed from the one central city of Rome, by the great citizens of Rome.

The Roman Empire is the most wonderful the world has ever known: not because of its size, but because of its strange unity and singleness. The world will surely never again see such a wonder. And the Romans achieved this by their power for holding together and working together in one purpose; they kept their empire by making roads *immediately*, and by establishing permanent military and civil colonies; they maintained their greatness because of their natural love of justice. There was at the bottom of every Roman heart a passion for simple, actual *truth* : even the trial of Jesus shows us this. They loved to feel they rested upon the plain truth of *facts*. Individually, they might be vain and unscrupulous. But in their social acts, in that which concerned justice and the freedom of a man, they had always this strange and beautiful craving for fairness between man and man, for justice between a man and the State, for the whole truth in any question under dispute. Even whilst the emperors and governors were the most cruel or foolish of men, still, as a rule, they could see what was true or right, though they did not choose to act upon it.

But an empire which is established on military power must at length be governed by one man, even as an army must be under the supreme command of one general : for a military empire is in truth a great army. The Romans struggled to keep their freedom, the splendid freedom of a Roman citizen, a civilian. But as the empire extended, more and more men had been admitted to the citizenship, men of every nation and country. St. Paul, as we know, was a Roman citizen. How could these millions of citizens meet in council to decide questions of peace or war, and to elect their great consuls ? And therefore, since men had not discovered how to choose their own representative by vote, the bulk of the citizens were not represented : they were dumb, they had no say.

Thus the army had to take control, and the greatest men were the generals of the army. Pompey and Julius Caesar, two of the world's greatest soldiers, were both consuls, prime ministers of the empire. The masters of the army became masters of the civil life as well. But in the year 50 B.C. the armies of the empire had two masters, Pompey in the east, Caesar in the west. The two fought for supremacy, and Caesar defeated Pompey, who was murdered in Egypt, to which land he had fled. Caesar was now alone master of the world. He was made absolute ruler of the empire. He sat in the senate on a golden throne, wearing the purple mantle of a general in his triumph. But the Romans would not have him named king. They hated the very thought of a king who would rule them. So Caesar took the title of Imperator— Emperor—which meant at that time master of the army.

Still the great Romans were angry. They did not want such an overlord. Even though they loved the great Julius, they could not bear that he should have permanent power over them, and over all free Romans. Rome must be governed by her citizens. Therefore, on the Ides of March, 44 B.C., the first and greatest citizens of Rome, led by Caius Cassius and Marcus Junius Brutus, murdered Caesar in the senate, by his golden throne.

It was terrible to good men like Brutus to have a share in such a thing. They did it for the freedom of their country. Yet they utterly failed. The young Caesar Octavianus became master of the world in the year 31 B.C., after defeating Mark Antony and Cleopatra in the battle of Actium. Octavian was the adopted son of Julius Caesar, and his full name was Caius Julius Caesar Octavianus. Later on he added the name of Augustus, by which he is now known. The period of the rule of Augustus is the greatest in Roman history—the Augustan age. During this age lived the greatest Roman writers and thinkers, the empire was prosperous and splendid. In the time of Augustus, also, Christ was born.

And Augustus had some of the beauty and noble gentleness of Christ. He was not like Julius Caesar, chiefly a fighter, a commander whom nothing could resist. He loved peace, and the happiness of the people. He carefully settled the government of the great empire. But, while he *said* that he restored the Republic, it turned out, as a matter of fact, that he had inaugurated that imperial form of government which was the first cause of the downfall of the empire. The rule of the *one man* made the rest of the citizens indifferent, irresponsible. They had no share in the empire; the Caesars and emperors swallowed up everything. So the citizens and great men began to care about their own little lives and nothing else. It is a free, proud people which keeps a nation alive. So that when the Romans ceased to feel themselves free and responsible, Rome became as it were flabby, a huge but flabby power.

Augustus died in the year 14 A.D. He had never heard of Jesus, who was one day to be executed in a distant province as an insignificant agitator and disturber of the peace. After Augustus come a string of Caesars famous for their extravagance and wickedness, which was not so terrible after all. When these Caesars came to the throne they took the name of Augustus, which thus became a title even higher than that of Emperor, for Augustus had had himself placed among the gods. Jupiter, Juno, Venus, Mars, Mercury, Augustus, all these gods had their temples and altars.

Augustus was followed by Tiberius, who first began to tyrannise over the Romans. He is supposed to have been very cruel. But the Romans themselves fawned before him, and betrayed one another to him. 'Oh! how anxious these people are to be slaves!' Tiberius said bitterly. He died in 37 A.D. After him came the mad Caligula, who wanted to have the statue of himself, as a god, put into the temple of Jerusalem and worshipped there. He hated the tiresome, turbulent, rather cowardly people of Rome, and said : 'I wish they had only one head, so that I could cut it off at a blow.' He was himself, however, soon murdered by an officer of the Praetorian Guard. In the year 54 Nero became emperor. He loved splendour, and built a gorgeous palace called the Golden House, where he gave astonishing feasts. Every one has heard the story that Rome, the enormous city, was set on fire at his bidding, so that he could enjoy, from his high grounds, a wonderful sight. Watching the sea of flames, which lasted for five or six days, he is said to have danced and sung with extravagant pleasure. Later the burnt quarters were built up again, and Nero said he found Rome a city of brick and wood, and left it a city of marble. At last his wild acts caused the leaders of the army to rise against him. He fled to a country house, and there he begged his faithful servant to kill him : which the man did, in grief and obedience. This was in the year 68.

It was no wonder these men were, or became, a little mad, for they were masters of a whole world, and they had the whole world at their feet, and all Rome cringing and squirming before them. We must remember Tiberius' saying : ' Oh ! how anxious these men are to be slaves ! ' It was the greatest citizens of Rome itself that sent the emperors mad with pride and extravagance, by utterly sinking their lives down to the will of the master.

After Nero emperors were chosen and destroyed again in quick succession. From the year 14, when Augustus died, to the year 96, in which Domitian was murdered, ten emperors rose and fell. In Domitian's time the conquest of Britain was accomplished, but the emperor was a base man, and he destroyed the great general Agricola out of jealousy.

Nero was the last of the true imperial line. After him, the succession depended not on birth but on chance, and the choice of the army. A victorious general, a notable citizen, might suddenly be raised to the throne. Later, even the sons of slaves or peasants or barbarians from Arabia or Hungary, were lifted up and invested with the imperial purple.

In the chaos and turmoil of the empire after Augustus, there was one splendid century, from 96 to 180, when Trajan, Hadrian, Antoninus Pius, and Marcus Aurelius were emperors. This is called ' the Age of the Antonines.' One great and noble ruler followed another, in succession. Within the empire there was peace and solid prosperity. The frontiers were established, the colonies grew rich and secure. Antoninus built the wall across Scotland, from Glasgow to Edinburgh. This was the northern boundary of the empire. And from this wall the Roman roads ran, with the single intervention of the Channel, straight and perfect to the other end of the empire, in Arabia or Meso potamia. There were post-houses and milestones all the way; and the Romans kept the account of the miles: from the wall of Antoninus to York, 222 Roman miles; from York to London 227; to Sandwich 67; crossing to Boulogne 45; to Rheims 174; to Lyons 330; Milan 324; Rome 426; Brindisi 360; the crossing to Dyracchium, or Durazzo, 40; Byzantium 711; Ancyra 283; Tarsus 301; Antioch 141; Tyre 252; Jerusalem 168. This makes 4080 Roman miles, which is 3740 English miles. So the Romans kept their itinerary.

This great empire remained solid owing to the excellence of the armies and of the magistrates. But it was too big. Once it was really established, it was bound to fall to pieces. And it fell naturally into two halves.

The old half of the empire was in Syria, Greece, North Africa; the new half was Gaul, Spain, Britain, and the countries of the Danube. The armies and the colonists of the empire of the west, Gaul, Britain, Spain, lived in northern countries, wild, cold in winter, peopled by fierce barbarians. But the colonists and armies of the eastern empire lived under burning suns, in ancient cities, older by far than Rome, and among a people delicate and luxurious. The great towns of the east, Smyrna, Ephesus, Antioch, were full of marble palaces and lovely temples whilst yet Rome was a rude little town. Alexandria in Egypt and Carthage in North Africa knew all the richness and delights of the Greeks and Phoenicians. And thus the millions of Romans in the East, living in a land of luxury and fruit, corn, pomegranates, dates, apricots, loved to be lazy, to dress in delicate clothes, to bathe and rub themselves with oil, to go to the theatre or the circus often, almost every day, to talk and feast and idle their lives away.

In the North it was different. There, men must watch

and act. In the North there were fine Roman towns—
Marseilles, Lyons, Treves, Vienna, York—many lovely
cities. But here men could not idle their lives away.
Here there was not any wine and oil, save what was
carried from afar off. And here were the great fierce races
of Germans near at hand, to keep one on the alert, or
the savage Caledonians. Here the Roman legions had to
contend with the bravest barbarians and the bitterest
cold. They were not like the softer armies of the East,
who fought the Persians in well-known, civilised warfare,
under hot skies.

Thus, gradually, there came a silent falling asunder in
the empire. After the year 180 a series of worthless emperors came to the throne. Rome itself became a centre of
shame and degradation. The great armies were hardly
ever in Italy. They were needed in Gaul, in Syria, in
Africa. The generals and the veterans away on the frontiers came to despise the noisy, foolish citizens of Rome,
and the Eternal City, Rome herself, Mistress of the World,
became an object of contempt. She kept her useless emperors and courtiers, her useless, extravagant mass of
inhabitants. But the real government, the real power,
was always in the hands of the great, far-off, permanent
armies, in Gaul, in the East, on the Danube, or in Britain.

II. Constantinople

As the years went on, the civilian citizens of Rome became weaker and more worthless. They were rich enough, but they had no spirit, no passion; they only considered their little pleasures and gratifications. The real Rome was in the great military camps on the Rhine and the Danube, and in the East.

A new phase began when, in 284, Diocletian, the general of the armies of the Danube, was chosen emperor by his soldiers. He came from poor people: perhaps his parents were slaves. But he was a great man. He found the empire too loose and rambling to be governed by one man, so he chose his own chief general Maximian, to share the honours of the empire with him. The fierce but brave Maximian was raised to the purple, and hailed as Caesar and Augustus along with Diocletian. He was the son of peasants, in Hungary. He was, however, a good leader, and he remained true to Diocletian.

But still the command was inefficient. The two emperors with their armies could not keep watch close enough over Europe and Asia. So they decided to make two new Caesars, and they chose the generals Constantius and Galerius. Constantius and Galerius were Caesars, but not emperors fully. They were not hailed Augustus. Diocletian and Maximian alone held this supreme title. But the four Caesars governed among them the four quarters of the empire.

The great Diocletian, the chief Augustus, kept for himself Asia Minor and Egypt, Greece, and the land we now call

Turkey—the lovely, rich old dominions.   Maximian Augustus had Italy and North Africa.   Galerius was stationed to defend the Danube, and to govern the Balkan Peninsula ; whilst Constantius Caesar had Gaul, Spain, Britain, defending the Rhine and the wall of Scotland.

So we see the choice of the greatest emperors leans to the old world—the rich, lovely East, the hot Africa, the proud old Greece and Italy.   The subordinate Caesars are given the northern regions, the savage lands.

When Diocletian and Maximian abdicated in 305, Galerius and Constantius, the two Caesars, took the title of Augustus.   Galerius became emperor in the East.   He was a violent, ambitious, unfriendly man.   Constantius, more gentle and more loved, kept command in the West, in Gaul and Britain.

Constantius had a son Constantine, the great Constantine, whom we like to claim as British-born.   The mother of Constantine, Helena, is said to have been the daughter of a British chieftain, whom Constantius married when he was a young officer in Britain.   So it is said that the famous Constantine was born in Britain.   But it is more probable that Helena was the daughter of an innkeeper, and that her son was born somewhere near the Danube.   However that may be, Helena was looked upon as a woman of humble origin.   When Constantius was raised to the rank of Caesar, it was necessary for him to have a noble wife, and a Roman.   So Helena was divorced. Constantine, her son, was at that time eighteen years old. He shared his mother's disgrace and downfall, and instead of finding himself the honoured son of the Caesar, he was left in a poor rank in the army of Galerius, in the East.

He was, however, brave and clever and lovable.   In appearance he was tall, dignified, handsome, and pleasant. The soldiers loved him, and he soon rose to be a leading officer.

Galerius, knowing his right of birth, was jealous of him from the first.   Seeing how the soldiers loved the young officer, and respected him in spite of all, Galerius was afraid of him as a dangerous rival. So the Emperor kept the young man in his own grasp in the East, ready to destroy him if anything happened.

Constantius, the Augustus in Gaul, was anxious for his son, kept so far off in the power of a rival. He sent message after message to Galerius, asking that Constantine might come to Gaul to visit his father. At last Galerius had to comply, for he was afraid of the armies.

Constantine was at this time in Nicomedia, just in Asia Minor, attending Galerius in the palace there. As soon as the young man received permission to go to Gaul, he made swift preparations. He left Nicomedia secretly the same night, and galloped along the road, from post-house to post-house, to the Bosphorus. There he was rowed over into Europe, and taking horse at the post again in Byzantium, he galloped northwards, travelling swiftly every day, taking a new horse at the post-house when the one he rode was tired, and thus journeying too quickly for any officer of Galerius to overtake him.

The emperor of the northern half of the empire was at Boulogne, ready to embark for an expedition against the Caledonians of Scotland. The troops of Gaul shouted with pleasure when Constantine galloped up and kissed his father.

Father and son passed into Britain, and the Caledonians were soon quieted. But it was the last expedition of Constantius. He died at York, begging his son to take care of the empire, and of the little children, his half-brothers and sisters.

The troops lamented their emperor, and felt the same dismay that troops always experience when they are left without a leader. The flower of the armies of Gaul had followed Constantius into Britain. They began to shout for Constantine.

But Constantine carefully kept himself out of sight of the troops, lest they should suddenly hail him Caesar

Augustus, and should force him to take the purple. He must be careful, for if anything unusual happened, the Emperor Galerius would denounce him as a rebel and a usurper, and rouse all the armies against him.

The officers, however, were all friends to Constantine. They addressed the legions, asking them, would they tamely wait till some stranger was sent by Galerius from the east, to take command, or would they choose the honour of placing at their head the son of their late beloved emperor. The troops as one man chose Constantine. He, however, still delayed, till he had written a letter telling Galerius the whole state of affairs. And then, at York, Constantine was clothed with the purple robe of the Augustus, and with the purple buskins. This sacred purple of the Romans was what we should call deep, rich crimson, it was not violet. No man might wear it but Caesar.

Galerius was furious when he heard what had happened, for he wanted to be sole emperor. But he was afraid of the northern army. He sent his royal messenger to Constantine, with an imperial mandate, allowing the young man to take command of the troops of Gaul, but forbidding him to take the title of Caesar.

To this Constantine and his soldiers would not agree. War followed. Different Caesars were raised up by different armies, till at one time six emperors were reigning in the empire, of whom Constantine and Galerius were only two. However, Constantine marched with a small but experienced army over the Alps, and defeated a great host in North Italy. He had now the chance of marching on Rome. The Aemilian and Flaminian roads stretched before him, from Milan running south. But he had not yet defeated all his enemies.

At last, the armies in Italy were all broken. In 312 Constantine came to Rome, the great mother-city, and was hailed as emperor. To make friends for himself, he wisely pronounced an act of oblivion, stating that all the deeds of enmity committed by the Romans against him in the past should be considered as forgotten, buried in oblivion. This reassured many frightened people, who fully expected to lose their lives for having sided against the conqueror, and it brought many to his side. He then destroyed the Praetorian Camp, the stronghold of hostile and insolent Roman guards. He also issued an edict of religious toleration, in 313, which allowed all Romans to worship as they pleased. This was a great boon to the trembling Christians.

There were still hostile armies, however. It was necessary to march against the troops of Licinius, on the Danube, then down from the Danube to the Bosphorus. There Constantine besieged the gate-town of Byzantium, a strong fortification. Licinius fled into Asia. Constantine pursued him, defeated him, and at last executed him in Nicomedia.

Thus, in 325, Constantine became master of the world. In the same year he issued letters exhorting his subjects to accept Christianity. But he allowed freedom of worship to all.

Constantine felt himself to be not only the master of the empire, but the founder of a new era : which, indeed, he was. With Constantine the old pagan Rome comes to an end. A new world was to begin, and Constantine wished to give it its new centre. He disliked Rome, the old, terrible mistress of the past. She was too much stained with blood and violence. The Capitol, the very centre of the old world, was crowned with the temples of the old gods, and these old gods could not soon be forgotten. Their spirit filled the old city. Then, too, there had been so much strife, so much violence, so much cruelty and splendour in the Eternal City by the Tiber, the City on the Seven Hills.

The later emperors nearly all disliked Rome. They were strangers, born far off. They depended on far-off armies. They found the Romans conceited and impudent and troublesome. Diocletian would not live in the capital. He preferred even Milan. And he loved Nicomedia, just in Asia. He retired away into Dalmatia, near the further coasts of the Adriatic, to die.

Constantine determined to build a new capital, so that he need not trouble about Rome any more. He wanted a city of his own, where a new life should begin, more peaceful, more congenial, less masterful. So he cast round in his mind for a site. It delighted him to think of raising his own new bright city. He knew the empire from end to end. And he chose Byzantium, at the gate of Europe and Asia, on the Bosphorus.

Constantine said that when he was besieging Byzantium, in the war against Licinius, he had dreamed a curious dream. An old woman came to him and stood by his side. He turned and looked at her, wondering who she was, when suddenly, under his gaze, she was transformed into a young, lovely girl, and he found himself placing the tiara of royalty on her head.

This dream he took to be a sign that the old Greek fortress-town of Byzantium should become a lovely and imperial city at his hands. He told the dream to his attendants. And he went out on the hills to look.

He looked towards Asia, and saw himself almost surrounded by waters. In front of him, looking east, the land narrowed to a blunt point, past which ran the swift blue waters of the Bosphorus, pouring rapidly through winding straits from the Black Sea into the Sea of Marmora, towards the Mediterranean. On his right-hand side, southwards, lay the waters of the Sea of Marmora, then called the Propontis, washing the sunny foot of the land ; and on his left-hand side, a mile or two away, like a wide river, curved the beautiful inlet from the Bosphorus, now called the Golden Horn, the harbour to the town, shining and clear, receiving a little river from the hills. In the harbour lay the winged ships, near the steep walls of the fortified Byzantium. And far off to the south he could see broad, dark, and white, and ruddy sails winging away to the Isles of Greece, across the space of the Propontis, whilst down the blue, winding waters in front of him to the north, came ships from the Black Sea, with corn from the Danube.

Behind him lay Europe, unseen. At his feet lay the hills and orchards and field patches, surrounding the little fortress-town, that held the ships to its side. Everywhere temples and shrines rose from the trees by the sea. And across, shining gold in the afternoon light, were the slopes of Asia, the pillared temples among the trees, the white, glittering walls of the opposite port, the white roads winding away among the olive-trees and vineyards, and past the corn of the valleys, on towards Nicomedia, to Ephesus, to Antioch, to Jerusalem. That was the East, where Jesus was born, the East, that loves to be still and dreamy, dreaming of the past. There was a grey dimness of olive trees, and a glitter of white and pink villas, a golden soil, faint tufts of palm-trees, dark groves of orange and lemon and myrtle.

Here Constantine determined to build his city, the centre of the new world, looking to Asia. He was getting old. This was the year 326, and he was born in 272. He had spent his life in the camp, and in moving from province to province. Now he would make a new centre for a new world, and have peace.

Constantine appointed a day for tracing the boundaries of the city. On two sides were the arms of the sea, enclosing the wide, blunt angle of the land. Clothed in the purple, with a lance in his hand, and at the head of a glittering throng, Constantine set out to trace the third side, the base of this wide triangle. He moved slowly forward, drawing the line with his lance. Attendants followed, surveyors, taking accurate mark. Then came the great throng of courtiers and people and soldiers, for it was high holiday. On and on went Constantine, past fields and orchards and vineyards, olive woods, and groves of laurel and pine, over little brooks and up the hillside. The people followed slowly, amazed at the immense space Constantine was enclosing. They murmured among themselves, and at last one ventured to remark that already the Emperor had enclosed more space than was necessary for the most ample city. ' I shall go on,' replied Constantine, ' till He, the invisible Guide, who marches before me, thinks proper to stop.' Thus he continued towards the sea again, enclosing five hills within his line.

And now, immediately, the great work began. Millions of slaves were at work. In the little isle of Proconessus blocks of white marble stood by the shore, the boats deep in the water with their heavy white cargo steered away to the Golden Horn, to the quays of the town, whilst from the North came the timber boats of the Black Sea. There was a great smoke of kilns burning lime for the mortar, and a great sound of thousands of slaves digging, carrying, levelling. Surveyors and architects moved here and there, the builders worked quickly, served by slaves. And the Emperor, in person, wearing his imperial cloak of deep crimson, went to the harbour to see the ships unlade, thousands of men heaving and hauling, or to the hills to see the foundations dug, or to the level places to see the first streets laid out, or to the river to see the aqueduct begun, or to the outskirts to see the deep foss dug out for the city walls. Ship after ship came from Africa with corn, from the isles with grapes and cattle, from Asia with fruits and oil. There were great kitchens, great meals of thousands of busy, excited workmen and women.

The great walls, with their gates, began slowly to rise. On the second hill, where Constantine had pitched his tent outside Byzantium, in the siege, there the chief Forum or market-place was laid out, a vast oval. He longed to see the two great arches, at the opposite ends of the oval space, rise up and be finished in their magnificence, to see the lovely pillared porticoes complete round about the open, elliptical market-place. Then came slow wagons toiling with mysterious heavy objects carefully packed and wrapped in cloths. These were unpacked, and proved to be lovely statues, brought from old Greece or from Asia to set in the porticoes. But most wonderful of all, a sight that thrilled Constantine, was the scaffolding in the centre of this great, grand, elliptical space. There the poles and pulleys rose to a great height, there were masses of slaves and oxen and ropes. And at last, when all the scaffolding was taken away, there stood a huge and lofty naked column, of marble and porphyry, rising a hundred and twenty feet from the ground, and bearing aloft the colossal bronze statue of Apollo, magnificent work of the old, dead masters of Greece.

So the town grew—great circuses, churches, baths, and palaces, marble and sumptuous. Streets were made, with big buildings where the poor would live, each family in one or two rooms. There were open places with fountains, and beautiful gardens with palm-trees, and fine streets leading down to the sea. Unfortunately, such quick building was not very sound, and in a few years' time several palaces began to fall. But still, it all seemed splendid.

Then, as things began to be ready, Constantine invited rich Roman senators and citizens from the cities of Europe and Asia and Africa, to come and take up their abode in the new palaces. They had to come, at the Emperor's bidding. They arrived by sea and land, huge trains of slaves and servants, ox-wagons, mules and horses laden with goods. Soon the town was full. The narrow streets were thronged with crowds of people, carriages, horses, mules, litters—there was hardly room to pass. Constantine gave away great quantities of food—African corn and Syrian oil and wine. There was a great profusion and plenty. There were splendid processions, and displays in the circus and theatre. Thousands of people enjoyed the pleasure of a new home, in a new, sunny, lovely climate by the sea, the beginning of a new life.

This removal of the centre of the civilised world, from
West to East, from Rome to Constantinople, took place
about the year 334.   It was the end of the old Rome, and
the beginning of Europe.   The Byzantine Empire belongs
to the East rather than to Europe.   Constantinople looks
to Asia.   Europe was left alone, confused, violent, turbulent, disordered, to face the darkness of her Middle
Ages.   The real light of culture and civilisation was withdrawn, lapsing back to the East.   The West would have
to struggle through a long obscure twilight, into her own
day, the day of modern Europe.

Rome, the city, lost her power.   Later she became the
home of the popes, but her empire was really over.   Till
after the conquest of the Goths there continued a shaky
Roman Empire of the West.   But it was an empire which
could only tumble into nothingness.

The Byzantine Empire continued in Constantinople,
however, right into the fifteenth century.   It is curious
that, though it was a purely Christian state, yet Constantine had really established an oriental form of government.   The Emperor was a Christian, yet he accounted
himself *divine*, and supreme above all men.   He was as
absolute as any Persian tyrant, for he was beyond all laws
and all criticism.   The people, the state, were at his mercy.
And so they continued for a thousand years.   This was
the way of life the Byzantines preferred.   It was a curious
form of oriental Christianity, all the pride and glory
centring in one man, himself a servant of Jesus.   This
eastern form of Christianity spread to Russia, where the
orthodox Church is the Greek Church.   The Greek Church
is the Church of Constantinople, for very soon Greek was
the language of Constantinople, of emperors and people
alike.   And this Greek Church keeps much of the mystery
of eastern religion, it seems to teach that strange, passionate
humility which makes a people prostrate itself before an
emperor as before a beautiful god, so that millions willingly
leave their lives in the hands of one man.   Contrasting

with this, there is a savage ferocity which hates the thing or being it has so humbly adored.

So the empire of Constantinople, called the Byzantine Empire, continued for a thousand years after the death of Constantine the Great. Its people were alternately humble to baseness, and inhumanly ferocious, until they were finally destroyed by the Turks in 1453.

III. Christianity

THE Greeks and Romans were pagans. They had many gods—gods of war, of harvest, of health, of marriage, of family, of the hearth and threshold, of the grove and fount and the sea. Everything that was wonderful or important or special had its presiding deity. The mystery of the passion of war was represented in the god Mars, the mystery of the deep, active sea was embodied in the god Neptune. To all the great gods temples were built, beautiful buildings of marble, with pillared fronts, and interiors decorated with carving and with statues, with gold and silver and ivory. There was always the altar, where the fire burned, and sacrifice was offered. Often there was a figure or statue of the god of the temple, sometimes exposed, sometimes veiled. The hill of temples in Rome was the Capitol. Here, on the Capitoline Hill, was the temple of Capitoline Jove, the greatest of the Roman gods. But the lesser gods had simple shrines, perhaps just a niche in the rock by a stream, or a plain altar among the trees of a grove.

There were really no settled priests in the pagan world. Some influential man in the neighbourhood was given the charge of a temple or sacred building, which he often had to take care of at his own expense. He had also to perform the sacred rites, as we nowadays get an important personage to perform the rite of laying a foundation-stone. Some very rich man was usually given the responsibility for the great games—which often cost him large sums of money—so there was no sacred profession, no special beings were set apart, like our clergy. All were men alike, none was more sacred than another. The richest and most important man in any district usually was responsible for the temple, that was all. There were certain *servants* of the temple, who attended to funerals and so on. But these were not priests—they were just servants of a different sort.

Thus there was no preaching, no praying, no talk about sin or salvation, no service at all. The people just came to the temple by themselves; or on special days they came to see the rites performed, the sacrifices offered, the acts of the ritual gone through. After the sacrifice the officiating priests — priests for the moment — might sprinkle the crowds with water, or the blood of the offerings, as a sign of purification. And then there was usually dancing and festivity, or perhaps public mourning. On feast days the people were crowned with flowers, or with leaves, or with ears of corn, according to the god of the day. People just cast a few grains of incense on the fire, in token of offering. And on certain days they made gay processions, the dancers going in front, dancing for the gods. And of course the great games were an offering to the gods also; there was a special ritual sacrifice and special songs were sung. But it was all part of the active, actual, everyday, normal life—not something apart. In the country the peasant people loved to take flowers, or a little cake, or a gift, to the shrine of some nymph by the fountain, to the god Pan among the trees, to Priapus in the orchard, to some fauns or nymphs in a cave. There would perhaps be a statue of Pan, with a stone altar; perhaps only an altar; perhaps a mere stone; or simply a tree or grove or spring of water; and offerings would be hung on the trees or laid on the rocks around. But there was no priest. It simply pleased the people to visit these little sacred places, and sometimes to make processions through the fields, the women carrying garlands and corn, one leading the kid that would be sacrificed, the boys playing on flutes or whistles, and dancing in front. Then when they came to the sacred place they imagined a god or nymph was hidden there, inside the trees or deep in the running spring. So they offered gifts and made little songs or speeches or dances to the hidden deity.

Since everything that was wonderful had its god, the Greeks and Romans were not jealous of strange gods. Rather they were anxious to sacrifice on the altars of strange gods also, for this would bring an added blessing. They would leave out no deity if they could help it. St. Paul tells how he saw an altar in Athens inscribed to the Unknown God. This was so that no god, lacking an altar, should in anger take revenge on the remiss men of the town. The Romans did not hate the Ephesian Diana, the Asiatic many-breasted mother, or the bull-slaying Persian sun god. They even welcomed them to Rome, these strange deities, and built them new temples.

But, if they freely respected all gods, they expected the same free reverence for their own shrines from all strangers. If the Romans exterminated the Druids of Gaul, it was because the Druids were a curious, special priesthood, who inflamed the people to rebellion, not because of their worship. The Romans, indeed, never understood the worship of the Druids, which was a worship of the mysterious tree of life, the dark, inhuman mysteries of the beginning of creation. The Romans could only understand human things. They could not comprehend the Druid inhuman creed, and they were filled with vague horror. They disliked the secret, powerful priests, who had such power over the people. In their own pagan world it was different. If there were priests in Egypt or Syria, they were no longer very important. There was an amiable equality between diverse gods. Only the Druids were a hostile priesthood. And only the God of the Jews was a jealous God. Only the Jews showed their hatred and horror of the free-and-easy pagan worship. Augustus very politely gave orders and gifts to have sacrifices made in the temple of Jerusalem to Jehovah, that Jehovah might not forget him, Augustus Cæsar. This was very flattering to the Jews, to think that the Roman emperor acknowledged their God. None the less they scorned even Augustus for worshipping his own great Jove on the Capitol of Rome. They thought even Augustus an abomination, an idolater, one not fit to live in the sight of Jehovah. Continually, when in Palestine the Romans celebrated the festivals of their own gods, the Jews, looking on with black hatred and horror, could not refrain from breaking out into fury, trying to stone to death these hated idolaters and their idols. It inflamed the Jews to such fury, to see the temples and shrines of the strange gods in their land, and to see the Roman processions, with their flute-playing and their garlands and their dancers and their dressing-up, moving in the streets of Jerusalem, that they rose again and again, great crowds of Jews killing the surprised Romans, and breaking the altars. When Caligula tried to put his statue in the Temple of Jerusalem, the Jews turned as one man, and it was taken away by the wise Roman governors. But while ever there were idols in Zion, no Jew could rest, insurrections were continual.

The Romans at first were puzzled. Why should not all gods be polite and respectful to one another, as civilised men are polite and respectful to each other, they wondered ? But at length they were irritated, and finally infuriated against these uncouth, jealous, vindictive Jews, who were so unreasonable in their hatred. Why should this stubborn and fanatic people disturb the world with their hatred ? the Romans asked themselves.

At last there was a general rising, and the Roman government had to fight for its own existence in the land of Israel. When Vespasian was emperor, Titus, his son, besieged Jerusalem. The rebellious Jews made the most obstinate resistance. The Romans, however, took the town and killed the people in front of them. The streets were heaped with dead Jews. But the last defenders were

still at bay, in the Temple precincts. After terrible fighting,
the defenders saw that the Holy of Holies must be taken.
So the Jews themselves set fire to the great Temple, to
prevent its falling into the hands of the enemy, and heaps
of the faithful defenders preferred to die in the flames,
rather than by the swords of the Romans. The Temple
burned furiously, a great conflagration. Yet the Romans
got much treasure, and holy relics like the Ark, the seven-
branched candlesticks, the sacred vessels. And these
they took to Rome to adorn the triumph of Titus. Away
there in Rome the citizens were not much impressed by
these most holy relics of the Jews. But they had satisfaction in seeing them, for already the Jews were beginning
to be detested, because of their fanatical pride, the pride
of the Chosen People.

The burning of the Temple took place in the year 70 A.D.,
forty years or so after the death of Christ. There were at
this time already many Christians, most of whom, naturally,
were Jews of Jerusalem. They were called Nazarenes.
They did not cease from their old religion when they
accepted Christ. They still went to the Temple, and took
their children as Jesus was taken, to be circumcised ; went,
as Joseph and Mary went, to the holy feast of the Passover ;
they observed the Jewish Sabbath, and the Jewish rites,
eating no unclean meat, such as we now eat. They were
Jews who believed also in Jesus.

These Nazarenes founded the first Christian congregation, which is called the Church of Jerusalem. Their first
fifteen bishops were circumcised Jews. Thus the Romans,
who did not care about details of religious belief, knew no
difference between Christians and Jews, in Jerusalem. At
the same time, in the great cities Antioch and Ephesus in
Syria, Alexandria in Egypt, Corinth in Greece, even in
Rome, Christianity was quietly spreading among Gentiles
who did *not* keep the feast of the Passover, or any of the
Jewish observances. So that already, before the fall of
Jerusalem, there were two kinds of Christians : Nazarenes,

or judaising Christians, and gentile Christians. There was the Nazarene Church of Jerusalem, and there were the gentile Churches of Antioch, Ephesus, and so on.

When the Temple was destroyed, and Jerusalem ruined, the poor Nazarenes were desolate. They retired away beyond Jordan to the little town of Pella, and there they remained, lonely and disconsolate. But still they could make many comforting visits to the Holy City, returning at the appointed times. For they had a passion for their old observances, their old solemn feasts. They longed for the day when the Temple would be re-built, and Jerusalem restored as it was before. They were still the chosen people, more important than any one in the world, according to their own idea; and now most important even among Jews, since they had their Messiah.

Again, however, in the time of the Emperor Hadrian, about fifty years after the fall of Jerusalem, the Jews rose once more in a terrible rebellion, all over Palestine. A new town had been re-built in place of the destroyed Jerusalem. The Romans gave it the new name of Aelia Capitolina. And on Mount Moriah they erected a temple to the Roman Jupiter. This last offence caused the last, fatal insurrection of all the Jews.

Hadrian was merciless this time. His soldiers fought, and spared none. They took towns and villages, and reduced them to ashes. It is said that about 600,000 Jews were destroyed, and a thousand towns and villages. For now the Roman hatred of Jews was confirmed.

Hadrian built up Jerusalem this time as a purely Roman city. The very name of Jerusalem was abolished, and that of Aelia put in its place—just as St. Petersburg has become Petrograd. Moreover, no Jew was allowed even to approach within sight of the town. Hadrian's soldiers kept strict watch, and any native found creeping back to the passionately-loved hills of the Holy City, now crowned with Roman temples, was either hanged or crucified or otherwise severely punished.

So, the Jewish nation was broken and scattered—and for ever ; thrown out into the world, where for more than a thousand years it still refused to mix with the world.

The Nazarenes at Pella were heart-broken by this new disaster. They felt they were not Jews in religion. Yet they must suffer. They at last took the only wise course. They chose a Latin bishop, Marcus, a Gentile. And Marcus gradually persuaded the congregation to renounce the Mosaic law. This they did, reluctantly. But once it was done, they were free from the taint of Judaism. They appealed to the Romans, saying that they were not Jews at all any more, but Gentile Christians. And finally, the Romans allowed them to return to Aelia. For it was recognised that a Jew was not a Jew because of his nation, but because of his religion. Nationality or citizenship or race made a Greek or a Roman or a Gaul. But religion made a Jew. So that when the Nazarenes abandoned the Judaic religion, they ceased to be Jews. In a little while they were permitted to restore the old-time name to Jerusalem. But the Temple was no more re-built, Zion which kept the Feast of the Passover did not exist any more. And bitterly did the true Jews now hate the Christian Jews, traitors to the old faith.

Thus Christianity became a Gentile religion. It spread rapidly in the Roman Empire. Almost everybody in the Eastern Empire spoke Greek, many spoke Latin also : in the West Latin was spoken. Preachers and teachers went everywhere, speaking Greek in Asia, Latin in Italy, and telling that there was but one God, whose Son was Jesus ; telling that through *love* men should have everlasting life, in immortal happiness. They had to go quietly, secretly, for they had many enemies, the bitterest being Jews. But they found many hearers ; particularly many Roman soldiers and officers listened closely. For soldiers have time to think.

Now, in a world weary of strife and excitement, and clogged with slavery, the thought of peace and innocent love, and of a life of still, gentle, everlasting happiness, was most beautiful. So many people in the world of that day were weary of the continual fighting, the continual excitement of wild combats in the circuses, wild or pompous displays, and the stifling physical luxury of the daily warm baths, the daily feasts, or long evening banquets which lasted from afternoon till sleeping-time, a long meal of talking and eating and drinking wine, and telling stories or reciting poems. For the well-to-do people it was a life all of one sort, stifling. And for the slaves it was a life of ignominy. On both hands, men were tired.

What could a slave want more than to be told that in the sight of God all men were equal, were brothers : and that all those who believed in Jesus would spend eternity with the Son of God, in continual happiness ? And what could the tired, satiated soldiers and citizens of Rome want more than to realise that this fighting, this feasting, this excitement, this continual warm luxury of baths, was nothing but a clog on the spirit : that the spirit of Jesus did away with all this barrenness, and left men free from bodily necessities, unhampered as the angels or the beams of the sun, eternal as these ?

Gradually, these beliefs became enlarged. The Christian Romans turned with dislike from the theatres and circuses and baths. They disliked physical luxury, all the plea-sures of the body became hateful to them, for they had had too much of such gratification. Their spirits wanted to be free, infinite, their bodies were a drag and a burden. So they kept strictly away from the temples, the feasts, the games ; they were quiet and inspired with holy, spiritual desires. They began to dream of the Second Coming of Christ, which was prophesied, and regarded as near at hand. Christ would come soon, and destroy the kingdom of the world, and make the kingdom of bliss on earth. The Judgment Day was near at hand, and after that, the Millennium, the era of bliss, when men would walk the shining streets of the new city, here on earth, at peace and

in shining concord with all men. Every one would be good
and pure. When these happy days should come, there
would be no more luxurious feeding and drinking and
dressing, and no fighting and no hard work. All would
wear pure white, none would need more than a little pure
food and drink, there would be no rich, no poor, no hungry
people and none greedy. There would be sufficient of all
things for all, and men and women, shining and beautiful
in their clean clothes, would walk the streets of the New
Jerusalem, the New Rome, bright as flowers, blissful in
the bliss of love, speaking gently, and coming to the
throne of Jesus to sit near Him. For Jesus would reign
like a Caesar, all majesty and love.

All Christians believed in this Millennium—but for the
slaves it was pure transportation. Then, *they too* would
walk the streets of gold, and sit with the King of Kings :
they too would wear pure white robes, and Jesus would
love them even more than the rest, because they had been
despised and oppressed on earth.

It was calculated when the Second Coming would take
place. The Six Days of Creation, when God made the
world, were taken to mean six thousand years. On the
seventh day the Lord rested—and He blessed that day.
Therefore when the seventh thousand of years should
approach, the Lord would look at His works, judge them,
and prepare for the Millennium of rest and blessedness.
Now the primitive Church at Antioch calculated that
from the days of Adam to their own day, that is, to the
year 100 or 150 A.D., would be just 6000 years. Therefore
the Second Coming must be at hand. Jesus Himself had
spoken of it, St. Paul had warned them.

These early Christians went in daily expectation of the
terrible event. They had been told that famine and
earthquake would precede the Second Advent, and that
fire would fall from heaven. Famine and pestilence came,
as well as earthquakes. In Vespasian's reign a great fire,
that raged for three days, again gutted a large part of

Rome. And then, in the year 79 came the terrible eruption of Vesuvius which buried Pompeii, Herculaneum and Stabiae in a rain of fire and lava and ash. Clearly these were the signs of the Second Coming, when Christ would judge the world.

The Christians trembled, and purified themselves. Their lives were rigidly holy. As darkness fell, at evening, they quivered, thinking that perhaps that night the heavens would break, and Christ with His angels and prophets would appear, summoning all men alike to His footstool. The slaves, as they silently submitted to their masters, and the poor men, as they saw the Roman ladies borne through the streets in golden litters, thought to themselves : ' Ah, if they but knew, these proud and vainglorious Romans ! If they but knew the sword that even now is unsheathed in the sky, ready to strike ! If they could know, how, in a short time, a short time now, they will be cast down into eternal punishment. Their Rome will be wiped out, and I shall be walking the bright streets of glass in the New Jerusalem, the New Rome, with the Saviour, the King of Kings. He who is greater than any Caesar is coming down upon Rome—ah, if they knew this, they would change their behaviour. They would cease to command so proudly, they would get down from their litters . . .'

The Romans could feel some secret working against them. They could feel, as it were, a silent threat in these people who were so quiet and humble and mysterious. They tried to fathom the mystery, but could not. For the Romans knew nothing about Christians, they thought them just a sect of the detested Jews.

It is surprising how little the Romans knew about the new religion. A famous man, named Pliny, was sent to be governor of Bithynia in the year 111. There, some men were brought before him, charged with the crime of being Christians. But Pliny knew nothing about the sect nor the crime. He had heard the name of Christians

merely—but what were they ?   And how was he to proceed against criminals whose crime he did not in the least
understand ?

He made a careful examination of the Christians, and
sent to his friend and master, the Emperor Trajan, a
curious account of the new sect.   Pliny was in some ways
very favourable to the Christians.   He disliked, with
true Roman fairness, to prosecute people whose guilt he
could not perceive.   Yet he lamented that the temples
in Bithynia were almost deserted, and that the sacred
victims, birds, kids, found hardly any purchasers, and
that even the ignorant country people were infected with
the new superstition.   Bithynia was the province just
across from Constantinople, in Asia, along the shores of
the Black Sea.   It is evident there were more Christians
there than in Rome.

Now Pliny was a great and famous man, and a lawyer.
He must have known about the trials of all the criminals
in Rome.   He must have known the proceedings of all
the more important cases.   Yet it is quite evident he
knew nothing of Christianity when he went to Bithynia,
and that he had before him no laws, and no previous cases
against Christians, to guide him.   He was quite at a loss.
And he showed no dislike of the new people : it only
troubled him that they refused to be Romans as well as
Christians.

This shows us that the educated Romans were ignorant
of what the Christians were ; that there cannot have been
any real legal prosecution ; and that the Church in Rome
either was not very large, or was very secret, or did not
extend into the upper classes, at the end of the first
century.   We are forced to think that the early Christians,
from the days of Paul, were very secret, like a secret
society, very cautious in revealing their mysteries : particularly that mystery of the Second Coming.

The Romans must have *heard* of the Christians, because
of the famous prosecution under Nero, in the year 64.

Now just at the time that Pliny went to Bithynia, Tacitus the Roman was writing his famous history. This was some forty years after the fire of Rome, which, as we know, Nero is suspected of causing, in order to enjoy the spectacle. Tacitus writes that Nero wanted to find some people on whom to lay the blame of this great fire : ' Consequently, to get rid of the report, Nero fastened the guilt on a class hated for their abominations, called Christians by the common people. Christus, from whom the name had its origin, suffered the extreme penalty during the reign of Tiberius at the hands of one of our procurators, Pontius Pilatus, and a most mischievous superstition, thus checked for a moment, again broke out, not only in Judaea, but even in Rome, where all things hideous and shameful from every part of the world find their centre and become popular. Accordingly, an arrest was first made of all who pleaded guilty ; then, upon their information, an immense multitude was convicted, not so much of the crime of firing the city, as of hatred against mankind. Mockery of every sort was added to their deaths. Covered with the skins of beasts, they were torn by dogs, and perished ; or they were nailed on crosses ; or they were doomed to the flames, and burnt, to serve as a nightly illumination, when daylight had expired.

' Nero offered his garden for the spectacle, while he mingled with the people in the dress of a charioteer, or stood aloft on a car. The guilt of the Christians deserved, indeed, the most extreme punishment, but there arose a feeling of compassion in the people ; for it was not, as it seemed, for the public good that they were sacrificed, but to glut one man's cruelty.'

This is all Tacitus says about the Christians : and it is probably all he knew. Pliny seems to have known no more. Yet why should Nero suddenly have fallen on these obscure people ? We cannot say. Only we do know that the Christians were confused with the Jews ; that the Romans truly believed the Jews hated mankind ;

and that Nero hated the Jews. But Poppaea, Nero's favourite wife, was a Jewess, and his favourite player was a Jew. And the Jews have always been accused of betraying the Christians, when they themselves were in danger. For of all their enemies, the Jews hated the Christians most. So perhaps it was suggested to Nero that certain persons, Christians, were the vilest and most evil of all Jewish sectaries.

However that may be, it is certain that a terrible fate befell these poor Christians. But we may be almost as certain that the persecution was as short as it was sharp and sudden. Nero had probably forgotten in a month's time that there were such people as Christians.

We see, however, both from Tacitus and Pliny, that there was current a vague but deep hatred of the Christians. Why should Tacitus think that the guilt of the poor creatures deserved the most extreme punishment ? What was the guilt ? All he says, is that they are convicted of *hating mankind*.

Now we can understand how the Romans came to imagine that the Christians hated mankind. In the first place, they considered the Christians were simply a set of Jews, and the Jews, the Chosen People, really did hate or despise all who were not of their own race. And then the Romans believed, above all, in the social, public life—men living usefully and openly together ; and the Christians shunned the social and public life of the Roman world. The Roman was interested most of all in the State, in the affairs of the empire. The Christians turned darkly away from such affairs, and would have nothing to do with them. They were a secret people. They held their meetings at night, in underground places. But this was probably because the poorer Christians, such as slaves, were only free at night ; and also because the congregations could not meet without being disturbed, save in some remote place, such as the catacombs.

The Romans detested secrecy, and at once suspected

evil. No matter how a Roman came unawares on these Christian meetings, he could never find an idol or a statue, no sign of a god, no sacred ornaments, no ritual going on, no altar with its fire, no sacrificial objects. The places of worship were bare. And therefore, said the Romans, the Christians must be devilishly cunning. They hid all their objects of worship. They had horrible secret rites. The tale went round, how a convert when he joined the Christian community was taken into a dark room, and given a knife, and made to strike : and how, under the heap of flour which he struck, was a hidden babe, on whose blood he was made to swear to keep secrets—and so on. These are tales which men always make up out of darkness and ignorance.

The vulgar populace of Rome hated the Christians, because they could feel the strange exulting secret of the Second Coming burning in Christian breasts. They hated them also because this secret people would not mix in with the rest. But the Christians could not mix in with the rest. Religion in those days was not a private matter that concerned a man's private soul only. It was part of every act of public life. If a man went out to dinner, he must spill wine to the gods, and call on the deities of the house, and the deities of hospitality, to witness his service and his thanks. If a family moved to a new house, the house must be devoted to the family gods, and blessed, with a whole festival and a sacred ritual. At a wedding, a funeral, a christening, the gods were supposed to be present, men made sacrifice and wore special emblems. On certain days, all doorways must be decked with laurel, men must all wear crowns of leaves. On other days, processions with dancing passed through the streets. The great games were dedicated to the gods. Men attended the altars beforehand, brought offerings or threw sweet incense on the fire, and were sprinkled with holy water or blood of victims.

From all these things the Christians kept gloomily

apart, afraid to offend their own God. They could not
go to the houses of their pagan friends and relatives, nor
to a wedding or funeral, nor to any festival, nor to the
games. They could hardly walk in the streets without
being required to pay some attention to some pagan god,
throw incense on some altar. They kept gloomily and
unsociably apart, they looked upon the great show of
Roman daily life with dark eyes of reproach and fore-
boding. This gradually infuriated the sociable Romans,
who lived all their life out of doors, in the porticoes of the
Forum, in the baths, in the streets—or, at evening, sociably
reclining round the table.

Yet the Christians were bound to keep apart. They
had a curious belief that the Roman gods were really
powerful demons. When Lucifer, or Satan, the bright
angel, rebelled against God, and was cast out with all his
rebellious host, he fell down to earth and to hell. But he
had the power of appearing in disguise to the souls of men.
Thus it was the great angelic demon, Lucifer, who appeared
to the Greeks or Romans as the great god, the Jupiter or
Jove of the Capitol. Jupiter was not a mere nothing.
He was Satan himself, terribly powerful, whom the Romans
worshipped. And it was Satan, under the name of Jupiter,
who had given the Romans their terrible, but evil power
over the world. And Satan possessed the soul of every
Roman who worshipped him, or who worshipped any
other of the great powerful demons, under any name—
Venus, or Mars, or Neptune, or Pan, or Priapus.

So the Christians believed. And they were terribly
afraid of putting their souls into the power of these living
demons, the pagan gods. Men used to swear then, more
solemnly than they swear now, by the name of Jupiter, or
Jove. If a Christian caught himself saying, in the common
fashion, ' By Jove ! ' then he must stop himself, and pray
to Jesus to save him from this same terrible Jove. The
Romans said, ' Jupiter bless you ' quite commonly. But
if a pagan said it to a Christian friend, the Christian must

lift his hand to ward off the evil influence, and protest that Jupiter was *not* God.

Thus naturally there grew up in Rome a great dislike of these quiet, silent Christians, with their distant manners and humble bearing and their patient looks of reproach, and their air of secret power. And the Christians became more secret. They had various signs, amongst themselves, whereby they knew one another. If a Christian were talking with another Roman, of whom he was not sure, he might carelessly, as if unheeding, draw the shape of a fish in the dust with his toe. Then he would wait to see if the other noticed. If not, the Christian would smear out the sign. For the fish was the symbol of Jesus.

Secrecy grew on the one hand, hatred on the other. It was the vulgar crowds who hated the Christians most. And the greatest troubles came when the greatest crowds gathered together. If the Christians were timid, they trembled as the days of the great games approached. If they were fervent and fanatic, they looked forward to a chance of martyrdom. For on these days the great mob of citizens, after serving at the altars, and being inflamed with wine, would remember the silent mystery and threat of the absent Christians. For the Christians taught that men should turn away from the world, particularly the world of Rome ; and this maddened the Romans. If there had been a flood, or an earthquake, or a famine some one would suggest that the Christians had caused it by their secret magic. Then up would go the great howl of a mob, a vast herd of vulgar people—' The Christians—the Christians—to the lions with the evil-working Christians ! ' In this torrent of vulgar frenzy the governors were helpless, and many Christians were martyred.

The Roman government almost always tried to be just. But even the magistrates disliked the Christians, not for their crimes, but for their opposition to the government. The will of the father was sacred in Rome—all authority was established upon it. But if a father bade a

Christian son or daughter attend any pagan festival, the youth or maiden quietly refused, which horrified the Romans. If a master bade his Christian slave attend him to the temple, the slave refused. The Christians would take no part in the government whatsoever. Even the soldiers threw away their arms, even officers threw away their swords and helmets, and loudly declared they would serve no pagan master whose soul was destined for hell, but only Christ the Lord. Such soldiers were promptly tried by martial law, and executed—as they would be to-day. But the pagan Romans were shocked. The magistrates felt that a great secret body of people was working to undermine the State altogether, and bring it down in ruin. They felt the danger. And, of course, it was a real danger. For surely it was the Christian religion finally which brought down the great pagan world into nothingness.

Still the magistrates and governors wanted to be fair. It was the people themselves who were violent and base— the great mob. When Pliny asked the Emperor Trajan how he should proceed, Trajan made these two wise conditions concerning the prosecution of Christians : first, that there should be no search or inquiry made about any citizen, to find out whether he were guilty of the crime of Christianity ; and secondly, any person who accused another man of this crime falsely, should pay a heavy forfeit. So that, as far as the government went, the Christians were fairly safe. And again, the magistrates did not *want* to punish. They admitted that the lives of Christians were blameless, as far as could be proved. Later, they admired the charity of the sect, their care of the poor and helpless. They only wanted the Christians not to persevere in *opposing* the great Roman State. If they could only persuade a Christian prisoner to cast a few grains of incense on the altar of one of the gods, as a sign of respect for the old gods, and for the great State these gods represented, then the magistrates dismissed the accused man with praise. But alas! the Christians often preferred martyrdom—nay, they even *claimed* the honour of martyrdom, which would raise them up to be saints in glory. And this astonished and repelled the pagan magistrates, who could not understand, and who detested, such an attitude.

As the Christian Church grew in numbers and power, the Roman government felt the danger more, and became more strict. At first, each congregation of Christians humbly and quietly elected from their own community a minister, or presbyter, to lead them and guide them. Then, as congregations grew larger and more numerous, there must be some authority to keep them all together. So the worshippers elected from among the presbyters a wise, capable leader, called an episcopal presbyter, which really means an inspector. These inspectors held meetings among themselves, settling all disputes among congregations, and governing all equally. But then it was necessary to have a head even of these meetings of inspectors. So at last they decided to choose one of the oldest and wisest of the episcopal presbyters, and make him the episcopal leader or governor, for life. And thus bishops first came into being, governing the communities of Christians.

But for more than a hundred years the Christian communities were mildly and wisely governed by the humble bishops, who accounted themselves just simple Christians, with special duties to perform. They settled all troubles, and they wrote famous letters, like those of St. Paul, to the Christian groups in other great cities, Alexandria, Corinth, Antioch. So the whole Christian community kept closely in touch, and was really strong, however it was hidden and obscured under the brilliant Roman Empire.

By the end of the second century there was a large community in Italy called the Church in Italy, another in Syria, another in Africa, another in Greece. These great provinces each had its own Church, or community of Christians. It was arranged that the episcopal presbyters should meet regularly in the chief town of the province—Rome, Corinth, Antioch, as it might be—and hold councils. These councils were called synods. And at these councils the laws of the Church, called canons, were drawn up, saying how a presbyter should be elected, and how a bishop; how the Church service should be conducted, what the priest or minister should do, and what the congregation should do; also exactly what they should believe; also how the large sums of money given to the Church by the Christians should be used.

At first each town or community in Italy sent its bishop to Rome, to the synod, and all bishops were equal. But again it was inevitable that there should be one among them who stood first. And it was inevitable that this should be the bishop of the chief city, the metropolis. It came to pass that the metropolitan bishop—that is, in Italy, the bishop of the Christians in Rome; in Egypt, the bishop of the Alexandrian Christians—should be the leading Christian in the whole province. And soon, instead of advising and entreating his brother bishops, his brother Christians, the metropolitan bishop began to command them, to instruct them what they should do. He became a dictator, with a great deal of power and pride.

The Churches of the different provinces kept closely together, under the ban of the Roman Empire. But they disputed which was the leading Church. And again Rome claimed the lead. She claimed two apostles—St. Peter and St. Paul, both martyred in Rome. No other city could claim more than one. And on the merits of St. Peter the Romans established their Church, using the phrase from the Bible—' Thou art Peter, and on this rock I will build my church '—as their justification. Rome claimed the lead. Her primate, or metropolitan, was the first of the bishops. The episcopal office, the established office of the bishop, had made each bishop equal. But now the primates or metropolitans rose above the simple bishops, and the Primate of Rome rose above the metropolitans. This took place about the end of the third century. Gradually the metropolitans became powerful as princes, and the Primate of Rome, the Father, or Papa, Pope, in time came to be almost as powerful as an emperor —indeed, at certain periods much more powerful. So there came into being an established priesthood or clergy, such as the Roman and Greek world had not known ; an order of men set apart in life, having a separate, if very great power in their hands, the so-called spiritual power, or power of the Church.

Even as early as 260, Paul of Samosata, metropolitan of Antioch, aroused the indignation of the East by his rich living, palaces, slaves, splendour—his haughty pride, and his scandalous deeds. So soon was the simple, humble Christian Church changed. And as early as the third century terrible disputes tore the Churches of the East and West, Rome and Antioch. This was concerning the time when Easter should be celebrated.

Following these came worse conflicts, quarrels as to matters of fact, and as to the meaning of the Trinity. The early history of the Church, particularly in Africa and the East, is horrible with warfare and massacres between contending parties of Christians. Certainly the Christians destroyed each other in far greater numbers, and with much more terrible ferocity, than they were ever destroyed in the pagan persecutions.

Yet as the Church grew richer and stronger, the Roman government grew more strict, more frightened, more vindictive, and the Roman mob more violent. In the time of the Emperor Maximian, who was a savage soldier, and half a barbarian, there was a horrible massacre of Christians—236 A.D. Just before this, however, under the reign of Severus, the Christians had been allowed to build their own public churches, and Christian bishops, for

the first time, had attended at the Roman court. But in
249 began such a fierce persecution, that the Christians
could not for two years elect a bishop of Rome, after
Fabianus their primate had been martyred in 250. The
emperors were now awaking to understand the strength
and power of Christianity, so that either they hated the
religion violently, and persecuted the Christians, or they
were attracted, and definitely friendly.

In the time of Diocletian began the great persecution
which the Church has called the Era of Martyrs. Yet for
eighteen years that famous emperor reigned in the spirit
of mildest and most liberal religious toleration. It was
Maximian and Galerius who really instituted the persecution. They were soldiers and originally ignorant
peasants. They became generals and emperors at a time
when Christian soldiers began publicly to throw away
their arms, and declare for Christ and martyrdom.
Maximian and Galerius naturally were mad with fury.
Then Diocletian became terrified. He saw the power
of the new sect : he knew that the Christians of that
day claimed supernatural power to perform miracles.
He believed they actually *did* perform the stupendous
miracles they claimed. It terrified him. He called it
magic, evil. And severe persecution began, about the
year 300.

All the property of the Church was to be taken away ;
all the Christian writings over all the Roman world were
to be delivered up, seized, and publicly burned ; churches
were to be levelled with the ground. When the edict
was published in Nicomedia, a Christian at once tore it
down, shouting his scorn of such tyrants. He was roasted
over a slow fire. This was in 303. Within ten days'
time, Diocletian's bed-chamber in Nicomedia was twice
in flames. The mind of the Emperor was filled with a
terrified horror of such people. Every mode of torture
was put into practice to discover which of the Christians
had committed the deed. Nothing could be extorted.

Even Galerius fled from Nicomedia. There was general terrible persecution.

But almost immediately Diocletian abdicated from the throne, weary of governing. Constantius and Galerius followed : Constantius always a friend of the Christians. And in 313, as we know, Constantine issued his edict of toleration. The favoured church in Constantinople was the Christian Church. Constantine was baptized just before he died.

Christianity had triumphed. For two short years, however, there was a relapse. The wise, clever, sad Julian the Apostate reigned in Constantinople from 361 to 363. He passionately wanted to restore paganism. He detested Christianity, though he was too humane to be a persecutor like Galerius. He was pierced with an arrow in the Persian war, and, dying, he is said to have grasped a handful of blood that flowed from the wound in his breast, and tossed it up to heaven, crying : ' Thou hast conquered, Galilean ! ' Julian is the last great pagan.

In 394 Christianity was established as the only religion of the empire. In Constantinople the Church sank before the power of the Emperor. In Rome the empire collapsed, and the curious, unstable power of the popes began. Everywhere the pagan religion was prohibited. But still in country places the simple people took offerings to the hidden shrines, groves, and springs.

The Christian Church now had two centres—Rome and Constantinople. In Constantinople was the Greek church, which had no images, only flat, quaint pictures of the Mother of Jesus : the priests of the Greek church also must marry, and wear a beard ; the ruler or chief of the church was called the Patriarch. The Patriarch never acquired in Constantinople such power as the popes acquired in Rome.

As the empire collapsed in Rome and Italy, the Christians became more unsettled. There were fierce conflicts between the parties in Rome, Alexandria, Constantinople, Antioch. But gradually the great religion of the new era established itself. Rome governed the Christians of Europe and North Africa, Constantinople was head of the Church in the East until the Mohammedans arose to break her power.

IV. The Germans

In Roman days the civilised world was exposed to great inrushes of wild, savage, or barbarian life. Floods of fierce, unknown people would suddenly pour in torrent over the settled, cultivated lands of the Mediterranean. They came from two directions, north and north-east. In the due east, Persia and India were civilised and settled. In the south, the ancient civilisations of Egypt and North Africa gave no signs of new life, and the negroes from beyond the Soudan never seem to have ventured from Africa. But north of Italy were vast, unknown lands, and away to the north-east, beyond the Danube, lay all the immense, terrifying wilderness of Tartary.

The first invasions the Romans had to suffer were from the Cimbri, who crossed the Alps from Gaul. Julius Caesar, however, conquered and subdued Gaul. And now the empire found its northern limit.

Two great reservoirs of human life lay beyond the Roman power. The greatest of these was Tartary, or Scythia, that immense region stretching from the Crimea to China, where dwelt innumerable hordes of dark, wild, horse-riding Asiatics. But the nearer reservoir was the Baltic Sea, which cradled the Germanic races.

The Romans of Latium were short, dark men of the wine-loving lands. Their great strength lay in their courage, and in their power of faithfulness, their intelligent, disciplined acting together for one united purpose. They conquered practically the whole civilised world of their day, and they seemed to have, as the Englishmen of this period, a constitution that would stand any climate, whether it was snowy Scotland or the burning sands of the East.

But the Romans never conquered Germany, their power never stretched far beyond the Rhine. The great Teutonic race seemed the indomitable opposite of the Romans. These short, energetic, dark-eyed men looked with astonishment at the huge, naked fair limbs of the men from the northern forests, at fresh, fierce faces with their blue eyes, and at the yellow hair—or the hair dyed bright red. These almost naked, big, white-skinned men lay and lounged about in an abandoned indolence, when no warfare was at hand : whereas the Romans were always spruce and aware of their conduct. So the latter looked with surprise and disgust at the sight of the great fair warriors lying about in the dirt, their limbs all soiled, their minds utterly indifferent and negligent. But still more impressed were the legions of Rome when these same huge, indolent warriors in warfare hurled forward like a great massive storm, flinging themselves with all their weight upon the wall of Roman iron, the locked shields, the swords and spears.

In the reign of Augustus the Romans suffered some terrible losses in the dark forests of Germany. But in the next reign the great general Germanicus inflicted severe defeats on the Germans. So the warfare went on, incessantly almost, for five hundred years. When it came to a battle, the Romans, with their iron-clad bodies and their perfect discipline, nearly always defeated the great naked hosts of Germans, destroying the barbarians in numbers. But when it came to following up these barbarians, through swamps and dark forests, to their homes, their camps, then the Romans were at a disadvantage. Brave as they were, the veterans were filled with mysterious fear when they found themselves in the dark, cold gloom of Germany, the northern savage land. They felt they had gone beyond their natural limits. So the Roman power never really extended across the Rhine.

The two opposite races of Europe had now met. The dark-eyed, swarthy, wine-loving men from the sunny lands met with the fierce, blue-eyed men, and the two could never understand one another, never meet and mix. It is as if the white-skinned men of the Germanic races were born from the northern sea, the heavy waters, the white snow, the yellow wintry sun, the perfect beautiful blue of ice. They had the fierceness and strength of the northern oceans, the keenness of ice. And thus they resisted the Romans, children of the sun.

The Romans first knew of Germany as the land whence the amber came : for in Rome amber was much esteemed. And as merchants are often the first explorers, so it was probably Roman and Phoenician traders who first penetrated the savage regions of Germany, even to the grey, forbidding shores of the Baltic, where amber was found in the greatest quantities. For amber is the fossilised resin of huge pine-trees that perished in one of the world's previous days. These traders no doubt gave presents to the wild Germans, of small bronze or iron ware—and then, if they returned alive, they came back rich men, having pieces of amber that would sell for a fortune in the markets of Rome. And they came back with strange stories of the unknown dark lands of the north.

By Germany, in that time, was meant all the land north of the Rhine. How far it stretched no one knew. But the Romans knew of a far-off northern sea, with great islands—beyond which lay the everlasting ice. Probably the northern sea was the Baltic, and the huge islands the Scandinavian Peninsula, and Jutland.

In the north of Germany were huge flat lands, often wet, swampy, impassable, through which wandered the great rivers Rhine or Rhenus Flux, Weser or Visurgis, and Elbe or Albis. To the south, however, the whole country was covered by a vast forest of dark fir and pine trees, tracts of which still remain. This Hercynian forest created the greatest impression on the Roman imagination.

No one knew how far it stretched. German-natives who had travelled through it had gone on for sixty days without coming to the end of it. In the illimitable shadow the pine-trunks rose up bare, the ground was brown with pine-needles, there was no undergrowth. A great silence pervaded everywhere, not broken by the dense whisper of the wind above. Between these shadowy trunks flitted deer, reindeer with branching horns ran in groups, or the great elk, with his massive antlers, stood darkly alone and pawed the ground, before he trotted away into the deepening shadow of trunks. In places fir-trees, like enormous Christmas-trees, stood packed close together, their dark green foliage impenetrable. Then the pines would begin again. Or there were beeches in great groves, and elder-bushes here and there : or again a stream or pond, where many bushes grew green and flowery, or big, heathy, half-open stretches covered with heather and whortleberries or cranberries. Across these spaces flew the wild swans, and the fierce, wild bull stood up to his knees in the swamp. Then the forest closed round again, the never-ending dark fir-trees, where the tusked wild boar ran rooting and bristling in the semi-darkness under the shadows, ready to fight for his life with the grey, shadowy wolves which would sometimes encircle him.

Winter came early. In October the first snow began to sprinkle down. And then for months the unending forests lay under snow, branches tore and cracked, reindeer pawed the snow to come at the moss or herbage, wolves ran in packs threading their way between the trunks, and the great bear lay curled up asleep in his hole. Meanwhile the perishing German natives would creep forth to hunt, braving the cold with their half-covered limbs.

It seems that the climate of North Europe was colder then than now. In those days great armies of Romans marched across the frozen Rhine, rolling their ponderous baggage-wagons on the ice. This could never happen now, the river does not freeze to this extent. The reindeer, also, which roamed the northern swamps and the Hercynian forests, now cannot live even round the southern Baltic. He must go much farther north, or he dies of warmth. Again, we are told that the wine of the Romans froze into lumps in the German camps. Now, in these very regions the vine grows. Perhaps the clearing of swamps and forests has made the difference, perhaps there is a change in the world.

In their camps along the Rhine the Roman soldiers, surrounded by the frozen, cracking darkness, told terrible stories of the land confronting them, stories of wolves, and growling bears, and the sudden, ferocious bull; stories of lurking, deadly Germans; stories of horrible sacrifices in groves dark as night; stories of demons that howled through the trees in the blackness, of wolves that turned into ghastly, blood-drinking women—and so on. So that tales of the black Hercynian forest thrilled the ears of the Romans, far off in Rome, in Antioch. The burning deserts of the East and the semi-tropical jungles did not impress the Roman imagination as did this northern forest.

Throughout the wild, icy Germany lived many separate tribes of Germans, some in the plains to the north, some among the hills, some deep in the forests. But wherever they were, they did not live in towns or close-clustered villages. The primitive German did not love his neighbours. He liked to have a space around himself. And therefore, between the tribes were wide border-lands of waste, dreary desert, swamps, or hills, or impenetrable forest, utterly uninhabited. So the tribes felt the pride of their own isolation.

And even individuals felt the same need for space or distance. When a German was going to build a house, he looked round for some pleasant spot, by a stream or spring—for he loved running water—or in a corner of a heath, or in a dry meadow among the swamps, and here, quite alone, he fixed his dwelling. With the help of his servants or slaves, and his women-folk, he made a round timber hut of poles driven into the ground, thatching this with straw or reeds, leaving a hole in the roof for the escape of the smoke. Here he lived with his family and his servants, until one wished to marry. Then the serf or slave would build a hut for himself at some little distance from his master. In the hut the man lay, in chilly weather when there was no fighting to be done, stretched out on the earth by the hearth; children rolled naked in the dirt, serfs' and masters' children all together, indistinguishable; the woman prepared food or spun flax, or idled likewise. When they were warm the men and young people went quite naked; the women had a long linen chemise that left the arms and breast bare. In colder weather all had a cloak, fastened with a pin or a thorn, leaving the rest of the body uncovered. But in very cold weather they wrapped cloths or skins around their limbs, binding them close with long crossed straps. The wealthiest often were clothed in linen trousers, wrapped close to their limbs with straps or coloured bands and tied close round the waist with another band, over a close shirt. The Germans, unlike the Romans, never wore long, loose robes, but liked a clothing that followed the form of the body. The women wore their hair long. In some tribes, the man must leave his hair and beard uncut, till he had slain his first foe, when he cut short his hair and shaved his beard. Some warriors kept a long, loose tail of hair, which they dyed red; some coiled their long hair carefully in a knot at the back of the head. Some were proud of their appearance, having beautifully sewn cloaks and garments of soft fur, soft fox-furs bordered by the spotted otter, or by ermine, white shirts with purple border-edges, and linen cloaks with colours. Some also plastered their houses with bright earths or colours in decoration.

Their wealth consisted in small, ugly cattle, horses, slaves, weapons. Weapons, slaves, horses: these were the dearest possessions, and they were bequeathed by a father, not to his eldest son, but to the bravest.

Slavery, however, was not in Germany what it was in Rome. In Germany a slave was a captive from another tribe, taken in war — or the child of such captives. But he was a free man living his own independent life, not a piece of human cattle, owned body and soul, as in Rome. A slave in Germany had his own house and family, his own possessions, he lived his own life. Merely he must do some work for his owner, pay some tribute of cheese or meat or leather, tend the cattle, and fight when called upon. Indeed he was more like a peasant than a slave.

Life was very careless. In summer the cattle roamed about feeding in the marshes or on the forest edge, and little patches of barley were grown. Then the people had meat, rough cheese, and a porridge of barley, and berries—there was no bread. The chief food was meat. In a bad winter, however, many cattle died of starvation, there was no corn, the people suffered. Then the warriors hunted, or lay inert by the hearth, drinking barley beer while it lasted, or gambling with one another in the chief's house, or lying motionless in a sort of despair. The poor often dug out underground dwellings where they could huddle in winter for warmth, lying long days without moving, when cold and starvation was upon them. But the wiser and richer made suitable provision of meat and barley, and could keep warm and merry in their houses.

The German love of freedom and separateness would not endure either service or control. What chiefs they had were war-leaders, chosen from among the bravest warriors. In times of peace the people did as they liked. They only had councils to decide what was to be done on some important occasion. To the council came the warriors, fully armed. They sat in a circle in the open air, drinking from wooden pots filled with beer, and listening to the chief, or the old wise man, or the priest, who was speaking in the centre. When the speech was warlike and fierce, they clashed their spears on their shields in approval. When it was peace-provoking, cowardly as they termed it, a low, harsh 'burrr . . .' of displeasure went round the circle. And so they settled the questions of war and peace, life and death.

War was the great business, fame the chief reward. The warriors cared little for possessions. They wanted to own famous weapons, good horses, a few slaves : for the rest, they kept hold on nothing. The land belonged to everybody and nobody, it was shared afresh every year. Agriculture was scorned. Fighting was the business of life : after that, hunting : after that, feasting and drinking and hearing songs of bravery. Nothing else mattered. Life was not made for producing. It was made for fierce contest and struggle of destruction, the glory of the struggle of opposition.

The women were the same as the men. Marriage was sacred, and the woman was deeply respected, even revered. But she, too, cared only for the glory won in battle. The greatest warrior, the man who had killed most enemies in battle, he was the greatest man, and to him the women looked with the greatest admiration or respect.

The warriors were by turns lazy and violent. Half their time they would lie by the hearth in the huts, or on the grass out of doors, drinking their beer till they were drunk, or gambling together, or feasting, eating huge masses of meat in the wooden hall of the chief man, or watching the naked youths dance amid sharp spears, swift and agile in the dangerous play. And then, at length, suddenly sick or surfeited of this stupid business, they would leap up, sound the horn, and dash out to the hunt of bears, boars, or deer ; or better still, they would gather for war.

Above all things, they loved fighting. They were wild with joy when the signal came, and they could gather together to go to war with some other tribe, or some other race, or with the Romans. Then, naked, or wearing little cloaks, and carrying the precious shield and spear, they marched through the forest tracks, or over the plains or hills. Their shields of wood or osier were painted bright in different colours, and were the most treasured possessions. If a warrior lost his shield he was disgraced for ever. He had far better lose his life. Spears also were valuable. Iron was scarce, and therefore a narrow, sharp spear-head was a thing to treasure.

Sometimes a number of warriors rode on their rough horses, to form the cavalry ; and if the journey was a long one, the wives with their children followed behind, to attend to their husbands. For the women were trained to be as brave and fierce as their warriors. Honour was everything ; and honour in a man meant having killed the greatest number of enemies. To be brave, to be feared as a terrible fighter, to have honourable wounds, this was the best a man could hope for. Nothing else really counted. The bravest and fiercest and most cunning in war were chosen chiefs, the young men served their chief with their lives. If he died they were all killed fighting round him. If he survived they went with him to his house, and feasted with him.

When they drew near the enemy they formed their battle-array. In front were all the picked youth of all the nation. These would fight on foot along with the cavalry. The army began to sound its battle chant, a loud, harsh kind of song, droning and rising to a loud roar. The warriors would put their concave shields to their mouths, to make the sound reverberate more fully. And then, with a great cry, suddenly they would fling their spears with wild force on the enemy, hurling themselves forward. The naked youths of the front were swift as the horses ; they leapt and swerved like the wind, darting and stabbing with their spears, and sheltering themselves with their shields, ever surging after the wild, fearless leader. But it is terrible to think what must have happened as they hurled their naked bodies against the iron wall of Roman shields,

and their spears against the iron helmets and cuirasses of
the legions. The wonder is that they achieved as much
success as they did, through their fearless, terrible daring,
and their onrush like the wind.

Feeling themselves repulsed, they would flee as swiftly
as they advanced, only to form again, and whirl once more
wildly to the attack. If they broke, however, and came
running towards the women and followers in the rear, then
the German wives would bare their bosoms and ask for
death rather than disgrace. They would drive their
husbands back to the battle, and even fight fiercely along
with the men. When it was over, wives and mothers
would command their husbands to show their wounds.
And the women rejoiced when they had to dress many
honourable wounds on the bodies of their fighters; they
mourned if their sons were unscathed.

These battles would sometimes follow one another in
swift succession, and the losses were enormous. How
could they be otherwise ! The naked dead piled the fields.
But there was little lamentation. It was honour, after
all, to die fighting. The men were silent, thinking of the
slain; the women wailed the death-song. But they did
not forget. In the long nights of winter, as they lay
round the hearth, the men spoke with praise and regret
of the brave dead.

Returning from battle to their homes, the council would
give cattle, horses, and land, or slaves, to the chief who
was bravest in the war. He, in his turn, would give the
blood-stained spear to his bravest young man, to another
a horse, or the clasp of a cloak. And the young warriors
lived and ate at the chief's large hut, sleeping on the floor
of his hall. This was all their reward, all their earning.
For there was no money or riches. The days lapsed into
sloth after war, for warriors never worked. They fought,
hunted, and feasted : it was for slaves, old people, women,
or weak men to labour, tilling the soil, tending cattle,
growing flax, making linen, preparing skins, food, fodder,

and fire-wood. The brave told tales of battle, or listened to a bard who could sing the stories of heroes. And they drank till they fell all drunk, and woke to drink again, to gamble, to sing, to hear stories, to watch the dance.

Gambling was the greatest vice—that and drunkenness. Men whose lives are not given to some form of production or creation must for ever live by risk, the chance of loss and danger. When the joy of war is taken from them, and they have no more the keen stimulant of the risk of losing their own lives, of taking another life, then they must fight the peaceful contest in gambling, risking their all for a chance of taking all. This is the passion of a non-producing, eternally-opposing people. And the German warriors in their peace days would gamble away house, horses, weapons, slaves, wife, children, clothes, then an arm, then a leg, till they had gambled everything, including their whole person, into slavery. And then they would serve as slaves, until perhaps the chance of war gave them freedom and property again.

Of the religion of the ancient Germans we do not know much. We know that they worshipped chiefly in dark groves, where on their rude altars they sacrificed victims, horses, and even men. Then they nailed the skulls of men and the hideous skulls of horses to the sacred trees. This was part of that great pre-historic tree-worship which seems to have been universal over Europe and even America, before our history begins. The dark groves with their blood-stained altars terrified and horrified the Romans, whether they found them near the Mediterranean, near Marseilles, or in Spain, Britain, or Germany.

The tree-worship, the worship of the Tree of Life seems always to have entailed human sacrifice. Life is the fruit of that Tree. But the Tree is dark and terrible, it de-mands life back again. With its branches spread it be-comes a Cross. And in our hymns, even to-day, we speak of Jesus ' hung on the Tree.'

The tree-worship was perhaps the central worship. But

there were other gods, gods of thunder, of the sun, of fertility—and to these temples were erected. In the North the great goddess of birth and production had her temple on an isle in the Baltic. This great mother is like the gentle cow which supports our life. Even the Mother of Jesus had with her in the stable the cows of peace and plenty, when Jesus was born. So every year the mysterious ' Mother,' an idol mysteriously veiled, was taken from her temple in the North, and, placed on a wagon drawn by cows, was led in slow procession sacredly through the land. And whilst this mysterious idol was moving in its procession, a holy peace must be kept throughout Germany, no man's hand must be lifted in violence, under pain of terrible penalty. So religion even then provided the breathing space of peace in the years of incessant fighting. Without such provision, men must have exterminated themselves.

It was the blue-eyed Teutons of the North, for ever unshaken in their opposition to the Roman spirit, who at last broke the empire. They were the great external opposing force. But when once Rome was broken, the German races mingled and mixed with the dark-eyed races, and it is from this intermingling of the two opposite spirits, two different and opposite streams of blood, that modern Europe has arisen. The fusion of the two opposites brought us the greatness of modern days : just as the hostility of the two brings disaster, now as in the old past.

V. The Goths and Vandals

THE great Germanic races were restless. Having no real purpose in their lives, only to fight and oppose one another, they became tired of home and needed adventure. Also, although the land was large, yet a few people occupied a big space, so that as the population grew there was not room.

Therefore from the dim lands of the northern seas, and from those vast regions far beyond the Elbe, from time to time came sudden overflowings of blue-eyed people pouring towards the Mediterranean like floods from a melting winter. The first hosts crossed the Rhine into Gaul. As early as 105 B.C. the Romans were startled and terrified by the appearance of hosts of fair-skinned barbarians, warriors with shields and spears, with clumsy wagons drawn by oxen, and accompanied by women and children. This was the first host of emigrants. They must have come from Germany. They threatened Italy, inflicted a terrible defeat on the Roman armies, then turned aside and wandered across France to Spain, then back again to the Rhone, slowly and uneasily migrating for several years before they were finally defeated and destroyed by the Roman Marius. These were the famous Cimbri.

After this Rome had only to repel invasions from Gaul, and when Gaul was finally conquered in 51 B.C., the Romans effectively barred the incursion of the Germans by placing a line of invincible forts along the Rhine, and keeping a great army there stationed. This outlet therefore was closed up to the Teutons. But behind the marshes and forests the nations were stirring. Out of the Baltic and from the northern sea-board sailed the long sharp ships of the first Northmen, rowing away to the Mediterranean to plunder, to fight. Some of these blue-eyed Northmen stayed in the Mediterranean lands.

But away in the North the Teutons were seething restlessly. They could not take ship in any great numbers. Yet they must burst out. The Rhine and the Rhinc frontiers were held fast. The sea lay to the west, northwards lay ice. The only way they could move was eastwards, behind Germany, as it were, traversing South Russia and approaching that other, opposite water, the Black Sea.

We do not know exactly what happened. We only know that in the middle of the second century great peoples or tribes called the Goths and Vandals were living in North Germany. The Goths were established to the east, about the mouth of the Vistula and the Gulf of Danzig, and eastward of them again, still on the Baltic, lay the Sclavonic or Celtic tribe of the Venedi or Wends. More westward in Germany, about the mouth of the Oder and south of the peninsula of Jutland, lay the Vandals, a nation of many tribes. West of these again lay the Langobardi, a famous tribe living on the lower Elbe, on the North Sea.

Some great impulse must have started these nations moving slowly eastwards, to Russia, then to the Black Sea, then southwards towards Constantinople and southeast towards Rome ; for each of the nations successively broke across the Danube into Roman territory, and came down to Italy. First came the Goths, then the Vandals, and lastly, the Langobardi.

First, we must consider the first-comers, the Goths. We know that in the year 150 or thereabouts they were still living in Germany. About the year 220 A.D. they appear by the Black Sea, harassing the Roman frontier-province of Dacia. Dacia lay between the Danube and the Dniester, where Roumania is now.

In the seventy years intervening between these two dates, the Gothic nations must have moved across South Russia and Poland, following the course of the rivers, travelling very slowly in migration, and carrying with them great numbers of men from tribes that lay in their way, such as the Venedi. The Ukraine was a rich fertile land supporting fine cattle and abounding in honey : for these were the wealth of a barbarous land, cattle and bees —milk and honey—and later, corn. This land the Goths must have enjoyed : yet they scorned the pastoral life ; they moved on in their wild poverty in search of adventure and war and plunder. So they came to the rich Roman colony of Dacia. There they turned south, crossed the Dniester, and plundered south to the Danube.

After a time they crossed the Danube into the peaceful Roman provinces, plundering and laying waste the land. They took and sacked the great city of Philippopolis, massacring the inhabitants. In this fatal year of 251 A.D. the Roman Emperor Decius marched against them with the flower of the Roman armies. In the great fight the Goths were victorious, Decius was killed, and his body must have been trampled down in the bog, for it was never recovered.

After this the Romans gave the barbarians great gifts, persuading them to retreat beyond the Danube. Then the Danube was fortified as the Rhine was fortified, and the Goths found themselves checked. They settled in the lands we now call Roumania and South Russia. But they must have adventure. They made themselves great flat-bottomed boats and sailed off on the Black Sea wildly southwards, through the Bosphorus into the Mediterranean. There they plundered and burned. On one expedition they sacked Athens. But in 269 the plundering·hosts were terribly defeated. The fleet was destroyed, there was great slaughter. Then pestilence fell on the Gothic hosts and wiped them out. Of those that remained the women were sold into slavery, the young men were enrolled into

the Roman army. The rest of the barbaric nation agreed
to remain beyond the Danube.

They remained quiet for fifty years. When they broke
out again it was in the great Constantine's reign. He
marched against them and punished them severely, in
322. After this the Goths turned against their savage
neighbours in the west. These were the Sarmatians, whom
we now call Cossacks. The Sarmatians were big, fair
like the Teutons, but they had the manners of Asiatic
Tartars. They wore loose robes of skins, lived in tents,
spent their lives on horseback, and fought with long
lances. A fierce wild tribe, with their shaggy beards and
their skin dresses, and their strange speech, they were
barbarians even to the Goths, and horrible to the Romans.

The Sarmatians lived in the plains of Hungary. They
appealed to Constantine. Constantine came with his
army and gave the Goths such a severe lesson, and yet
such a just peace, that the Gothic nation held the name
of Constantine in great reverence, respecting for his sake
even the noble emperor's weak descendants in the years
to come.

Constantine, as we know, shifted the capital of the empire
from Rome to Constantinople. The empire had now two
centres. Soon it had two separate emperors, an emperor
of the East, and an emperor of the West. And then there
was a ruinous division between the two halves.

Just as Rome was destroying herself internally, a
sinister event took place outside. The year 375 is marked
as an epoch in the world's history, for it was the year in
which the Huns, coming out of the vast unknown Asia,
crossed the Volga on their way to Europe.

The Gothic nation was more or less settled to the north
of the Danube. It comprised two great tribes, the Ostrogoths or East Goths, and the Visigoths or West Goths.
The ancient king of all the Goths, Hermanric, was an
Ostrogoth. He was a famous king, and the Gothic nation
was developing and becoming civilised.

Suddenly, as a volcano bursts and the lava pours down on a doomed people, the Huns burst out of Asia and came down in their black myriads upon the Goths. The Huns were hideous little people on horseback, savage, terribly fierce, and numerous like clouds of locusts. Hermanric tried to oppose them. He was killed, and the defeated Ostrogoths submitted to their hideous little enemies. The bulk of the Gothic nation, however, including nearly all the Visigoths, fled in supreme terror to the Danube, to escape the diabolic myriads of the enemy, who seemed to them more like baboons than men.

At the Danube the Romans were on the watch. The terrified Goths stretched out their hands and cried and implored to be allowed to cross. But the officers must wait for the imperial permission. At last came the fatal mandate : the Goths were to be brought over.

The river was a mile wide at the place where the Goths encamped, opposite a Roman camp, and it was rushing rapidly in flood. The large boats came over, but as they returned heavily laden they became unmanageable. Many were swept away, and great numbers of unfortunate families of Goths perished shrieking in the water. As the boatmen became more skilled, however, vessel after vessel crossed and returned with its load of human life. The Goths left on shore clamoured and cried. Sentries were posted to keep a watch to the north, the fires were kept burning at night. And meanwhile the great boats came and went without interruption, all through the day, and through the night, lighted over the black dark river in the night-time by great fires on opposite shores, by torches and fire-baskets fixed to the ships. The Goths, with women and children, stood packed in a solid mass, motionless in fear as the boat rocked and swung over the flood. Then they landed in safety on the southern shore. Day after day, night after night the transport continued, and still a crowd surged at the landing-place on the north shore. At last, however, it was nearly over. The warriors came down, the Gothic sentries left their posts, to be rowed across. The left bank seemed clear.

And now the Romans found themselves with vast hosts of refugees, covering the countryside in a thick, helpless encampment. There was no food, or not enough, and no shelter. The Goths began to starve, for the country could not support such a terrific influx. Starvation was worse than fear of the Huns, loud murmurs arose, then fights; the Roman garrison and populace were in danger of being overwhelmed.

At this juncture appeared on the left bank the king of the Ostrogoths, with the remainder of his people, imploring to be allowed to cross. The Romans were obdurate. They would not add to the danger and confusion of their own awful condition, overwhelmed as they were in a sea of homeless, ravenous refugees, great, powerful, wild people. The Ostrogoths in terror searched along the banks, and at last found a place where they could contrive to cross without Roman help.

Then terrible times followed. Famine came, women and children died of starvation, men like great gaunt wolves roamed seeking food. Romans were massacred for their supplies. The Goths spread out, hungrily devouring the land. The Romans tried to prevent them. And then war began.

The Goths united under the brave Fritigern. In 377 a great but indecisive battle left the plain of Salices white with the big bones of the Goths, the smaller, finer bones of the Romans. In 378 the Goths swept down the Balkan Peninsula to Hadrianople, not far from Constantinople itself. They were met by the Roman armies under the brave Emperor Valens. But the huge Goths in the frenzy of desperation swept yelling on the Roman ranks, the legions broke, the Emperor was wounded. He escaped, but whilst his wounds were being dressed in a cottage the shouting Goths surrounded the house. Unable to burst in the door, they shot burning arrows into the thatched roof: the house was soon in flames, consuming its inmates. Only one soldier dropped from a window to carry the awful news to Constantinople. Two-thirds of the Roman army was destroyed, and the empire received the first of her death-blows.

The Goths retreated from Hadrianople. Their hosts rolled slowly towards Constantinople, and from the hills of the suburbs the barbarians from the north looked in wonder on the lovely shining city girdled by the blue sea beyond them. Then they turned north, laden with plunder.

Terror and hatred of the Gothic name now filled all Roman hearts. Since Constantine there had been some friendliness between the two nations ; the Goths had been rapidly learning some of the arts of civilisation from the Romans, the Romans had been pleased to teach the great northern strangers. Consequently in the cities of Asia were very many Gothic youths, being brought up by the Romans and taught the Roman way of life. Now, in their terror and horror of the Goths, the Romans of the east made a plan. On a certain day, in all the eastern cities the Gothic youths of fourteen, sixteen, twenty years of age, tall, beautiful young men, educated, speaking Greek or Latin, and looking upon their Roman friends as brothers, were gathered together in the market-places as if for some game or show. Suddenly they were all slaughtered, every one, all in one day.

This made the breach between the two nations irreparable. But the Goths were never capable of long, disciplined efforts. They became weary, and then they abandoned all their plans. So, after the death of Fritigern, the armies crumbled away. Then the wise Emperor Theodosius made friends with the Gothic leaders, and persuaded the nation to settle in peace in the Balkan Peninsula. And in Constantinople, and in the Emperor's wonderful palace the barbarian chiefs were received and entertained as friends, till they became used to splendours and to civilisation, and lost some of their warlike passion.

But peace was only temporary. In 395, a few weeks
after Theodosius was dead, the Gothic nations were again
in arms. Seeking fresh fields of plunder, the chieftain
Alaric led his bands into Greece and ruined the land.
During this successful expedition he was raised on a
shield in front of the ranks and hailed by the warriors
' Alaric, King of the Visigoths.' Thus the nation again
united under one leader, and this one of the boldest and
most artful of men.

Rome was now in a state of weak, helpless terror. Alaric
saw that it was time to strike. In his panic the emperor
of the west, Honorius, gave orders for the calling home of
the frontier legions, from Britain, from the Rhine. The
fortresses of the Rhine, that had been held fast for hundreds
of years, were abandoned to the natives and to decay,
whilst the legions marched across Gaul to Italy. On the
great wall from the Forth to the Clyde the Roman sentries
took their last look at the misty Highland hills to the
north, then descended the towers to mount no more. The
wall was left to the fury of the Caledonians. And slowly,
not very surely, the legions converged towards Rome.

In the year 400 Alaric invaded Italy. With his swift
army, which was becoming accustomed to Roman lands,
he swept past Verona towards Milan, where the Emperor
Honorius lay terror-stricken. Honorius fled, pursued by
Gothic cavalry. He would have been taken but for the
advance of the Roman armies from the south, led by the
great general Stilicho.

Stilicho himself was a Vandal by birth. But he had
been brought up by the Romans, and was faithful to them.
He was a splendid general. He wished to take the enemy
at a disadvantage. Since their contact with the Romans
of the east, the Goths had become Christians. The barbarian army under Alaric rested near Turin, piously to
observe the most sacred days of Easter. Though a Christian himself, leading Christian armies, yet Stilicho decided
to take advantage of this circumstance. He fell on the

Goths whilst they were celebrating their most holy festival. The Goths were taken by surprise, though they soon recovered. They fought bravely, but were terribly defeated. This battle of Pollentia is famous as the great defeat of the Goths, the saving of Italy.

Alaric managed to escape into the Alps. He came down with another army, and was again defeated by Stilicho, and with difficulty extricated himself and retreated beyond the Adriatic. Italy breathed free again.

But now it seemed as if all Germany was breaking loose and pouring down on Italy. Clouds of Germans had been moving from the Baltic to the upper Danube, whence they were urged forward by the pressure of the Huns from behind. In 405 they broke through the Alps into Italy. Stilicho marched north and again won a great victory. Twelve thousand of the defeated Germans, who were of the tribes of Vandals, Burgundians, Suevi, took service with Rome, and Stilicho was again hailed ' Deliverer of Italy.' The rest of the barbarians were driven back into Gaul.

In 407, on the last dark day of the year, hosts of Germans marched over the Rhine, on the ice, into Gaul. They were never driven back again—the Roman frontier was broken for ever. The barriers between savage and civilised Europe were destroyed. The Roman frontiers along the Rhine had enjoyed a long peace. The land was beautiful with villas and gardens and exquisite Roman cities; a fair, cultivated landscape stretched away into Gaul.

Suddenly, the peaceful inhabitants, who had been used to ride and hunt in Germany, safe even in the Hercynian woods, and who were accustomed to see the tall Germans in the market-places and circuses of the Roman frontier towns, peaceful purchasers and sightseers, now, without warning, saw flames arise and spears flashing. The colonists were massacred, the land was blackened, the barbarians overran Gaul. It was in this year that the legions still in Britain revolted against the Roman rule, and declared themselves independent.

The Romans were not satisfied with trouble. In 408, for mere reasons of court jealousy and intrigue, they basely beheaded their great general Stilicho. The Roman court had established itself among the impassable marshes of Ravenna, on the Adriatic. There they felt secure in themselves, so they did not care what became of Italy. Honorius trembled and exulted. He agreed to the execution of Stilicho.

Alaric heard of the shameful death of his great rival. Then cunningly, smiling to himself, he began to negotiate with the foolish Honorius, thus keeping Ravenna quiet, whilst with his Gothic armies he marched past, down the Flaminian Way, straight to Rome. On he went, till he passed the stately arches, and pitched his camp under the walls of the great city. This was in 408. For six hundred and nineteen years, since the invasion of the Cimbri and Teutons, barbarians from the same lands the Goths came from, Rome had been inviolate. Now it was reduced by famine. But Alaric was a Christian, and declared himself no enemy of the sacred city. He demanded a ransom of all the gold and silver and costly furniture in Rome, and a surrender of all the German slaves. ' What have you left us ? ' asked the trembling Romans. ' Your lives,' said the contemptuous Visigoth. And he marched quietly away.

In 409 Alaric again besieged Rome. The Emperor Honorius and his court were still enjoying themselves in safety behind the marshes of Ravenna. Alaric sent bishops of the Italian towns into Rome, offering peace. But Rome would not accept Alaric as an ally. Still he did not attack the town, but marched down to the Port of Rome, and held up the food ships till Rome herself submitted.

Yet still the stupid Honorius would not come to terms with Alaric. Instead he actually sent a rival barbarian chieftain with an army against the great Goth. The third time, Rome paid for the cowardice of Ravenna. In the year 410 Alaric appeared in wrath before the city. At the hour of midnight the Salarian Gate was treacherously opened, and the fury of the tribes of Germany and Russia and Asia, Teutons and Celts and Slavs and Tartars, poured through the ancient, inviolate streets. Alaric, a Christian himself, exhorted his Christian Goths to spare life, but to seize treasure. This they no doubt did. But there was no controlling the fierce Slavonic Alani and Sarmatians, the bloodthirsty Huns, the still heathen Germans who found themselves in the vast, medley army. Terrible slaughter took place in the streets, in the houses, even in the churches. Rome had fallen, her pride was gone for ever.

For six days the barbarian armies occupied Rome. Then they proceeded to ravage Italy. After this they scattered, to enjoy their spoil. The rich Romans were dead. In their lovely villas by the sea the Germans sprawled their huge limbs, lying drinking, gambling, singing, feasting, as at home. But now they lay on warm, marble terraces, stretched on silken cushions, looking out past the orange and almond trees to the blue waves of the Mediterranean. Beautiful delicate slaves attended the huge warriors, bringing wine cooled with snow, and rare food, and exquisite sweetmeats made of honey, and apricots, and oranges, and raisins, also beautiful bunches of grapes, and peaches each one laid sweet and downy on its own leaf. There the savage heroes shouted and sang, telling stories of the far-off grey Baltic, or of the bleak steppes of Russia.

But Alaric died in 410, when he was preparing to cross to Sicily. He was only 34 years of age. It is said that the river Busento was turned aside by the Goths, and that Alaric with all his arms and treasure was buried in the river bed. The river was then brought back to its own course, so that it rolled its waves above the great Visigoth. And then the workmen and slaves were all killed, the secret kept for ever.

The Goths began to sicken with diseases in Italy. Ataulf, their new chief, made peace with Honorius and later married Placidia, the Emperor's sister. Then he led his hosts out of Italy, leaving the land at peace. He moved into Gaul, and then he decided to cross the Pyrenees.

The legions of Spain, like the legions of Britain, had revolted from their Roman allegiance, and in 407 they had invited into their lands the wild barbarians who had crossed the Rhine into Gaul. Of these the Vandals were the chief tribe. They were a much more ferocious, destructive race than the Goths, so that we still speak of an act of wilful destruction as an act of vandalism. Spain, a lovely and highly civilised Roman province, was lost when her treacherous legions invited the Vandals over the Pyrenees.

In 415, however, Ataulf, the successor of Alaric, being now friendly to Rome, determined to march with his Visigoths over the Pyrenees and dispossess the destructive Vandals. This he did, defeated the barbarians, and established his kingdom in North Spain, his capital in Barcelona. And thus began the Visigoth rule in Spain. The Visigoths in Spain became the nobility and freemen of Spain, as did the Normans in England, the natives forming the lower classes. Later the Moors came and overthrew the Visigoth rule, but after some hundreds of years the Moors were driven out, and the proud Spaniards, in whose veins runs the Gothic blood of Alaric, resumed their sway over the Peninsula.

Whilst the Visigoths settled themselves in North Spain, the Vandals still held the south. In 428 the Roman governor of North Africa rebelled against Rome. He sent across the Straits of Gibraltar and asked the fierce Vandals to come to his help. The Vandals, who were ready ship-builders, saw their chance. Under their king, Genseric, they sailed across to the lovely and rich North African provinces, once the granary of Rome. Genseric was a terrible, inhuman leader. The Vandals fell upon the sunny African cities like a cloud of death. Soon they had dispossessed the Romans, and then was established a powerful, sea-faring kingdom of Vandals in the lands we now call Tripoli, having the capital in Carthage, one of the ancient great cities of the world. This Vandal empire in Africa was not destroyed till 534.

Meanwhile Europe was in chaos. African Vandals ravaged the sea, Vandals landed in Italy and again sacked Rome, in 455. In Gaul the Visigoths under Theodoric had established a kingdom in the south of France, in the fair land known as Aquitaine. There they settled down to peace and prosperity, spreading their kingdom over Northern Spain, and ruling a splendid Visigoth realm. They were already Christians.

The Burgundians, another German tribe, settled down peacefully in the fertile fields on the Rhone, the Jura, and by the upper waters of the Rhine. They too became Christians. The Franks, also German, settled in the north of Gaul, around the Scheldt and Somme and the Moselle.

In 490 another Theodoric, the Ostrogoth, founded the Ostrogothic kingdom in Italy, and the Roman empire in the West disappeared. The empire in the East still persisted, governed from Constantinople. But it was hopelessly weak. About 540 the emperor of Constantinople invited the help of the Langobardi. This brought down the ferocious tribe of Lombards into Southern Europe, where their descendants still remain.

These are the real Dark Ages, when Europe was a welter of fighting barbarians. The splendour and peace of the Roman Empire utterly disappeared, Italy was almost depopulated by war and pestilence. The earth fell back into its wild state ; a traveller in the once smiling, wonderful Italian country might have imagined himself in a savage land, save for the ruins and presence of Roman buildings, Roman roads.

Still the tide of barbarians flowed over the Danube. But it was no longer German, but Slavonic or Asiatic. The warlike Bulgarians came down upon the Balkan Peninsula, followed by Slavonic tribes, tall, fair, like

Germans, but having Asiatic dress and manners, and a Slavonic speech.

So, as the great empire dwindled to the confines of Constantinople, the rest of Europe was flooded with barbarians from Germany, Russia, and Asia. These barbarians settled down at last, and, mingling or not mingling with the natives of the lands they occupied, formed the base of the great modern nations : English, French, Spanish, Lombard, Swiss, Bulgarian, and so on. All these are formed from a wild mixture of races, in which, except perhaps in the case of the Slavs, the Germanic element was dominant during the Dark Ages.

VI. The Huns

THE great flood of Germanic barbarians that broke over Europe in the decline of the Roman Empire changed for ever the disposition of Europe, and even changed or modified the very races of the different countries. Where the Germans stayed, they settled, and out of their rooting in the new lands rose in time the perfected civilisations of our history. Thus in England the Saxons, Danes, and Normans were all of Germanic blood, and the fusion of these tribes with the native Briton has resulted in our modern English race. In the south of France the Visigoth kingdom of Aquitaine soon developed into civilisation. Aquitaine was perhaps the most cultured land in Europe in the time of Richard Cœur de Lion. Spain had two distinct developments : in the north the Gothic, and in the south the Arabic or Moorish. In the end the Gothic triumphed and dominated Spain. In Italy we have the Langobardi in Lombardy, the Veneti in Venice, and later, the Northmen in Sicily and Naples. These are the races which, fused with the native Italian, brought Italy to her second and greatest flowering, in the fifteenth century. France had the more peaceful German Burgundian settled along the Rhone and the Jura, bringing the land into beautiful cultivation, whilst in the north the fiercer Franks, who gave their name to the whole country, occupied the land from the Rhine to the Loire.

Thus we see that from the distribution of German tribes among native nations, in the fourth, fifth, sixth centuries—even on to the eleventh—the modern nations of

Europe have arisen. There is one great barbarian race, however, which we have not considered, and this is the race whose name rang terror through the whole ancient world. We have said that the year 375 is marked as an epoch in the world's history, by the crossing of the Huns over the Volga. More startling than the name of Goth or Vandal is the name of Hun. Yet the Hunnish force was only the black hammer which smashed up the already broken Roman world; it did nothing towards building up a new world. The Germanic races entered in and formed the basis of a new Europe. The Hunnish force rolled away like a thunder-cloud that has burst and struck the land.

Beyond the Volga lie the vast tracts of Middle Asia, still hardly known to us. In Roman days this enormous region was one dim shadow, whose fringes alone were known. Out of this enormous unknown, from time to time there issued black clouds of human beings, savage and horrible. The black cloud burst on Europe, first on Russia, then on the Germanic lands beyond the Danube and the Vistula. And every time the black swarm broke out of the east, the white clouds of German and Slavonic barbarians came rolling over Europe to the south. And thus we say the Huns destroyed the Roman world, by displacing the German and Slavonic races and impelling them southwards.

For thousands of years the Huns must have roamed between China and the Volga, and between the Arctic regions and Persia, in that immeasurable basin of dreary land called Tartary or Scythia. They were of Tartar or Mongolian race, dark yellow in colour, Asiatic. The distinguishing marks of the Tartars were that they lived in tents, roaming from place to place : that they tilled no ground : that they lived on horseback : that they had no beards, and wore loose garments.

The Huns, however, were the most terrible of all Tartars. They lived together in families or clans. These families had, in course of time, grown enormous. Thousands of individuals kept together in one moving host, called a horde. When they pitched their round, black tents, made of horse-hair cloth stretched over a frame shaped like a bee-hive, or like a barrel, then the plain would be blackened for miles around with the vast encampment. Their cattle and horses were guarded in innumerable herds. They fed on the dreary plains surrounding the camp. Then, when all the grass was eaten, there would be a loud, buzzing activity, as of a world of bees. The black tents disappeared, wagons were harnessed, men on horseback were darting here and there over the plain like clouds of flies, and the great swarm moved on, on into the vast unknown, over the horizon.

The darting, horse-riding Hunnish men were dreaded on both sides of the world. Long before they troubled Europe, they had brought ruin on the beautiful, civilised empire of China. Twice they conquered the great, cultivated lands of China, and had to be paid off with enormous tribute. They even demanded every year a band of the fairest maidens of China : for the Tartar women were hideous and savage. Thus we have still a poem written by an unhappy Chinese princess who was given to a Tartar chief as tribute. She weeps and complains that she, who had been brought up so delicate, silken and flowery in the fair palace of her father in China, should be condemned to be carried off into far exile by a savage Tartar, mingled with his gruesome wives, her only food raw meat, her only drink sour milk, her only palace a tent of woven horse-hair, and her only music the shrill noise of Tartar speech. If she could but be a bird, she cries, and fly back to her dear home in China ! But no doubt the poor princess perished among the savages, carried hither and thither with the herds in Central Asia.

About the year 300 B.C. the Chinese began to build that wonder of the world, the Great Wall of China, to keep back these Tartars. But continually the pitiless Huns broke through, carrying devastation and slaughter into

the gentle lands.   At last, however, in the course of
centuries, the Chinese strengthened themselves against
this hated foe.   They drilled and perfected their armies,
and steeled their courage, till at last, about the year
300 A.D., six hundred years after the commencement of
the Great Wall, the Chinese armies began to inflict crushing
defeat upon the Tartars and Huns.   The victory was
carried away into Tartary, and far in the wastes, far beyond
the Wall the proud Chinese armies erected their trophies
of triumph, carven pillars which still exist, with their
record of battles won.

It was after this date that the Huns turned west.   Gradually those that refused to submit to Chinese rule gathered
and roved west, band after band.   The first hordes approached Europe.   They defeated the fierce Slavonic
Alani who dwelt along the Volga.   In 375 the hordes
crossed the Volga on rafts and flat boats.   And then we
know how they swept down on the Goths near the Danube,
and on the Germanic tribes by the Baltic.   On their
hideous, swift little horses the Huns overran the land in
an incredibly short time.

The Hunnish men were dreadful to look at.   They lived
on their horses, ate, drank, and even slept on horseback.
Whether they gathered their assemblies, or whether they
traded in a market-place, they were always seated on their
savage little steeds.   Mounted, they fought at a distance
with bows and arrows and spears, or close at hand, fiercely
wheeling and flying on horseback, with swords.

When a Hun did dismount and stand on the earth, he
was very ugly.   Bow-legged, he waddled as he walked.
He was little, short in build, but very broad and powerful.
His head was big and like an animal's, with coarse, straight
black hair.   Tiny black eyes sparkled deep in the flesh of
the flat face, the great wide mouth opened and shut.
There was no beard, only a few bristles here and there ;
for the practice of cutting their faces whilst young prevented the hair from growing.

These untamable people were like animals. They were very swift and sudden in their movements, and the first hordes seem to have been almost without human feelings. When they came down on the Goths they slaughtered indiscriminately, opening their wide mouths and slashing and slaying anything that was alive and was not Hunnish. They spoke with shrill, high voices, calling shrilly, using strange, savage gestures. And when they had finished killing, they collected all the booty they wanted, for they were very greedy, and then they set fire to all that would burn, and that they did not want.

No wonder the fleeing Goths were horrified. They felt that behind these fearful faces there was no human spirit. They felt that no human speech could reach these creatures. The Hunnish speech seemed like the shrill, neighing communication of animals. And the Huns were avaricious as demons.

The Christian Romans said that the Huns were not human. They were born of evil spirits who mated with witches in the dreary deserts of Asia.

Human or not, the Romans soon had to reckon with the Huns. The main body of the horde moved slowly. The women were in the great clumsy wagons, that were drawn by five or six yoke of oxen. There were huge wagon-loads of plunder, besides prisoners, slaves, who were on foot. Then there were the herds of cattle. So that the main tribe advanced at a slow pace.

The warriors were just as swift as the horde was slow. No one knew where they would turn up next. They carried no baggage. For food, they cut some slices of raw meat, and these, placed like a saddle, cooked a little between the heat of the horse's body and the warrior's thigh. This made strong, savage food. Beyond this, the horsemen carried little balls of hard curd cheese, which they broke, dissolved in water, and so ate. They could live for many days on this poor sustenance, if they found no other food.

Bands of Huns crossed the Danube and ravaged the land. Then they joined the Gothic and Vandal hosts against the common enemy Rome. At the taking of Rome by Alaric many Huns were present—indeed they formed part of almost every barbarian army. They despised the Romans, particularly the Byzantines. They would not deign to speak Greek. But both Goths and Huns were proud when they learned to speak the military Latin.

Whilst these bands roved, the bulk of the Hunnish nation stayed beyond the Danube. They occupied the great open plains of the land that is still theirs—or still bears their name—Hungary, the land of the Huns. There they roved and hunted, and in time they built large villages of wooden huts, where they dwelt more permanently, although still they would leave the village empty at times, and set off wandering.

Gradually, however, they learned from the Goths and the Romans. The Huns were quick and intelligent in their way; they very quickly picked up Latin, and learned Roman methods of life. But they kept their own habits. They loved money. They would go to the Roman markets over the Danube to sell cattle, cheese, hides, horse-hair, and to buy Roman goods. But they liked to sell more than they bought.

The Huns made themselves masters of the upper Danube. At places were stationed their great flat boats and their canoes made of hollowed tree-trunks. From time to time a chieftain would ride up with his bands and his wagons, out of Europe, bringing all his plunder. Then would be great excitement in the Hunnish villages. The Hun would bring with him fair women from Germany or Italy, as many as possible. Some of these he would keep for himself, some he would sell among his neighbours. Then he would bring fine cattle, fine furniture, gold, treasures of Roman villas, fruits, fine food, casks of wine. There would take place a great feasting and drinking. For the

Huns also loved to get drunk at times. In Tartary they made a strong drink called koumiss, from fermented mare's milk. But when they tasted wine, they liked this better, even as the Germans did not care for their own beer when they could get the wines of Italy.

So the Hunnish villages grew rich, and a little civilised. The Huns were not so terrible at home. They treated the slaves and the captured women kindly, if roughly. The men were not cruel, save only in the wild flare of war, when they killed and burned everything before them, as in an intoxication.

The nation was wild and lawless in itself, subject to no rule, but only willing to be led by a military leader or king. In the early fifth century the Hunnish king Rugilas sent his ambassadors or message-bearers both to the courts of Constantinople and of Ravenna. The Byzantine emperor paid a yearly tribute of 350 pounds weight of gold to the king of the Huns occupying the lands of the Danube and the river Theiss, allowing him also the title of Roman general. The Huns despised the Byzantines deeply. When Rugulas died in 433, his nephews Attila and Bleda immediately demanded an increased tribute, and the surrender of the Hunnish emigrants who had taken refuge in Constantinople. The Byzantines gave up the Huns, who were immediately crucified by their fellow-countrymen, for going to dwell in peace with the despised Romans of the East.

Attila is the greatest of the Huns. He was a squat, broad-backed man with a large head and a flat face. But his little eyes sparkled with tremendous passions, his body had great nervous energy. A haughty little creature, he had a prancing way of walking, and he rolled his eyes fiercely, filling the onlookers with terror, and enjoying the terror he inspired.

But he was exceedingly clever as well as powerful. He murdered his brother Bleda, and in 445 founded the great Hunnish kingdom that stretched from the Volga to the

Danube. He had a fine wooden palace in Hungary, in the midst of a wooden town. His palace was clean, it had carven pillars and fair halls, with apartments for his many wives.

Attila is perhaps the greatest barbarian conqueror that ever lived. His people loved him, worshipped him as a great magician. 'Attila, my Attila,' sang the warriors.

Attila first turned east. He subdued Russia, Germany, even Scandinavia—the very lands that Rome could never subdue. He spread east and came into contact with China, offering an alliance on equal terms with the emperor of that realm.

In 450, however, Attila set out from his wooden palace on the upper Danube. Genseric, the ferocious Vandal of Africa, had asked him to attack the Romans of Italy from the north. The Franks of Gaul had invited his aid. And, rapacious Hun that he was, he had heard from the Hunnish armies who had been fighting in Gaul how rich that land was. Therefore he took his dreaded title, 'Attila, the Scourge of God,' and moved with his bands across the lands we now call Austria, Bavaria, Switzerland, to the Rhine. There he summoned all the chiefs of Russia and Germany to his army.

Over the Rhine came thousands and thousands of the mixed host. Swift as clouds the hordes of Hunnish cavalry swept forward and ravaged Gaul. That rich and beautiful land thrilled with horror. Peasants in the country, people in the towns working peacefully and going their way looked up and saw horsemen appearing over the brow of the hill. In a few moments the forerunners became a dark swarm. Like a wind they came down. The towns might hastily shut their gates and hold out for a time. The trembling inhabitants looked over the walls and saw the host encamped. Then slowly over the hill-brow came the heavy wagons.

In a sudden unexpected rush the Huns would be on the

town. Grinning with war-excitement, the little men swarmed and slashed, killing every inhabitant in their glee of slaughter. They found priests and bishops hastily baptizing the infants, lest death should overtake the unchristened babies and their helpless souls be lost. This sight made the savage little Huns grin wider. Swiftly the priests and bishops were cut down, the babies tossed on spears. For the sight of the ceremonies of the Christian religion irritated the Huns extremely. Then the town was thoroughly pillaged, food and wine consumed. After the revel, when all was stripped, the retreating Huns fired the towns, and far-off Gauls knew by the redness of the sky what was happening. Cities burned to a blackened ruin, for even the stone buildings were usually supported by beams and pillars of timber; the poorer quarters were of wood.

Such was the fate of beautiful Roman cities like Metz and Trèves, and many others. The Huns advanced into Gaul, leaving the earth like a cinder behind them, strewn with the charred remains of men and women. It was said that wherever the horse of Attila set his foot, there the grass never grew again.

As the Huns attacked the sacred city of Orleans, they were threatened by the approach of the Romans, led by the famous general Aetius, who was himself a Tartar from Asia, and the Visigoths of Aquitaine led by the aged Theodoric. Attila moved off. He kept to the open country, for he had a horror of being shut up in a town. Slowly, retiring with his wagons, he was followed by the Romans and the Visigoths, to whose aid came the Burgundians from the Rhone, and the Franks under Merwig. So Attila retreated beyond the Seine. He wanted to find a plain where he could spread out his vast host.

At last, on the plain of Châlons, on the Marne, the two huge armies came together. On the one hand was Attila, with Huns, Goths, Burgundians, Saxons, Franks, Slavs, a countless host; on the other Aetius and Theodoric, with a vast army of Romans, Goths, Burgundians, Franks, Huns, bands from almost every tribe. It seemed as if one half of the barbaric world was camped against the other half.

There was one hill commanding the plain. Aetius, with his Roman Gauls, and Thorismond, son of Theodoric, with his Goths, seized this position. And then, in the afternoon, the battle began. There was no plan. The two hosts just rushed at one another, and unspeakable hand-to-hand murder went on for hours, among masses and masses of different men. At last the Visigoths decided the day. They drove back the Ostrogoths, who were on Attila's side, and attacked the startled Huns themselves on the flank. The Huns swerved in confusion, broke, and rushed to shelter behind their wall of chariots and wagons. The Goths also desisted. But the roaring bloody carnage went on, till night fell, and men could see to fight and kill no more.

In the morning there was a great scene in both camps. The Goths could not find their king. It was decided he must be slain, and at last his body was found under a heap of dead. With wild cries of lamentation, and clashing of shields, they raised up Thorismond upon the shield, and proclaimed him king. Meanwhile Attila with his Huns was entrenched behind his wagons. Most of his army was gone. It is said he made himself ready for death : he had piled up a huge funeral pyre of saddles. If the Romans attacked his camp he would mount it and be consumed in the roaring flames.

But Aetius with the Gallo-Romans was too exhausted to attack. He waited. Attila also waited. The days passed in suspense. At last suddenly Attila broke up his camp, and retreated east. Aetius followed. Attila moved northwards and re-crossed the Rhine. Gaul breathed free, and Europe was saved. For if, in 451, Attila had won this great battle of Châlons, on the Catalaunian plain beside the Marne, Europe would have fallen under Tartar sway, or at least would have suffered most terribly from the ' Scourge of God.'

It is sad that the great generals of that day were so shamefully treated. We know of the execution of the great Vandal Stilicho in 408. Now Aetius, the one man who could support the tottering world, was foully murdered by the hand of the emperor Valentinian himself; whilst the young Thorismond was slain by his own brothers.

Attila was not finished. He was angry at his defeat, and very much irritated by Rome. The barbarian king was exceedingly proud. He considered himself superior to any monarch or emperor in the world. Therefore he ought to number the highest princess in the world among his already numerous wives. Therefore he demanded the hand of the Princess Honoria, sister of Valentinian. Honoria herself, being unhappy and foolish, had sent a ring to Attila, asking him to espouse her. The Romans were horrified beyond measure. Honoria was closely imprisoned. Attila's demand was coldly refused.

The matter rankled in the mind of the Hun. He had already many wives, but he wanted to add to them this princess of ancient and haughty Rome. In 452 he marched down from his wooden capital, through the eastern Alps, towards the Adriatic Sea. At the head of the Adriatic stood a noble city, Aquileia, mistress of that sea, and the key to Italy by the eastern route.

In all his offended spite Attila fell upon Aquileia, and took it. Though it was a great and rich city, he destroyed it so savagely, so utterly, that thirty years later, men standing on the site of the town had to look hard to make out the ruins. The surrounding country was a neglected desert. Those people from Aquileia and the villages who had time to escape fled in terror deep into the marshes and islands of the shallow sea, made wretched huts, and miserably subsisted on fish and shell-fish. And this was the very beginning of that which later on became the world-famous city of Venice, built in the sea.

Attila marched on into the plains of the Po. Vicenza, Verona, Bergamo ran with blood and were stripped by the greedy, insatiable Huns. Milan and Pavia submitted without resistance. The whole of the north was Attila's. Milan was a royal city, a favourite with the later emperors. Attila took up his abode in the imperial palace.

In the palace was a large picture painted on the wall. It represented the Roman emperor sitting on his throne, whilst all the other kings, mostly barbarians, kneeled before him and offered the bags containing tribute. This Attila would not allow. He sent for the court painter and bade him change the figures. When this was done, Attila was seen sitting upon the throne, with all the kings, including the Roman emperor, kneeling before him, bringing their tribute. 'That is nearer the truth,' said Attila, as indeed it was.

Attila remained in Milan, Italy trembled helpless. At last, after much fear and despair, the Romans sent a solemn embassy, which fell prostrate at the feet of Attila. They offered, in the name of the Emperor and of Rome, all their treasures, if the king of the Huns would spare Italy from further attack.

Attila considered. He had been for some time in the sunny land. His men were spread about, feasting, drinking, living lives they were not accustomed to, and which were not natural to them. Disease and pestilence had broken out; the Huns were dying like flies. He must take them back into the cold, fresh air of the north.

Therefore he accepted great treasures, and withdrew, threatening horrible revenge if the Princess Honoria were not sent to him. He slowly crossed Italy and entered the Alps, threading his way northwards towards the head-waters of the Danube, making for his capital in Hungary. All submitted to him on the way.

As he passed he saw a princess of a barbarian tribe, and was pleased by her. So he took her with him. Crossing the Danube, he reached his palace, if we may call it such.

There he made a great feast, a bridal feast for his new bride, whom he married that day in Hunnish fashion, and a feast to celebrate his return in triumph.

The eating, the drinking, the singing, the praise were tremendous. At length all retired for the night. In the morning, it seemed the king lay very late. This was not his custom. The attendants began to listen. They could hear no sound. At last they knocked, and called to their king, but received no answer. Then they broke open the door.

They saw the bride, crouching trembling in a corner beside the bed, covering herself in a veil, speechless. On the bed lay Attila, in a pool of blood. His powerful blood had been too much for his veins. In the night he had burst an artery, and was dead.

This was in 453. The supreme power of the Huns passed with Attila, the Scourge of God—Attila, my Attila ! None the less the nation remained a danger to Europe. Still the clouds of little horsemen swept down on the settled lands. They came from Hungary and Austria, and followed the line of the Danube, bursting down on Bavaria, on Suabia, Germany, and France. This continued even till the tenth century. But the attacks became smaller and less perilous.

The Huns themselves were conquered time after time by fresh Asiatic tribes. First came the Tartar Avars, at the end of the sixth century. They established themselves in Hungary, and were overthrown by Charlemagne. Then came the Magyars, another Tartar nation, who settled in Hungary about the year 900. We speak of the Hungarians of to-day as Magyars, for they use the Magyar language, though their race is mixed. After the Magyars other Tartars and Mongols have conquered Hungary, last of all the Turks. But since the Huns this land has been occupied by Asiatics. Before the Huns it was Slavonic.

VII. Gaul

GADHEL was an ancient mythical hero of prehistoric Europe, about whom we know little save that he gave his name to a great race of people, the Gadhels or Gaels.

There are Gaels to-day in Great Britain. Their language, the Gaelic, is spoken in Scotland, Ireland, Wales, and Brittany. It was once the language of all France. France, Britain, Ireland, in the days before the Romans, were occupied by one great race, the Gaels, whom we call Celts.

The Romans knew the Gaels or Celts quite early, for this race occupied parts of North Italy and made invasions to the south. About 388 B.C. the small struggling city of Rome was sacked by a Gallic host, and for two hundred years after this it was all the growing republic could do to make headway northwards. However, before Caesar's time the Gauls of North Italy and of the Marseilles district had been subdued and Romanised.

The Romans could not pronounce the word *Gael*, so they made it *Gallus*. Gallus is not pleasant to an English tongue, so we turn it into Gaul. The land of the Gauls was named Gallia by the Romans. This is the great country occupied to-day by France, and stretching to the Rhine.

The Gauls or Celts were not savages. From very early times they had taken some part in the glowing life of the Mediterranean. In the south of Gaul was the great port of Massilia, now called Marseilles. Massilia was founded six hundred years before Christ, by settlers from the Eastern Mediterranean. It soon rose to importance, and became the rival of the superb Carthage, that wonderful city of the Phoenicians in North Africa, opposite the toe of Sicily. Massilia at length surpassed Tyre and Sidon and Carthage, and was itself surpassed only by the newer great city of Alexandria.

A great bustle of trade was carried on in Massilia long before Julius Caesar was born to change the world. Merchants arrived from Egypt, Greece, Syria, Africa, and Rome, disembarked on the quays, and loading their goods on horse-back—wine, iron goods, weapons, armour, spices, clothing—passed through the land of Gaul. Since Gaul was in constant communication with Britain, no doubt these merchants crossed into our island with their goods, though not many would find their way so far. In return, Gaul exported to Rome and Africa her woollen robes, her fine cured hams, her mountain cheeses, her great dogs. So that the land of Gaul, though wild and disorderly and barbaric, was by no means savage or primitive.

The Gauls south of the Seine were middle-sized men, taller than the short Romans. They had long fair hair, blue eyes, ruddy, round, blunt faces. Their heads, too, were round, bullet-shaped. They wore linen clothes, close breeches and a close tunic. The Gauls were famous for their breeches, which were disgraceful to Roman eyes.

North of the Seine dwelt the Belgae, another race of Gauls or Celts. They differed from their southern neighbours only in their stature, for they were taller, in the long shape of their heads, and in their fiercer, more stubborn tempers. Perhaps in the Celtic blood of the Belgae was mingled a stream of German blood, for the Rhine made no unsurpassable barrier between Belgae and Germans.

It is supposed that the Gauls had been in earlier days much more powerful and civilised than they were when Caesar advanced upon them. We know from the Celtic legends, and the legends of King Arthur, that once they had fine companies of knights, all equal like a brother-hood, sitting at a round table. In those days the Celtic freemen were under no man's heel, they feared none, unless it were the Druids. The Druids were the religious body. They were three classes: the Ouadd or sacrificing priest, who performed sacrifices and did the lowest priestly work; then the bards who, filled with holy inspiration, sang the glowing chants and records which moved the souls of the knights and listeners in the banqueting halls; then the holy Druid himself, who dwelt in the dim groves of the forest, and was rarely seen by the world. In the shadow of his oak retreat the Druid lived like a hermit, meditating on the sacred mysteries, trying to find out the will of that great God called the Terrible, the Unknown. In these dark groves he gave education to the young men of good birth. From him they learned the long poems or psalms or legends in which all the knowledge of the Celtic race was embodied. And then at times the Druid came forth, when some awful sacrifice was to be performed, perhaps in the great stone circles like Stonehenge, or in the oak groves. Again he was seen on the most solemn day when the mistletoe was cut. Only the Druid himself might approach the sacred mistletoe. At due time he advanced from the solemn procession, having purified himself, fasted, and prayed. The great oak-tree rose before him, the terrible Tree sacred to the One Supreme God. On the oak, between the clefts, grew the golden bough, the delicate fountain, the holy mistletoe. In deep reverence before the awful tree, the Druid trembled with mystery as he reached to cut the golden bough, the mistle-toe, the golden child of the Almighty Tree, the fair Son of the terrible Father.

Thus we see that the centre of the ancient life of the Celts was the Druid. It was he who knew all that there was to be known: he knew of the sun and the stars, and their motions, of the seasons and their changes; he knew of the processes of birth and the mysteries of death; and also he was acquainted with the chief knights in the land, and fully informed concerning the dangerous enemies without. It was he who prophesied, counselled, sent forth orders, suggested war and plans of battle, and controlled justice, and made condemnation. Indeed, from his dark secret retreats the Druid governed the Celtic world : for the priests were all united under the Arch-Druid. The knights and chiefs or kings whom the knights elected from among themselves reverenced the Druid, obeyed him implicitly, and dreaded above all things the terrible threat of excommunication. And since the bards sang in the halls of the knights, and sang as they were informed by the Druid, so the mind of the knight was formed under the influence of the mystic priest, even without his knowing it.

When Julius Caesar came to Gaul, however, this unity of priestly and knightly order was dying out. Druids were losing their strong influence, becoming more worldly and shallow, the knights became greedy and conceited, the freemen became servile followers. Scorning the priests, the knights seized power and made themselves absolute kings. Some chiefs ruled over villages or little towns placed for safety on a hill, beside a river, or behind a marsh; other chiefs were masters of quite large towns, where were many low, wooden halls, dark, with heavy pillars of wood inside, and also streets of round wattle huts with their large, pointed, thatched roofs. In the larger towns lived merchants and weavers, as well as numerous slaves and hangers-on of the chiefs, soldiers, and peasant freemen. The Gaul was not like the German : he hated to be alone. His huts clustered close together. But he lived a dirty, irregular life, careless of everything except his own quarrels and those of his clan. For if he could not live alone, he could not live in company, since his life was consumed in brawls and jealousies.

Each knight, if possible, had a little town to himself and his clan : for like the Tartars, the Celts lived in families or clans. At this town watchmen were always on the look-out, for every clan quarrelled with every other, and the chiefs were like strutting cocks crowing out challenges and flying in each other's faces. Outside the town were the fields where the slaves and freemen worked in a half-hearted fashion, for they thought it more manly to crow challenge and fight and steal. Round the huts lay half-naked children, rolling in the dirt, and ragged, unkempt women peered out suspiciously. Pigs grunted around, a goat was tied to a pole. Inside the hall, not far off, a knight sat at table with dozens of his retainers, listening to his own praises sung to the sound of the harp by a degenerate bard, whilst all his company of clansmen shouted applause and flattery. Then they would come outside and do noisy military exercises.

Notwithstanding their squalor and their quarrelsome, impoverished lives the Gauls were very fond of fine clothing, and of a bragging, swaggering appearance. It was they who invented gaudy tartans—and imitation silver. A chief often used up the substance of his clan in buying grand showy armour of silver and gold, fine horses, silver chariots. For some of the bigger chiefs were rich, they were masters of large clans, they received the tribute of innumerable people, and gathered wealth from their towns. It was the chief business of these lords to be proud and splendid. They provided for their knights, watched the honour of their clan, saw that none of the clansmen actually starved, that is, if food were to be had, and led the clan to battle with neighbours. In time of peace, however, it was the pride of these chieftains to dash along in a silver chariot drawn by fiery horses, and driven by a handsome charioteer, whilst the lord himself stood upright and motionless with his weapons, glittering in splendid armour, his plumes and his coloured cloak flying, thrilling the crowd like a god. Slaves ran beside him or behind him, ragged freemen hailed him as he passed. It was a glitter of arrogance and bravery, and a humbling of all people for their glorification in one man. Of course it was the people who chose this.

The Druids meanwhile still occupied the groves. But these gaudy chiefs took hardly any notice of them, and the Druids took care not to offend the chiefs. The bards had become mere hangers-on in the halls of the knights, singing shameful flattery. The nation was broken up into innumerable quarrelsome clans, each seeking its own glorification; the mass of the people among themselves were squalid, spiteful, enslaved. In some large clans, however, the Druids maintained their power, and these clans were the hardest to beat.

Britain was accounted the home of the Druids. There the luxury and folly of the knights was held in check, there the Druid still governed. No doubt Britain knew all about the doings of the Romans in Gaul; the Druids had prepared for the coming of Caesar. Merchants and priests sailed back and forth across the English Channel. But the two nations of Britain and Gaul no longer held together.

Caesar was made proconsul of Gaul in 58 B.C., and he remained so until 49 B.C. At this time the Romans held sway over south-east Gaul, the Germans over the north. Caesar marched from Rome to Geneva in eight days to stop the advance of the Celtic Helvetians into Gaul. He broke the Rhone bridge, and held them back. Having subdued the Helvetians, he turned north. There the German chieftain Ariovistus was defeated, and the flow of Germans into Gaul was stopped. Next year Caesar marched against the Belgae. The tribe called the Remi, out of jealousy of the other tribes, opened the gates of their capital, Rheims, to the Romans, and so Caesar had a stronghold in the north. It was always so. By using one tribe of jealous Celts against another, the Roman won his victories. They could never have been won if the Gauls had but united.

In 55 B.C. Caesar came to Britain, to sever the connection between the two countries, and smite a blow at the holy land of the Gauls, for Britain was the home of the Gallic faith. Next year he came again, received the pretended submission of Cassivelaunus, and returned with a few pearls and slaves. But he really did nothing in Britain : it was beyond him.

This attack on their holy land roused all the defeated Gauls into revolt. There was at last a union among them —but too late. Summoned by the Druids, they met in lonely places at night, to form their plans. The Romans were afraid. In 53 B.C. Caesar gathered a great army of ten legions, and ravaged the lands of the north.

Then came forward the last and greatest of the Gallic chieftains, Vercingetorix. He fought bravely, and won a splendid victory over Caesar. This was the only real defeat Caesar suffered. And shortly he had his revenge. Vercingetorix was beaten and the Gallic spirit broken in a battle near Dijon.

Vercingetorix with his small force was encircled by the legions in the hills of Central France. Sorely besieged, he sent out the Gallic cavalry to rouse the land. The summons was answered. Gauls from all parts marched to the relief of the brave leader. But the relieving army was driven back, and Vercingetorix withdrew into his besieged town.

He knew the case was now hopeless. Calling his starving, faithful bands together, he told them he would save them. Then he bade his attendants dress him in his most splendid armour and apparel. Meanwhile, in the opposite camp Caesar was sitting in high tribunal amongst his officers. Suddenly there was shouting, a commotion. A chieftain in splendid glittering armour, with plumes waving from his helmet, bracelets of gold on his arms, his horse shining with silver and coloured cloths, galloped into his presence. He leaped from his horse. It was seen he was a Gaul, for he wore the close tartan breeches no Roman would put on. The guards stood round him. He flung himself at Caesar's feet, crying out that he yielded. It was Vercingetorix yielding himself up to save his beleaguered men.

Caesar attacked him with bitter words, bade the lictors seize him. Vercingetorix was sent to Rome to be paraded in Caesar's triumph; then he was kept for six years in prison, fretting his noble soul; then at last beheaded.

By 51 B.C. all Gaul was at Caesar's feet. At once the attitude of the conqueror changed. He really liked the dashing, swaggering Gauls. He enrolled a Gallic legion, the Alauda or Larks. He repressed the Druids, and forbade human sacrifices. He tried to make the people freer, lightening the tribute.

And thus began the great change. The Gauls admired their conquerors immensely, they thought the Romans wonderful. So they began to imitate them. Quick and changeable by nature, the Gallic chiefs or knights, wherever they came into contact with the newcomers, quickly picked up some Latin speech, some Roman manners. Of this they were very proud. The Gallic soldiers and freemen imitated their chiefs.

It is said that in Gaul Caesar fought against three million people : one million perished ; one million were enslaved ; one million remained free. So a million slaves had new masters. For the rest, most of the chieftains swore submission to Rome, and were left in possession of their houses, with what slaves or clansmen remained to them. Then life began again. The race quickly increased, for the Gauls were a fruitful people.

The south-eastern part of the country, the old 'Province,' was already Roman and civilised. Many of the people wore Roman dress and spoke Latin. For many generations ships arriving in Massilia had brought goods and men from Tyre, Carthage, Athens, the greatest sea-cities of the old world. These had brought the arts of Greece and Syria to the south of Gaul, so that the fair cities there, Massilia, Narbonne, Toulouse, Arles, were already educated and cultured whilst the north of Gaul lay semi-barbaric, and Paris did not exist.

It was not till the days of Augustus, however, that the

'Province' took the lead in Gaul, for Caesar quarrelled with the Provincials. Augustus wanted to make the Gauls forget their old race, their old religion, and imagine themselves Roman. He removed the Druids, and tried to draw away the clans from their allegiance to the patriotic chiefs. Many chieftains were invited to Italy. Where there was an ancient Gallic town, sacred in the native eyes, Augustus caused the old influence to be broken by establishing a new city in the neighbourhood. So Lyons was founded on the Rhone a few miles away from the old Gallic town of Vienne, and soon people ceased to look to Vienne as their centre. The centrality was transferred to Lyons. When a new city was not established, the old town was given a new name, just as Jerusalem was changed to Aelia. Then the whole country was divided into four provinces, and the provinces arranged to cut across the old race distinctions. Thus the Belgae were not all together in one province. Some were in Belgica, some were in the province of Lyons.

Augustus built the Roman capital of Gaul central between the four provinces. He wished to turn the country into a great Roman state, with a Roman capital. Architects and surveyors studied the land, and a little village on the Rhone was taken as the site. Innumerable slaves and workmen were set to work. In fifteen years' time the splendid capital stood proudly where the village had been; the great city of Lyons had risen. Craftsmen, scholars, merchants, lawyers, patricians had been invited from Italy, throngs of Romans laughed in the broad streets. There was a great market-place, and a mint for making the Gallic money, a splendid central temple of Gaul, built just where the Saône joins the Rhone, and dedicated to Augustus and Roma; besides this, shops, booksellers' shops, schools of rhetoric and eloquence, villas, workrooms. From far around the Gauls came to the great market, or to the theatres or the schools; boats sailed up and down the Rhone; Gallic chieftains who were rich enough built themselves villas in the town; Gallic chariots drove through the streets noisily, their owners proud to be in this fine place.

In the great temple stood the altar of Augustus, surrounded by sixty-four statues representing the Gallic counties or cantons. A second altar belonged to the goddess of Rome. Every year delegates came from each ' city ' or canton to Lyons. They solemnly celebrated the sacrifice in honour of the Emperor and the goddess, and afterwards they met as a kind of national council or parliament, to discuss the government of the country.

Lyons was also the centre of the great road system. Coming from Italy, the Roman road led over the Alps straight into its market-place. From Switzerland or Helvetia came the road through Geneva to Lyons. And then out of the market-place led the four great Augustan roads of Gaul. The first ran north, through Metz, Trèves, to Coblenz on the Rhine ; the second went sheer north-west to Boulogne, and this was the road to Britain ; the third went due west to the Bay of Biscay ; the fourth ran south to Massilia (Marseilles) and Narbonne, on the Mediterranean.

On these roads stood the new Roman cities of Gaul, and from city to city passed constant traffic : the legions marching to the Rhine or to Britain, followed by the baggage-wagons ; Gallic nobles glittering along in their chariots ; slaves or messengers trotting steadily ; colonists marching or riding wearily out of Italy, making for a new home in Gaul ; merchants with strings of pack-horses, workmen with packs, slaves with burdens, strangers from Germany, Britain, Africa, Asia, all met and exchanged greetings on these firm roads. The common language was the vulgar Latin, which everybody learned to speak more or less.

Thus the land became completely Romanised. In place of their wooden halls the Gallic chiefs and the rich freemen built villas such as the Romans had erected for themselves in the countryside. The villas were beautiful open houses of stone or brick, one storey high, with terraces and sometimes a low square tower. High walls ran round the courtyard and gardens. At the back were stables and barracks for the slaves, as well as granaries, barns, cattle-sheds. All around stretched the cultivated lands, smiling and fruitful. This land was tilled by gangs of slaves, who went out in the morning with an overseer and worked till evening, then returned to their quarters, where they were locked up at night.

But still the Gallic freemen lived in their own villages, worked their own land, or wove wool. They were still numerous, although the villas and richer houses seemed to cover a great deal of the country. The rich Gauls began to leave off the native 'breeks,' and wore the Roman toga, speaking only Latin, or a provincial dialect of Latin. Many of the common people also used this provincial Latin. Districts were ruled by Roman governors, magistrates administered the Roman law. All seemed fair and Roman. But in the more remote districts the Gallic peasants still clung together in clans, and held fast to the memory of the Druids. Only the old Province, or Provence as we call it, became more Italian than Italy herself. There great Roman buildings arose; the land was cultivated in the Italian manner; the landscape, the very people looked Italian. Things Gallic were scorned and almost forgotten. Massilia proudly held her Greek schools, a true cosmopolitan city of the old world, a centre of Greek learning.

All this splendid settlement and governing of Gaul cost money. Taxation was very heavy. Even from the first the peasant freemen and artisans groaned. Taxation was always the curse of Gaul. But as time went on, and the vicious emperors allowed the taxes to be farmed out, selling the privilege of collecting taxes to the highest bidder, then the exactions became impossible, and risings took place. Save for this the land knew many happy years; Gaul was one of the most smiling provinces of the empire till the end of the second century after Christ.

Trouble was bound to come. As the Gauls were absorbed by Rome, the Germans were roused to opposition. In 214 the Allemanni, a group of German tribes, made themselves troublesome in the north-east. In 241 great hosts of Franks began to enter Gaul, passing through the whole length of the land to ravage Spain. Many Germans settled in the north as peasants. Gaul lay between Italy and Germany, between the hammer and the anvil. When Germany was weak, Rome came down on Gaul. As Rome weakened, the Germans smote the Gallic land, broke the nation to atoms.

Meanwhile, as the barbarians stirred in the north, Christianity began to work in the south. Christians came from the east, from Greece, Antioch, Joppa, sailing to Massilia and up the Rhone to Lyons. In these days Greek was the universal language of the east. It was St. Paul's language. Small communities of Greek-speaking Christians grew up in Gaul. The new gospel spread. And then in 244 the Church in Rome sent forth a Latin mission. This had great success. The Gauls were already accustomed, from Druid worship, to revere One Supreme God. They could not take the dozens of Roman deities seriously. Now came Christianity, which seemed much more natural to them. They embraced it readily, especially in the towns.

Seven bishops came from Rome to Gaul. They would not touch at Massilia, for that great city adhered too firmly to the old culture. They landed at Narbo, and spread into Central Gaul, establishing the gospel there. In 251 Dionysius with eleven brethren settled at Lutetia (Paris), and founded the Church of Northern France. From this time Christianity spread swiftly. Before a hundred years were past all Gaul was Christian. Indeed Gaul, not Italy, led the way in the new religion.

In the happy days of the empire, all citizens were free and equal, Romans and Gauls, rich and poor alike. They

all were safe from oppression, they all had justice at the
hands of the good magistrates.   But as the empire at Rome
grew rotten, freedom disappeared.   Men were all scheming
and contriving for money and power.   In this scheming
the poor were at the mercy of the more cunning upper
classes, those with money to begin with.   And thus taxes
were imposed beyond reason, poor freemen were taxed
and fined and conscripted till they were driven to despair.
No one was safe but the rich and cunning.   The wretched
freemen saw the slaves of the wealthy remain safe and
sound, whilst they themselves were seized for horrible
foreign wars, or starved to death when the tax-gatherers
had taken all they owned.   It was better to be the slave
of a rich man, than to be free and at the mercy of every
greedy bully, count or duke or official.   For the rich men
protected themselves and their possessions either by bribes
or by armed force or by obtaining a share in the government.   So in despair one after another of the freemen
went and surrendered himself and his family into slavery,
under some rich chieftain or Roman, some greedy, unscrupulous person of wealth.   Then he could no longer be
seized and sent off to war, or seized and tortured to pay
taxes.

This cruel business went on till more than three-quarters
of the people in Gaul were mere slaves, three-quarters of
the human life of the country mere property of weak, vain,
foolish nobles.   These nobles all kept bands of vicious
soldiers, besides those kept by the vile government in
Gaul.   These soldiers devoured and destroyed substance.
So the land was sinking to degradation.   The splendid
central power of Rome was gone ; Gaul was far weaker than
in old Gallic days, and yet richer, fatter, more supine, a
prostrate land.

' Where the carcase is, the eagles will be.'   For years
the lands of the Gallic freemen had been passing into
desolation, for years the German peasants had been
filtering in, settling on the deserted fields.   Now the

German eagles began to hover over helpless Gaul.   On the last night of the year 406 myriads of Vandals, Huns, Goths, Alans crossed the Rhine and poured over Gaul. We know how the cities suffered.   Whilst things were so bad, from time to time the miserable peasants rose in terrible murderous uprisings, slaying and burning devil-ishly, then starving and dying themselves, then sinking back to a condition worse than before.

In 412 the Visigoths, already half Roman in their ways, came and occupied the southern region.   They merely took half the forest land and gardens, two-thirds of all the cultivated lands, and worked these mostly with the Gauls or Provincials already established there.   The big, good-natured Burgundians did the same on the Rhone. So that the Visigoths and Burgundians were really a blessing to south and east Gaul.   They saved the land from enemies, they destroyed nothing, they were amiable masters and neighbours, they left the natives working as before, and only took a good portion of the produce.

Then in 451 came Attila with the Huns.   Attila was defeated at Châlons, but Gaul was ruined.   The north was gutted, and Theodoric was dead.   After the death of their king the Goths broke into horrible civil war.   Peace was restored for a time, but by the end of the century their land too was destroyed, smashed up.   Everywhere, in Bur-gundy the same, there was murderous fighting, destruc-tion, desolation.   The whole country was swamped in ruin. 'The ocean sweeping over it could not have added to the desolation.'   Cattle had been killed or driven off, man exterminated; fields returned into heath-land and forest; wolves and bears lurked in the ruined streets of Roman cities.   Gaul was a desert of desolation.   Italy was not much better.   The weakness of the Romans and the ferocity of the barbarians had gutted civilised Europe.

Through all this only the light of Christianity flickered. Dukes, counts, governors, these annihilated one another. The government was wiped out.   All was howling, welter-ing insecurity. Only the Christian bishops and clergy kept their souls clear and their minds strong. In the spoiled cities the bishops took authority, to prevent the whole place turning into a den of thieves and murderers, wolves and bears. The Roman law-courts, called basilicas, became Christian churches, and in these buildings the clergy exhorted and commanded the demoralised people. Even Attila had been forced to reverence one bishop, Lupus, Bishop of Troyes, for the fierce Hun found this Christian leader such a noble, commanding presence, unafraid.

Rome was ended, Gaul was left a waste, stranded region, with only the Christian bishops keeping their heads erect in the wreckage. New power must come from somewhere, new life, new force, new strength to build up another Gaul. And where was the force to come from ? Not from the south, for the south was spent. The bishops quite rightly looked to the north. They looked carefully to the most powerful of the tribes of northern Germans. These tribes were the Franks. The bishops had now to look to the Franks as masters or servants. They must depend on the fierce but manly barbarians of the north, and forget the corrupt, foolish Romans.

VIII. The Franks and Charlemagne

In the darkest ages of the fifth and sixth centuries Christianity alone kept hope alive. In the terrible welter and insecurity of Gaul, some men were weary to death of fighting, robbing, burning, thieving, snatching; they wanted peace and the stillness of the soul above all things. Then the monastic life suggested itself. Men seeking the life of the mind and spirit gathered together in the religious houses, or monasteries, where, shut off from the howling desert world, they could think, and write, and pray, and hope. They worked in their fields and kept some spots on the earth sunny and clear. They went among the people, helping, encouraging, teaching, keeping the soul alive and preventing men from sinking back into brutish emptiness. Their lives were a continued protest against the degraded, hopeless slavery of Roman Gaul. Man cannot live without hope, and it was the monks and priests who kept the hope alive in the countryside, the bishops and clergy who fed it in the towns.

At the same time the people mingled all kinds of superstitions with the Christian beliefs. If they had worshipped some strange pagan goddess at a well, a goddess to whom they brought flowers, then they put a statue of the Virgin Mary in place of the idol of the goddess, and it was Mary who performed miracles with the water, and whose voice was heard at night from the bubbling of the spring, and to whom flowers or even other sacrifices were offered. Many sacred trees of the Druids were cut down. But at other times a crucifix was nailed to a bough, and Jesus became the Son of the mystic Tree ; or else a little chapel or shrine was built in the shade of the oak, and here the gifts to the terrible deity of the Druids were hung up in offering to the new God, the new golden bough, the golden Jesus. So the mistletoe was sacred to Jesus. And even now it is the symbol of the kiss of love and increase in our Christmas festivities. So the old and new religions mingled in the Gallic Christianity, the two spirits became one, Jesus is the fruit of the Tree.

Even this measure of peace was to be disturbed again. In the south the Visigothic and the Burgundian kingdoms were Christian, but they belonged to the eastern Christianity, not the Roman. In the north the German Franks were still pagan. The Franks had long been friends and allies of the Roman people. As allies of the Romans for many years they defended the left bank of the Rhine. As Roman power faded away, they came to possess these lands of the left side of the Rhine. These were the first Frankish lands, and always the centre of the Frankish people, the territories we now call Alsace, Lorraine, Luxemburg, Belgium. For the Franks did not like emigrating far from the Rhine.

The Franks were not a single tribe, but probably a confederacy of Germans from many tribes. Frank means a man armed with a franciscus, or axe : a German axe-fighter. They were a loose, brave, barbarous, pagan people, hardly united at all. One of their tribes to the north was the Salian. They were settled by the marshy Rhine mouths. The Salians were very brave, and had caused endless trouble by their ceaseless raids into Northern Gaul. They became the most important of the Franks. Their chiefs were the Merwings, one of the most considerable families in all the confederation. We know that a Merwig or Merwing led the Franks against Attila, and watched that king from the north, until he crossed the Rhine.

In the year 481 a boy of fifteen, Clovis, became heir to

the kingship of the Salian Franks. His tribe was small, counting four thousand fighting men, but very brave, sprung from those Batavian Germans whom the Romans respected so deeply. Clovis was faithfully followed, and made headway. By the time he was twenty he was head of a large army of Franks, his own Salians forming the core of the fighting force.

At Soissons the shadow of the Roman name was kept up in the court of Syagrius. All Gaul was in the hands of barbarians, except Armorica (Brittany), and the land stretching from Brittany to the Frankish borders. Armorica was a free Gallic republic. Syagrius, in the Roman name, ruled over the broad district between the Loire and the Meuse, the district of which Paris is the real centre, but which Syagrius feebly governed from Soissons. He administered justice between the Germans and the Gauls, and hoped one day to gather all the north into a kingdom.

This was not destined to take place. In 486 the young Frank Clovis fell upon Syagrius. Syagrius fled south for his life, to Toulouse, the capital of the young Visigothic king Alaric. Clovis sent messengers and warriors down to the Mediterranean, to Alaric in Toulouse, demanding the surrender of Syagrius. Alaric, not seeing what a deadly neighbour he was bringing himself, delivered up Syagrius, who was promptly slain by Clovis.

The Franks now occupied the territories of the unfortunate Syagrius, and Clovis was possessed of a large district, bounded by the Rhine on the north, the Loire on the south, Burgundy on the east, and Armorica on the west. Gaul was now swallowed up by barbarians, the Gallo-Romans had no land of their own. Only Armorica, a corner, remained free.

The Roman Church of Gaul was established in the north, in the territories of Syagrius. Rheims was the most famous bishopric. The bishops had now a new power to encounter; the Franks were upon them. The Franks were pagan, but then the bishops always had hopes of the wild, uncivilised Germanic tribes, for if they could convert them, they would have great influence over them. So the great desire of the Gallic bishops was to convert the Franks. If they could convert them they could use them, and establish the power of the Gallic Church upon them.

Remigius, Bishop of Rheims, was an astute man. Whilst Clovis was still very young, he had been very friendly to him. The friendship continued, but still Remigius dared not press the young pagan to desert his old faith. At last Clovis, having become more powerful, wished to marry, and to marry a princess. Remigius no doubt artfully suggested the fair Clotilde, a Christian of the Roman Church, and niece to the king of Burgundy. So Clovis married Clotilde.

Remigius had taught Clotilde carefully. He knew the Germans were always very soft and pliant towards their young wives. He knew also that women in his time depended on Christianity for their freedom and equality, for all pagans kept their wives in the background. If Clotilde had a Christian husband she would be a free Christian woman. If not, she would be an obscure pagan wife. It was no wonder that women were the most ardent missionaries in private life, in the first days.

But Clovis was still only a petty prince among the Franks. In 496 the Allemanni, the All-men, the famous German confederacy who had their home about the head-waters of the Rhine, pushed towards Gaul, and pressed on the Franks in Alsace. The Franks of the south called on the Franks of the north. Clovis came down with his Salian army. A great battle took place between the united Franks and the Allemanni. The battle was going against the Franks. In his wild excitement, feeling that he was losing, in the midst of battle Clovis thought of his queen at home. Without knowing what he was doing, he cried out as he fought that if the God of his Clotilde would grant him victory, he would accept her faith. So he swept on in a new rush, the tide of battle turned, the Allemanni were utterly routed.

In their joy nearly all the tribes in the confederation of Franks submitted to the overlordship of Clovis, and he had a great people under him. Now came the time to fulfil his vow. But in his cool mind he was unwilling to do so. He hesitated. Clotilde and Remigius persuaded and persuaded him. At last he consented. He was baptized in Rheims Cathedral, with three thousand of his warriors, whom he had commanded or exhorted to accept the new faith along with him. Remigius, or St. Remy as we now call him, was delighted. He performed the ceremony with all possible splendour, and it seemed to the barbarians as if they were entering heaven itself.

The bishops now handed over the relics of the old Roman legions, their standards and trophies, to Clovis, and Clovis became master of Northern Gaul, save only for Armorica. He was a Christian of the true Latin or Roman Church, as were all the Gallic clergy. But the Burgundians and the Goths were heretic Arians, belonging to the eastern form of Christianity. So the bishops hated them.

Clovis was the drawn sword of the bishops. First he attacked the Burgundians, and defeated their king Gondebald in 500. Then he ravaged Provence, the old Roman province just round Marseilles, and gave it to a friend, Theodoric the Ostrogoth. Then he looked at the great kingdom of the Goths, stretching away from the south to the Bay of Biscay and the Loire, a rich land.

' It much displeases me,' said Clovis in 507, ' that the Goths, being Arians, should own a part of Gaul. Let us go and, God helping, seize their land.' So they swooped down, the Frankish hosts on the Visigoths. Clovis met Alaric in single combat. Alaric was slain, his army routed. The Franks began to ravage the country. Theodoric the Ostrogoth came against his former friend, and saved just a strip of the Visigothic kingdom along the Mediterranean

round Narbonne to the Pyrenees. This the Visigoths
kept for three centuries longer. It was called Septimania.

The Franks treated the Visigothic land shamefully, and
then, when weary of it, retired north, carrying off rich
spoil and countless captives. The Gallo-Romans of Aquitaine, amazed at their orthodox friends from the north,
conceived a hatred against them that lasted for hundreds
of years, a hatred far surpassing anything they ever felt
for their more humane conquerors the Goths.

Meanwhile the Emperor of the East had sent an embassy
to Clovis, bearing orders to confer the title of Consul
Romanus on the barbarian. Clovis was pleased. With
great pomp he celebrated the investiture. In the cathedral
of Tours, Martin, Bishop of Tours, invested the Frankish
chieftain with the purple tunic and mantle, and with a
diadem. So Clovis rode through the streets, amid the
acclamations of the people. He was a Roman Consul, as
Julius Caesar had been before him. The Gallo-Romans
were much moved, for they ever looked back to their days
of Roman greatness.

Clovis was now raised above any other Germanic chief
or king. He tried to establish himself more securely by
killing off any head of a tribe he could lay his hands on.
One after another he murdered them, and made himself
king of their tribes. At last all the Meroving chiefs had
perished, Clovis' own relations, and he was sole head of
the Franks, acknowledged by all.

' Woe is me ! ' he said at last, ' for I am left as a sojourner
in the midst of strangers. I have now no kinsman to help
me, if misfortune comes.' But he said this like a cunning
fox, hoping to draw forward any man who pretended to
belong to his royal house. If any had come forward,
Clovis would at once have dispatched him. But there
was none to come.

Clovis and his Franks were no governors. They could
not rule a country. They could only spoil it. The Gallic
bishops clustered round his throne flattering him and

cunningly using him. The Franks paid to their bishops all the reverential homage they had yielded to their mysterious pagan priests in the past. Clovis loaded the Church with gifts and lands, till it was said the Gallo-Romans recovered through their clergy what they lost through the wars. For the clergy and bishops were all Gallo-Romans. No Frank would dream of taking holy orders. A Frank would live by his sword. So the Gallo-Romans had the Church of Gaul entirely in their own hands, and in this indirect way they governed their own country. For bishops advised and instructed the Frankish princes.

So, in the towns, and on the great Church estates all over the country the Gallic bishops erected their palaces. Just as counts and dukes had had the cities in their power in late Roman days, so the bishops had them now. The bishops were the sole rulers, magistrates, protectors of the towns. They were the established landed aristocracy. They really had the warlike, barbarian kings in their power. They became a proud, worldly, domineering race, most unchristian.

Clovis died in 511, and the territories in Gaul were roughly divided among his three sons. The settlement of the land went on slowly, for the Franks were very German in feeling; they kept returning to their old homes by the Rhine, and new bodies of Franks continually passed into Gaul.

When the Franks did settle it was in a very irregular manner. They avoided towns, for they disliked being crowded and shut up. The Gallo-Romans had the cities to themselves. The Franks dispersed themselves in little knots or groups in the countryside, each group almost separate and independent of all the others. The kings had great territories. On these lands they owned certain manor-houses, and with his whole court the king rode from one big farm to another. When he had exhausted the hunting and the provision of one manor or villa, he and his following mounted horse and rode away to camp in another. They caroused, gambled and hunted all day long, when no fighting was to be done. They also practised military sports, that kept them busy.

The king as we know gave large tracts of land to the bishops and to the Church. He also granted fiefs or estates to his friends, the warriors who fought with him, or the men whom he liked. The greater chiefs, however, who had followed the king independently, took greater lands for themselves, and assumed full, free power over it. So that after Clovis' time we have the kings moving about to their various houses on their own territories, to hunt and sport; we have the more independent chiefs living with their own following on other territories; and we have the smaller estates which the king had given to his friends, and which he might any time take back again.

The Franks, indeed all the Germans, did not attach themselves to land. They counted the man everything, the land nothing. The Frankish king would not deign to call himself king of France or Francia. He was a king of men, king of the Franks. The land was only the hunting-ground and the provision-field of men.

So the king paid not the slightest heed to the cultivation of his territories. On the land which he reserved as his own, the Gallo-Romans were living and working. Most of these were left as they were, and only compelled to give tribute, to provide the king with all he wanted. It was the same on the territories of the great chiefs. Many of the Gallo-Roman gentlemen and freemen remained as they were, in their villas or huts, but they had to give tribute to the Frankish chieftain, yield up corn and cattle and service at his demand. Real tribute meant personal service, labour in the fields of the overlord. When a Frank was given a farm or manor of his own, if it were not occupied he took possession. If it were occupied he got rid of the occupant, installed himself, and worked the land with his captives or slaves. This Frank, having received his land from the king as reward for fighting services, was still a king's man. He must fight for the king. But he paid no tribute, unless it were in certain provisions. He was almost independent. Only the great independent chiefs held their lands without paying any tribute at all. The commoner Franks who came into Gaul took their share of what they could get—captives, cattle, goods, money. With these they sheltered themselves under a great chieftain, and either asked him to give them a farm, for which they would pay tribute, or else some post in his household. Some of them sank very low, became mere servants or serfs; some remained free farmers.

The Franks kept the land in some sort of order, by the help of the clergy. Councils were held from time to time. There were courts of justice in each district, presided over by a count, whom the king appointed. But as a rule each great landlord made his men bring their disputes before him, and he settled all matters, with the help of his clerk or priest. The chiefs took no notice of the king's court. Life was wild and disorderly. A good deal of land fell out of cultivation.

The Gallo-Romans were really better off under the Franks than under the later Roman government. The Franks never extorted exorbitant, ruinous taxes. They depended on free gifts. Again, the Germans had always a higher sense of individual freedom than the southerners. They never had personal slaves. They disliked slaves in their household, they could not endure the personal service of slaves. The sight of fields being worked by gangs of men under an overseer was displeasing to them. Already, when the Roman power broke down, the Gallo-Romans had begun to be afraid of their slave-gangs. Already much land was divided into plots, with cottages or huts.

Now the old Roman villa with its splendours and its barracks for slaves disappeared. The manor-house took its place, with a dove-cot, a church near by, and then the cluster of huts where the labourers lived. The land round

about the manor-house belonged to the lord of the manor.
Beyond this, the estate was broken up into little plots,
and each plot was worked by a freeman or a slave, or even
by a poor Frank. So we see that the condition of the
slave was much improved, he had his own house for himself and his family, and his own possessions, few as they
were, and his own life to himself. But the condition of
the freeman sank. Just like a slave, the freeman had
to go to work in his master's fields. For the master or
lord kept no labourers. The broad lands round the manor
were tilled by the men who lived in the village. Before
they touched their own fields they must all, slave, freeman
and poor Frank alike, put in so many days of work on the
master's estate. When the manor lands were finished,
then the serf might begin on his own.

Still, each man had a soul of his own. The priests were
all Gallo-Romans, as were most of the workers on the land.
They helped their fellow-countrymen where they could.
The Franks were careless task-masters. All went well in
years of plenty. In times of bad harvest, many serfs
with their families starved to death.

Thus the Gauls possessed their own land again, they
had their own huts, each a piece of his mother-earth. But
they were serfs. And they were to remain so for hundreds
of years. The spirit of German independence and individual liberty had combined with the old Roman ideal
of social unity, and the first signs of real European life
appeared. But it was all crude and low.

The division of the country among the three sons of
Clovis was a misfortune, for these three quarrelled. The
Frankish kings even strove to keep up the war-spirit, for
they despised a settled life as being fit only for women and
churchmen. With their long yellow hair and their fierce
ways, these kings were either warrior chiefs or nothing.
So the fierce and endless fighting went on, trampling the
face of Gaul, which might else have been a pleasant land
again. For a hundred years the weary wreckage con-

tinued, whilst the Gallo-Romans laboured and the priests and bishops tried to keep some order. But the bishops were almost as bad as the nobles, so greedy for land, so arrogant, so fierce and eager to make war.

In 628 the good king Dagobert became king of all Gaul, and pacified the land. When he died the old turmoil went on. The king of the north-east, Neustria, fought the king of the north-west, Austrasia. Further south, kings went for nothing, the nobles smashed at one another in endless fray. The land was weary and war-tattered.

In these days the first rude castles were built. The pleasant country houses and villas and open manors that remained from Gallo-Roman days were no use. The Frankish nobles built themselves strongholds with thick walls and unbreakable towers, dark, ugly dens with no windows and no warmth, bitter cold and unhealthy to live in, but secure. Most of the old pleasant houses were destroyed. New ugly buildings frowned from some strong position, huts clustered at their base or by the road not far off.

Churches also were built, and fine abbeys, in a new style, in which the Roman manner was modified by the German spirit. Everywhere the German spirit was pervading old forms, to give birth to a new world. More monasteries arose, refuge for war-weary mortals. But these had to be built strong as fortresses, since bishops and abbots fought as ferociously as dukes and counts.

In 687 Pippin of Heristal won the battle of Testry, over the western Franks, the Neustrians, and became chief of all the Frankish nation. He was a good fighter, and wise. He favoured the monks against the too-greedy and impudent bishops, and he proceeded to pacify the land. But no sooner was internal fighting hushed, than external enemies appeared. First the ferocious, pagan Saxons broke over the Rhine. Then the Mohammedans appeared.

The Franks were still German in speech, German in spirit and in manners. Indeed, from the banks of the

Rhine to the Seine the land was rather West Germany than Northern France. The Gallo-Romans of the south hated the northerners. But the worst enemies of the Franks were no longer the Visigoth of the south or the Burgundian of the east, but the wild Saxon of the north, and the Mohammedan from Spain.

Again Gaul was between two fires. No sooner were the Saxons driven over the Rhine than the Mohammedans appeared over the Pyrenees. By 718 the Arabs or Moors had finally defeated the Visigoths in Spain. Then the dark armies poured into Southern Gaul. They defeated the Visigoths there, sacked Bordeaux, marched on Tours.

Charles Martel, chief of all the Franks, came down to Aquitaine against the great Arab general Abd-el-Rahman. Behind Abd-el-Rahman the Arabs were drawn up on their swift and beautiful horses, glittering with armour of fine, thin steel, their faces dark and fierce, their dark beards flowing. They were a great, beautiful host. Behind Charles Martel stood the ranks of tall, blond Franks, Germans, armed with their huge battle-axes. The dark sons of Arabia and Africa faced the young power of Europe. The long and bloody battle of Tours was fought between the two. But the light Arabs with their scimitars could not stand against the whirling battle-axes of the Franks. There was monstrous slaughter, and the Arabs fell back towards the south. But they were not driven out of France. For years they held the south of Aquitaine and Septimania, along the Mediterranean.

In 768 Charles, afterwards called Charlemagne, became king of the Franks. Charlemagne is one of the most famous figures in all history. He was a true Frankish-German, tall, with beautiful bright hair and fresh colouring. German was his native tongue, German the language of his household. But he spoke Latin, and understood Greek. He wore the Frankish dress : that is, a linen shirt and drawers next his skin ; above these, a tunic with a silken hem, and breeches of the same stuff as the tunic ;

then he wrapped his knees and legs down to the ankles with strips of linen ; in winter he had a loose overcoat of fur, ermine or otter, short but warm ; and over this he wore a coloured Frankish cloak, and slung across him by a gold or silver belt, a scabbarded sword. He hated foreign dress. He lived and ate among the Franks just as one of themselves, without show.

Yet he was one of the greatest of men. As a fighter and vast conqueror he is to be compared only with Alexander, Caesar, or Napoleon. He fought against twelve nations, and spread his great empire from the Elbe to the Pyrenees, and away south down Italy as far as Rome. The great Haroun el Raschid, greatest of the Arab Caliphs, wished to be the friend of so splendid a conqueror, though he despised all other Europeans.

But Charlemagne was great in many ways. He was learned, and did all he could for education in Francia. He built many fine buildings, bridges, roads. He tried to encourage agriculture, and prevent famine. He was much beloved by all his subjects ; and he seemed to stand alone in the world in his greatness. Only the great Haroun el Raschid could compare with him, of all men living at that day.

Amid the squalor of misery and discord in Italy in the Dark Ages, the popes, bishops of Rome, gradually rose to power. The Pope was head of the Church, and in every land the Church was growing stronger and stronger. Kings depended on bishops, and were afraid of them. The Frankish kings, wisely, had been friends of the popes.

In 799, however, the Roman citizens rose against Pope Leo III., and would have destroyed him for his many crimes. Leo had already shown himself submissive to the Frankish king. Now he fled to Charles. The king received him gladly, and they agreed to give one another kindness for kindness. Charles with his armies restored the Pope to Rome. In return, whilst he was celebrating mass at the

Vatican on Christmas Day of the year 800, Pope Leo suddenly stepped forward, poured a vial of oil over Charles's head, and crowned him with a golden crown. All the greatest Franks and Romans were present. No doubt they knew what was to happen, for immediately they cried aloud: 'Hail, Charles Augustus, crowned of God, great and peaceful Emperor of the Romans! Long life and victory!'

Thus once more a great leader was hailed as Augustus in Rome. The empire of the West had vanished. There was nothing truly Roman left. And yet, in Rome itself, a Christian priest crowned a German soldier, and gave him the title that Nero and Hadrian had borne. This strange event shows what power Rome still had over the minds of men. This was really the beginning, also, of the Holy Roman Empire, which lasted almost to our own day.

Charles was now the Emperor Charles the Great. He ruled as emperor over a great part of Europe. And the rest of his reign passed fairly quietly. He had to go out against the Northmen or Danes, who were ravaging North Germany. He repressed them so strongly that the Danes were forced to depend more on their ships, and thus began their invasions of Britain, France, and the Mediterranean lands.

The Emperor tried hard to settle his land of France peacefully and well. Every town had its two governors, the bishop and the count, whilst through the country were sent commissioners, before whom all wrong could be laid. They judged even the counts. Charlemagne made himself head of the Church, to keep the bishops in check.

But it was not much use. The poorer freemen were at the mercy of the greedy, fighting chieftains and bishops. The poorer Franks, who had come to Gaul as free warriors, and who had remained proud and independent, having free farms or small estates of their own, now sank again. Many

were killed in the wars.   Those remaining were threatened
all the time by rich landowners.   So they put themselves
under the protection of some lord, and paid tribute of
service.   The same was the case with Gallic freemen.
They all became bond, sinking down towards serfdom.
This process seemed inevitable in the Dark Ages.   It
seemed as if the mass of men must be serfs or slaves, at
the mercy of the few.   In Charlemagne's day nine-tenths
of the people of Gaul were serfs, one-tenth only were free,
and many of these were priests and monks.   When Charles
gave the learned Englishman Alcuin the present of an
estate, we learn that 20,000 serfs went with the land, and
were included in the gift.   Yet this was not a large estate.
So low was the value of men.

The serfs on the estates of churchmen and on the king's
own land were not so badly off.   They were not badly
treated, some even came to hold property and to be deemed
worthy to be warriors.   In years of plenty they were
content.   But agriculture was very badly managed, and
some years there was terrible scarcity.   In 805 and 806
thousands of serfs with their families just starved to death.
During times like these, many men begged to be admitted
into monasteries, to become monks : so many, indeed, that
the king had to forbid further admissions.

We are bound to feel that these Gallo-Romans, ancestors
of the modern French, were during this period spiritless,
made for slavery.   The Franks never levied armies from
the Gallic people—evidently considering them unfit for
military purposes.   Charlemagne struggled to improve
the condition of the great servile masses of these serfs or
villeins.   But they were too apathetic, and the Franks
were too contemptuous of them altogether to trouble
about them.   The Gallo-Romans dragged on their degraded existence, caring nothing for freedom, filled with
strange and sometimes horrible superstitions, loving to
make pilgrimages to shrines, neglecting all work, desiring
to inflict strange penances on themselves, and performing

mysterious rites before trees and groves and springs, using charms and practising magic, and willing to commit strange crimes.

Charlemagne died in 814, and was buried in his own town of Aix-la-Chapelle. His great empire soon fell to pieces, the old darkness sank over the lands. Great lords warred on one another, the lesser lords were killed off. The descendants of Charlemagne, emperors they called themselves, tried to reign. But they were weak and effortless.

Gradually the Franks dropped their German speech. The bishops and clergy, the teachers, the instructors, were all Gallo-Romans, and spoke a sort of Latin. It was easier for the Franks to learn the Gallic language, the ' Romana Rustica ' as it was called, the Rustic Latin, than for the Gauls to learn the difficult German. At one time all intelligent Franks spoke both languages. Then gradually the German was forgotten ; by 850 or 900 the Romance language was the language of the Franks in Gaul, as well as of the Gallo-Romans.

As kings grew weaker, dukes and counts grew stronger, till they were really independent lords of their own great lands. Great dukes of Gothia, Gascony, Burgundy, Brittany, Aquitaine, counts of Toulouse, Flanders, Vermandois—these were stronger than any poor Caroling king, in their own regions. Thus the Feudal System begins. In the ninth century the terrible Northmen began to invade France, and the dukes and lords began to build the huge feudal castles against them. In the tenth century the Northmen settled along the Seine. Their land became Normandy : there was a new duke, Duke of Normandy : and soon the Normans were speaking French, they were more French than the Frenchmen. Yet they were pure Germans by blood, Danes.

An adventurer, Robert the Strong, became Duke of France, that is of the small middle region round Paris. In 987 the Carolingian line died out and Hugh Capet, Duke of France, was proclaimed King of France : that is, he was mere war-leader or war-lord of all the dukes and counts, who remained independent as before. And so now at last, with Hugh Capet, the real kingdom of France begins, separate from Germany altogether, separate from Italy and Rome, the French lords having one head, one leader.

IX. The Popes and the Emperors

AT first, as we know, the popes were only bishops of Rome, without any power in the world, save over their clergy and congregations. But as the Christian Church grew, and Christians became numerous, the bishop became master of the considerable moneys of the Church, and of the increasing property in land and goods. So that soon he was important in Rome, having great authority over the people in the city.

After the departure of the emperors from Rome, the bishops were left supreme in the capital. They claimed that they were the successors of St. Peter, and that Jesus had put the government of the souls of men into the hands of Peter : therefore they, the bishops of Rome, were governors of the spiritual life of Christians. And as the spiritual life is much higher than the temporal life, so the governors of the spiritual realm are much greater than the governors of the world : thus the Bishop of the Christians, the Papa, or Pope, as he came to be called, was much higher in authority than an emperor. So the Pope Leo preached in 446, and so the Pope Gelasius plainly wrote to the Emperor Anastasius at Constantinople, in 494.

In the time of Gregory the Great, 590-604, the Roman world in Italy was already in ruins, and the Christian Church was the only organised power. In Italy, in Sicily, even in farther provinces, the Church had acquired rich lands, looked after by deacons or subdeacons, and ruled by bishops. But as yet the bishops were ministers of peace. The rents and produce of the Church estates were brought to the mouth of the Tiber, and on the four great sacred festivals, the Pope divided their quarterly allowance to the clergy, to his domestics, to the monasteries, the churches, the places of burial, the alms-houses, and the hospitals of Rome and of the diocese of Rome. On the first day of the month he distributed to the poor, according to season, their allowance of corn, wine, cheese, oil, vegetables, fish, cloth, and money, and such was the misery of Italy at that time that many nobles were glad to accept the Pope's bounty, for they had nothing left of their own. The sick, the helpless, pilgrims, and strangers were relieved every hour, and Gregory was not in vain called the Father of his Country. For he had to stand alone against the terrible attacks of the Lombards on Rome, reasoning with them and persuading them. Besides all this, he sent out missionaries, and England was converted by his means.

But as the years went on, the civil life of Italy grew more chaotic. The city of Rome had no defences, and no real government. The senators and chief citizens elected the Pope, and when they were displeased with him, murdered him or drove him out or forced him to his knees. The country round Rome was turned into wilderness.

The Church of Constantinople, moreover, now called the Greek Church, was very antagonistic to the Roman Church. The Patriarch of Constantinople proudly called himself the Universal Bishop, and tried to make the Bishop of Rome submit to his authority, which the popes of Rome refused to do. At the same time the emperors at Constantinople still claimed to rule over Italy, incapable as they often were. About 730 the Emperor in Constantinople began a great quarrel with the Italian Church, about the use of images. The Roman Christians loved their statues of the Mother of Jesus, and the Infant, their statues of Jesus, and their Crucifixes. The Byzantine rulers wanted these images abolished and destroyed. There was a tremendous struggle again between East and West, religious this time. The bishops of Rome stuck to

their images, crucifixes and shrines, and the western
Christians loved them for it. So the Roman Church
triumphed, the Byzantines were driven back, to spread
their Greek Church up the Black Sea to Russia, leaving
Western Europe alone.

The popes became more popular, the bishops grew
stronger. But the times were wretched, there was no
security anywhere. The rich bishops in Gaul, ruling like
princes, often forgot or ignored the distracted popes at
Rome. Then the Mohammedan power rose up. It had
begun its first attacks on Eastern Christendom in 630,
and it spread victorious along the Mediterranean. Christians must fight Moslems, and the Pope, the great head
of Christendom, must stand clear to his people. Again,
the Frankish princes, Charles Martel, Pippin, Charlemagne,
found that they needed some support, some stay in the
disordered world. They made themselves firm friends with
the tempest-tossed popes of Rome, and the popes helped
the princes in return to the kingly and the imperial crown.
So the popes became established as powerful heads of
Christendom.

After Charlemagne, however, the Frankish Empire went
to pieces, and the Frankish emperors dwindled and became
more foolish and feeble till they ended in the insane Charles
the Fat, and then the imperial name more or less died out.
France became a welter of princes and dukes. The remains
of Charlemagne's empire continued in the dukedoms of
Germany, Franconia, and Lorraine.

The disappearance of the Carolings, as the House of
Charlemagne was called, had a disastrous effect on Italy,
where the Frankish emperors had ruled and kept some sort
of connection with the Pope. Popes were set up and
thrown down by the robber knights of the Campagna,
who called themselves senators or consuls, till the power
of the papacy even came into the hands of loose women,
and popes were the creatures of rich, reckless mistresses.

Germany at this time consisted of six great duchies:

Saxony, Franconia, Thuringia, Suabia, Bavaria and Lorraine. These duchies were practically independent, but they recognised a king. The House of Charlemagne had come to an end. There was no heir to the old Frankish name. In 919, at an assembly of the Saxon and Franconian peoples, Henry, Duke of Saxony, was chosen King of the Germans. He is usually called Henry the Fowler. He was a strong, active man. He fought against the Norman Vikings, and against the Slavonic peoples who threatened Germany in the east, but chiefly against the wild Huns and Magyars who came up from the Middle Danube, invading Europe about this time. Henry the Fowler won the allegiance of the other great dukes of Germany, so that when he died they elected his son Otto, king. Otto fought against the Slavonic Prussians, pushed his power over the Elbe, and established the great bishopric of Magdeburg as a strong centre in the east. He also established border-governments called Palatinates and Marks. In 955 he inflicted a crushing defeat on the Magyars, so that they retreated to Hungary, where they live to this day.

Otto was never safe from the great dukes of Germany, who were jealous of him. So he made friends with the bishops. The bishops of Germany were far from Rome. They were the only educated people in the land. They were rich and powerful as princes. So into their hands Otto put the administration of the land, and the great bishops of Cologne, Mainz, Worms, Magdeburg were now collecting taxes, holding law-courts, and organising armies in Germany, whilst the dukes fought and plundered and made havoc.

But Italy has always had a fatal fascination for the Germans, ever since the first barbarians came against Rome. Otto could not bear to think of the degradation and shame of the popes. He depended on the bishops of Germany. And how could any bishops be respected if their chief, the Holy Father, were a creature of shame?

Moreover the powerful Archbishop of Mainz already refused to serve Otto very willingly. So the king thought
that if he marched into Italy and set the Pope straight
there, he should be master of his clergy at home.

He came down over the Alps and easily mastered North
Italy. He occupied Rome, and rescued the Pope John
from his enemies. In 962, Otto was crowned Emperor of
Rome, by the grace of God and the Pope. And so the
Holy Roman Empire was really established. It became
one of the greatest institutions of the Middle Ages. And so
also began the most important relationship between Pope
and Emperor. Henceforth the German kings were filled
with the fatal passion to rule in Italy, to stretch a great
empire from the Baltic over the Alps to the extremes of
Sicily and Calabria. And this was never possible, for the
peoples of Italy and Germany are so vitally different. If
Rome could not rule Germany, how could Germany rule
Rome ? Yet the two extreme nations of Europe never
ceased to be fascinated the one by the other, pitched
against one another.

Another sign of the fascination which Italy exerted over
the Germanic mind is seen in the conquest of Sicily and
South Italy by the Normans. We know that the Normans
from Norway and Denmark, fierce Vikings, raided Europe
and England in the time of Charlemagne. We know that
they settled in the Seine valley, and established the Dukedom of Normandy, soon becoming more French than the
French. We know that from Normandy they conquered
England in 1066. In 1040 a little band of Normans were
fighting as free lances in the south of Italy. In Normandy,
in the castle of Hauteville, was a Norman knight named
Tancred, who had twelve sons. These sons must ride to
seek their fortune. Some came south to Calabria. One
of these sons was called Robert, Robert Guiscard, or
Wiscard, Wiseacre. He was a tall, splendid Viking with
long, flaxen beard flying, and blue eyes sparking fire. He
joined his countrymen in the south, where the Greeks from

Constantinople were fighting the Pope. Ultimately the Pope made Robert Guiscard Duke of Apulia and Calabria, and of such lands in Sicily and Italy as he could win from the perfidious Greeks. This was in 1060, six years before the Conquest of England. And this was the beginning of the famous Norman kingdom of Sicily and Naples, which lasted so long, and was such a power in the Mediterranean and such a thorn in the side of the popes. Normans emigrated in great numbers, in their ships, like Vikings of old, and settled in Sicily under Robert. So that once more the North settles and possesses the South.

On the one side the Pope had the Normans for neighbours. To the north of him lay Tuscany, and beyond that the great towns of Lombardy, just rising to new independence and new strength—Milan, Bologna, Florence, Verona, Pisa, Genoa.

In 1073 Hildebrand, a monk, was raised to the papal throne, becoming Gregory VII. He was a small man, but impressive. The people loved him, the monks and many of the bishops and nobles were on his side. And he was determined to be the chief power in Christendom. 'The Roman Pontiff is unique in the world. He alone can depose or reconcile bishops. He can be judged by no one. The Roman Church never has been deceived and never can be deceived. The Roman Pontiff has the right to depose emperors. Human pride has created the power of the kings, God's mercy has created the power of the bishops. The Pope is the master of emperors.' This is Hildebrand's declaration.

There was bound to be trouble between him and the Emperor. Henry IV. was a clever emperor. It was his custom, and the custom of the nobles, to create bishops in Germany, giving them the ring and crozier as symbols of their office. This distinctly meant that the bishops were to obey the Emperor first, and the Pope afterwards. To this Hildebrand could never agree.

In 1075 Hildebrand declared that 'If any emperor,

king, duke, marquis or count, or any lay person or power
has the presumption to grant investiture, let him know
that he is excommunicated.' So the Pope announced his
intention to take away from the Emperor the bishops, on
whom the Emperor depended for the administering of his
kingdom. Henry soon answered.

' Henry, King, not through usurpation but through the
holy ordination of God, to Hildebrand, at present not
Pope but false monk—descend and relinquish the chair
which thou hast usurped. Let another ascend the throne
of Saint Peter, who shall not practise violence under the
cloak of religion, but shall teach the sound doctrine of
Saint Peter. I, Henry, King by the Grace of God, do say
to thee descend, descend, to be damned throughout all
ages.'

The Pope's reply begins : ' O Saint Peter, chief of the
apostles, incline to us, I beg, thy holy ears and hear me,
thy servant, whom thou hast nourished from infancy and
whom until this day thou hast freed from the hand of
the wicked who have hated and do hate me,' . . . and
it ends, ' I absolve all Christians from the bonds of the
oath which they have made to Henry, the Emperor, and
I forbid any one to serve him as king. And since he
has scorned to obey as a Christian, and has not returned
to God whom he deserted, I bind him with the chain of
anathema.'

Nearly all Italy came to the side of the Pope, the Normans, Matilda of Tuscany, and the great Lombard towns.
Hildebrand made friends even in Henry's Germany.
Henry had to struggle against his own nobles. In a
council or diet of the empire of Germany, in 1077, they
spoke against him to his face, hoping that the Pope would
come to Augsburg, to attend the next diet, and depose
Henry from the throne.

The Emperor thought he had better make himself safe.
He crossed the Alps in winter-time. Hildebrand was
residing at the castle of Canossa, guest of Matilda of Tus-

cany. Canossa is on the northern slopes of the Apennines. The weather was cold, snow lay on the ground. The Emperor sent messengers, asking to be allowed to present himself before the Pope, to sue for pardon. Hildebrand refused. On three consecutive days the Emperor came humbly to the door of the castle, barefooted and penitent in the snow, and three times Hildebrand had him driven away. But at last Matilda persuaded the Pope to receive the Emperor. Henry was admitted. He threw himself at the feet of Hildebrand, was raised and pardoned. ' Conquered by the persistency of his compunction and by the constant supplications of all those who were present, we loosed the chain of the anathema and at length received him into the favour of communion, and into the life of the holy mother Church.' So says Hildebrand, Pope Gregory VII.

But Henry was not as humble as he seemed. He had saved himself in Germany by this submission. He went home, gathered his power, and again defied the Pope. He was again deposed. Then Henry in his turn declared Hildebrand to be no longer pope, and bestowed the title on a German bishop. Then he marched with a great German army over the mountains and passes of the Tyrol, entering Italy by way of Verona. He advanced to the walls of Rome, but owing to malaria in his army was forced to retire. But three years later, in 1084, he was again before the gates of Rome. He took the city, and besieged the Pope in the castle of St. Angelo. Hildebrand appealed wildly to Robert Guiscard and the Normans. Robert, who did not want an emperor in Rome, hastily advanced from besieging Durazzo on the Adriatic, and saved the Pope. But the German host of the Emperor plundered Rome as it had never before been plundered, neither by the Goths under Alaric nor by the Vandals under Genseric.

For bringing this upon them, the Roman people turned with hate on their Pope, so he departed, and shortly died in Salerno. 'I have loved righteousness and hated iniquity,' he said, ' and therefore I die in exile.'

Henry IV. died in 1106, but the struggle went on. In the Concordat of Worms, 1122, it was agreed that the election of the bishops should be left in the hands of the Church, that the ring and the crozier should be bestowed by the Pope. But the Emperor or his representative was to be present at all elections, and disputed elections were to be referred to him. All bishops, moreover, were to do homage to the Emperor for the lands they held in his dominions. This left the Emperor, in Germany at least, lord of his bishops still.

This, however, was not an end to the struggle between Pope and Emperor. The Emperor of the Holy Roman Empire claimed, by his very title, a sort of universal sovereignty. And the Pope claimed the highest authority of all. So how could these opposite claims be settled by settling this investiture of bishops ? And yet the early emperors were good Catholics, they loved the popes, in their way; and the popes respected the greatness of the emperors. It was again the great power of Germany balancing the power of Rome. But this time it was not nation against nation, but the spiritual power against the military. Hildebrand had united his Church over the whole of Europe, as if it were one great monastery which he governed. The clergy owed their allegiance to God and the Pope, nothing to the Emperor, the kings or barons. All over Europe one language, Latin, was spoken by the clergy, one doctrine taught. At the same time the church lands were wide and rich as the lands of the empire, though the estates of the Church were scattered over every country. It was Hildebrand's idea to use kings and their soldiers, all the kings of Europe, as servants of the Church. It was Henry's idea to make the clergy serve the interests of the empire.

We must not imagine that Germany was a kingdom such as we understand kingdoms. It was a confederacy of great independent dukedoms. When one king died, the next was chosen by the great dukes, from among themselves. And just as the king was chiefly a duke, so the emperor was, in the first place, duke of his own lands, then elected king of Germany, then crowned emperor by the Pope. Germany was growing. Austria was the great Mark or border province to the east, Brandenburg to the north. New dukes, margraves and counts arose, new electors.

In 1152 Frederick, called Barbarossa, or Red Beard, was elected King of Germany and then crowned Emperor of the Holy Roman Empire. He was, in the first place, Duke of Franconia and Suabia : that is of South Germany, from the Lake of Constance northwards to Lorraine. He was Frederick Hohenstaufen, of the Castle of Wibelin, in Suabia. His House was called the Hohenstaufen, his faction was called the Ghibelin by the Italians, who could not pronounce Wibelin. Another great man in Germany at this time was Henry the Lion, Duke of Saxony. He came of the Bavarian House of Welf, called Guelph by the Italians. Frederick and Henry represent the two great factions of Guelph and Ghibelin, which fought one another for so many hundreds of years in Germany and Italy.

Frederick, when he became emperor, knew he must keep Henry the Lion friendly, otherwise this fierce duke would cause a revolution in Germany. So he gave him the dukedom of Bavaria, and Henry remained true to the cause of the Emperor. To the north Saxony was shut off from the Baltic. Henry, who was powerful and practically an independent king, seized Bremen from its owners, the military archbishops, and secured Lübeck from Adolph of Holstein. In these and other cities of the Baltic seaboard he started the great Baltic trade, with Denmark, Sweden, Norway, and even England. The land edging the Baltic was marshy : he invited hosts of settlers from Flanders and Holland, and set them to work draining and clearing the land, for farming. Then he united with the

king of Denmark and smashed the Slavonic pirates who
preyed on the Baltic trade.   Wherever he could he ousted
the Slavs from North Germany.   When he could not oust
them, he converted them to Christianity, sending the
monks to preach to them.   Thus the Slavs in Prussia
and Mecklenburg and Pomerania became subject.   He
captured the Holy Isle of Rugen, which was the centre
of the mysterious Slavonic worship, and destroyed its
most sacred temple.   Then he created bishoprics in his
new towns, Schwerin, Mecklenburg, Oldenburg, etc., and
the bishops were fighting vassals of his.   Thus he had a
vast kingdom in Germany, many towns he owned, active
in trade, and an important sea-power.   But the people
hated him, because he trampled over them brutally.   He
became so proud, that when the Emperor Frederick called
to him for help, he calmly refused to send any men to
Italy, in answer to the summons.   But in 1181 he had to
submit to the Emperor, because the other dukes and
counts went against him.

In Germany Frederick Barbarossa tried to make some
order.   The dukes and counts and nobles were always
fighting among themselves.   Along the Rhine, that great
river of commerce, and along the chief roads rose impregnable castles of robber knights who preyed upon the
surrounding country.   He issued a General Peace Constitution, establishing agreements among neighbouring
lords to keep the peace.   He cleared away many robber
knights, he encouraged trade, he held great Diets or
Councils to establish laws.   The country became more
prosperous, education began to spread, poets sprang up,
and the new songs and ballads were sung, in the German
tongue, from one end of the land to the other.   Then
Frederick, who had gathered large estates for himself, had
his son crowned King of Rome, so that the empire should
pass from father to son, and not be subject to election.

None the less, Barbarossa could not stay in Germany.
He must try to rule Italy.   Over the Alps he went, with

his train of attendants and soldiers, and in 1154 descended with his numerous host in Lombardy. He still imagined himself ruler of the great Roman Empire of Hadrian or Diocletian. Frederick was crowned in Rome by Adrian IV., once called Nicolas Breakspear, the English Pope. All was very fine and splendid. But before Frederick left Italy, Pope and Emperor had definitely quarrelled, over the question of precedence. Would Frederick hold the bridle of the Pope's horse? Barbarossa said no, for he was greatest. The Pope claimed supremacy for himself. The old quarrel at once began.

Adrian died, and the Pope Alexander III. was set up. Alexander had insulted the Emperor. Therefore Barbarossa refused to acknowledge him, and set up Victor IV., the anti-Pope. War followed. The Pope Alexander was chased about Italy by the armies of Frederick. But the great Lombard cities stood solid against the Emperor. He besieged Milan for three years, till it yielded to starvation. Then he razed it to the ground, in 1162. He drove Alexander into France, after which he himself departed for Germany. Alexander at once returned to Rome, Milan was rebuilt, and in 1166 Frederick was once more forced to march down with a great army to Italy.

Again he drove the Pope from the Holy City. Alexander fled to the Normans of Sicily. But a terrible pestilence broke out in the German armies, as so often happened, and thousands of the soldiers fell into the grave. Frederick returned to Germany, forced to leave Italy to herself, for the cities of the Lombard league were too strong against him.

The famous cities built the strong fortress, called Alessandria, in honour of their Pope, south-west of Milan, to protect that city. In 1174 Barbarossa came to subdue Alessandria. The siege went on till 1175. Then relieving armies came. It was at this time that Frederick sent to Germany, to Henry the Lion, for help, which Henry refused.

Frederick decided to march on Milan. The cities of the League determined to stop him. They went swiftly against him, and met him at Legnano in 1176. A picked body of the soldiers of the League, called the Company of Death, surrounded the wagon on which their standard stood, determined to fight to the last gasp rather than give in to this emperor from the north. Frederick nearly succeeded in cutting his way through to the wagon, but he was unhorsed, and all the efforts of his German knights were powerless. He was badly defeated, and fled, almost alone, to his faithful town of Pavia.

This is the famous battle of Legnano, when we see towns, and townspeople, not dukes or counts, coming forth to fight for their freedom and their rights.

In July 1177, exactly a century since Henry IV. had humbled himself at Canossa before Hildebrand, Frederick threw himself at the feet of Alexander, in St. Mark's, Venice, in a solemn ceremony of reconciliation. At Venice the Emperor gave up all claim to the patrimony and temporal power of St. Peter. In 1183, in his final treaty of Constance, with the Lombard League, he gave up his claim to rule Lombardy, and the cities were allowed to govern themselves.

But again, the Emperor was not as humble as he seemed. The Lombard cities quarrelled among themselves, and he soon obtained power among them. In 1186 he married his son Henry to Constance, heiress of the Norman kingdom of Sicily. Now, with the strong kingdom of Sicily and Naples added on to the empire, the Pope was caught on the flank. This is a new turn in the contest.

In 1189 the old Emperor set off on a crusade to Palestine. Next year he was drowned whilst bathing in a river in Asia Minor. Thus ended one of the greatest and most energetic Germans.

Henry VI., Barbarossa's son, made terrible work in South Italy. He died, however, in 1197, leaving a baby son to succeed him. In 1198 Innocent III., the great pope

of the Middle Ages, was elected to the papacy. Innocent
was of a noble Italian family, and a lawyer. He believed,
like Hildebrand, that the papacy should exercise a spiritual
rule over all Europe. But he saw that to have spiritual
rule, the Church must have power, and to have power she
must have a kingdom of her own, a real kingdom, with its
centre and capital at Rome. So he set himself to work
to put kings and princes in their places, and virtually to
rule all Europe as if it were one big country. He was a
wise and good man. He did not like the cruelties and
extravagance of war. He wanted to establish a good,
moral rule. And he failed, as Hildebrand had failed,
because in the end it is impossible to rule mankind, at
least in any great region, without the sword.

In the turmoil that followed Henry vi.'s death, Innocent
tried to interfere. He had interfered in England, trying
to force on the chapters the bishops he had elected himself— as in the case of Stephen Langton. He had brought
King John to his knees, and exacted much tribute from
England. All the time he wanted to uphold the cause of
the righteous and the poor, and yet he only succeeded in
rousing the deepest antagonism in the people. It was the
same in Germany. There the bishops and archbishops
were powerful great princes, very German in their ways,
very lordly and worldly in their living, caring for their
own bishopric and their own German power, but very
little for far-off Rome. They were the most un-Roman
and independent of all the clergy. The Pope wanted to
correct this, to make them more humble and Christian-
like. They stood against him with all their might, and
all the Germans, clergy, princes, poor alike detested the
Pope for his interfering. The songs and ballads of the
time curse the name of Innocent, and call the Pope a
stirrer-up of strife and hate, a devil seeking his own power.
Yet he only wanted to do what was right, strictly, according to the Catholic conception.

Innocent did great work. He tried to enforce a cosmo-

politan authority over Europe, when people wanted
to act separately and nationally. But he tried all the
time to make nations and princes wiser, more just, better
in their dealings. His great Lateran Council of 1215,
which was attended by 400 bishops, 800 abbots, and
ambassadors from every great power, was one of the most
splendid councils Europe has ever seen. It reformed the
Church, and brought in new church laws, or canons, all
wise and broad, forbidding, for example, the cruel trials by
ordeal, or by duel, substituting methods of true justice.

But in the young Frederick was growing up one who
would bring both papacy and empire to the brink of destruction. Frederick was only three years old when his
father, Henry vi., died. The little boy remained with his
mother, Constance, in Sicily or South Italy, under the
protection of the Pope. He was red-haired, a real Hohenstaufen, but rather small and puny looking. He had for
his tutor Honorius, who became Pope later on.

Frederick was perhaps the cleverest man of the Middle
Ages. He was King of Sicily and Naples from the time
he was four years old, and had all advantages. At court
he usually spoke the Romance language, a kind of early
Italian or French. He loved the minstrels and jongleurs
who made poetry and sang to the harp, the troubadours.
So when he was quite young he too learned to sing and
make poems; and he was a good poet. Italian was his
native language. At the Sicilian court too were Moors
or Arabs. The Moors had established powerful kingdoms
in Spain and Sicily. They were on the whole more
educated, more civilised than the Europeans. They were
the best mathematicians, astronomists, physicians, and bot-
anists in the world, besides that they had a beautiful literature and architecture. Sicily of that day was a wonderful
island, the meeting-place of East and West, the flower of
civilisation. And of all this Frederick had full advantage.
He studied philosophy and religion, and understood more
than the popes. He wrote a book on hawking, which

remained for centuries the best book on the subject. He made a collection of wild animals at Palermo, established a school of medicine at Salerno, and founded the university of Naples. He was perhaps the most cultured man in Europe, but Italian, hardly a German any more. His contemporaries called him the Wonder of the World.

In his ambition, and his war-like activity, he was like Napoleon. Napoleon too was born on an Italian island, and was emperor of a strange people. But Frederick had not the stubborn heart and fixed purpose of Napoleon, though he had a much more brilliant personality.

Frederick's mother died in 1198, when he was still a baby, and she left him under the guardianship of Pope Innocent III. In 1211, a group of princes in Germany, the King of Bohemia, the Duke of Austria, the Duke of Bavaria, and others, hating the Guelphs, elected the boy Frederick, who was away in Sicily, King of Germany. In 1212, Frederick, being only fifteen years old, made a bold dash into Germany, and soon raised a great following against the Guelph Emperor Otto. In 1214 he got the upper hand; Otto IV. was defeated, Frederick was solemnly crowned emperor in the portico of Charlemagne's basilica at Aix-la-Chapelle. Soon after he departed to Italy again, and only paid two more visits to Germany, in 1235 and in 1236. They were not very important. Frederick was a thorough Italian, though German by blood.

Innocent III. had helped Frederick against Otto IV., hoping to get a humble, dependent emperor. There was peace between the two till Innocent died, in 1216. After Innocent came Honorius III., who had been Frederick's tutor. He was a mild, learned man, and the two remained friendly. In 1220 Frederick was crowned emperor at Rome, and for once the Romans did not raise the disturbance they usually made at the crowning of the hated foreign emperors. Innocent's desire had been that the northern empire and the kingdom of Sicily should not be joined, under the Emperor, for if they were the Papacy would be placed between them as between the two blades of a pair of scissors. Unfortunately Honorius agreed that Frederick should unite both domains. Now the Papacy was in the Emperor's fist.

The popes were very anxious to make Crusades, and Frederick was urged to go. For a long time he refused, and was threatened with excommunication. He thought Crusades foolish. But Honorius died in 1227, and Gregory, who was Pope after him, drove Frederick II. into setting sail from Brindisi. After a day or two at sea the Emperor fell ill, and returned. He was promptly excommunicated. ' Very well,' thought Frederick, ' I will now go to Palestine.' In 1228 he was already in the Holy Land. The Pope, who saw Frederick's mocking cleverness, excommunicated him again. It was no good. Frederick turned to the world, and said—' You see I am the champion of Christendom.' And all Europe applauded him. The people of Rome rose and drove out Gregory. The Emperor was delighted. He did not care a straw about Palestine and the Holy Places, but he had made his point.

Then, in Palestine, instead of wasting time fighting and squabbling, having a strong force at his back he made a treaty with the Sultan of Cairo, by which Jerusalem, Bethlehem, Nazareth, were yielded to the Christians, and all necessary means of communication with the coast. A campaign could not possibly have done so well. But the Pope was furious, and would have nothing to do with the success of an excommunicated man, declaring the whole treaty void. Frederick calmly had himself crowned King of Jerusalem, taking the crown himself from the altar, since no priest dared touch it. Then he wrote a friendly letter to the Pope, and Gregory was forced to agree to what had been done.

While Frederick was away, the Pope had stirred up Italy, and undone all the good work in Sicily. But in 1230 the two made friends, and the Emperor was relieved of the excommunication. Then Frederick set to work. He loved his Sicilian kingdom, and determined to make it a model to the world. He established a pure autocracy, almost a tyranny, and set up a rigid system of government. But it was all excellent, for it kept the peace and the land prospered marvellously. The court was brilliant and intellectual; science, education, building flourished; no country was in such an admirable state. All this Frederick was able to build up upon the work of the great Normans who had preceded him.

Then he turned to Italy. He fought the strong cities of the League, capturing them one after the other. In 1237 he won a brilliant victory over Milan, thus wiping out his father's disgrace at Legnano. By 1239 he had Italy in his hands, and began to organise it. Out of his Sicilian Court of Justice he made an Imperial Court for all Italy, and began to rule this southern empire, having crushed in Germany a revolt headed by his own son Henry, whom he imprisoned for life.

But there was bound to be perpetual war now, between the Emperor and the Pope, for the latter saw his kingdom, the States of the Church, encircled and ground down in the Italian grip of Frederick. In 1239 the Emperor was again excommunicated, and there began the final contest between the Papacy and the Hohenstaufen Empire.

' I will tear the mask from the face of this wolfish tyrant, and force him to lay aside worldly affairs and earthly pomp, and to tread in the holy footsteps of Christ,' wrote Frederick of the Pope. The Pope replied that Frederick was a heretic, that he disbelieved in the immortality of the soul, that he spoke of Moses, Abraham, and Christ as the three great impostors.

The struggle was now to the death. Both sides tried to draw all Europe into the conflict. The Pope tried to turn Germany against its emperor, and failed. He summoned a great number of cardinals and bishops from every land, to make a universal solemn condemnation of Frederick. But Frederick was lucky enough to capture

the twenty-two Genoese vessels that were conveying these
prelates to the Tiber mouth, and he chuckled and kept
them prisoners. All over Italy friars and wandering
preachers went about stirring up the people against the
infidel Emperor.

In 1241 Gregory died. Innocent IV. was elected. Some
attempt was made at reconciliation, but it failed. Innocent IV. extorted money from the Church in every land, to
keep up this vast struggle. In 1244 the Pope fled to Genoa,
and cried to the world that he was a martyr to the violence
of the evil Frederick. In 1245 he went to Lyons, called
a great Council, declared the Emperor excommunicated
and dethroned, deposed. He stirred up Germany, and
had an anti-emperor elected, Henry Raspe. Then he
declared a holy Crusade against the infidel Frederick.
Innocent IV. determined to exterminate the House of
Hohenstaufen, which had determined to exterminate the
power of the Papacy. Frederick was declared to be a
Pharaoh, a Herod, a Nero, who must be destroyed in
Christ's name.

The Emperor quickly replied. 'I hold my crown,' he
said, 'from God alone; neither the Pope, nor the Council
of Lyons, nor the devil shall rend it from me.' Then he
went on : ' Shall the pride of a man of low birth degrade
the Emperor, who has no superior nor equal on earth ? '

Italy now became the scene of a hideous conflict. In
the north, Eccelin da Romano, Frederick's lieutenant,
carried on a ruthless war which has given him a terrible
name in history. Frederick was active in the south.
But in 1247 Parma deserted to the Pope. Frederick
hurried to recover it. He settled down to a siege, and
built the city of Vittoria as a base of antagonism. But
the Parmesans, after a long siege, made a sudden sortie,
burnt Vittoria, utterly routed the Emperor, capturing even
his crown. It was the death-blow to Frederick's cause.
He became more wild, suspicious of his nearest friends :
a raving red beast, they called him. He was mad to destroy

the Papacy. Like Napoleon in later days, he said how happy Asia was, that she need fear no intrigues of popes. He almost declared himself another Prophet of God, like Mahomet. He wanted the divine honours of the Augustan emperors of old to be paid to his person. He proclaimed his own birthplace in Sicily sacred, and said that his great councillor Peter de la Vigne was the Peter, the Rock, on whom the Imperial Church was to be founded.

But all this was the frenzy of failure and mortal hatred of popes. In 1249 his Legate Enzio was defeated and imprisoned by the Bolognese. Frederick hurried north to relieve him. But on December 13, 1250, Frederick died, and the last hope of Hohenstaufen dominion in Italy vanished. Manfred, the Emperor's illegitimate son, fought bravely on, more or less holding Italy for twelve years, till he was slain in battle in 1266. Frederick's son Conrad had become emperor in Germany on his father's death, but he too speedily died, in 1254, leaving a little son Conradin. Conradin, who was a brave, capable youth, marched into Italy in 1268, two years after Manfred's death. He was defeated and captured and beheaded by the help of the French, and so ended the ' viper brood ' of Hohenstaufen, as the Pope and the French called them.

The Pope would seem to be victorious. But in fact the papal power was shattered. From this time it fell into the hands of the French, who rose up as the greatest nation. There was no central papal power in Europe any more. For many years the popes lived at Avignon in South France, while little emperors rose and fell in Germany, unimportant. Nations, states, cities now became separate and strong; the great oneness of the power of the Church was gone. So we approach the divided Europe of later days, leaving the Christendom of the Middle Ages.

X. The Crusades

In the early Middle Ages Europe was one great realm as it has never been since. It was not strictly Europe, but Christendom. There were so many little states that they did not matter. A man counted himself first a Christian, then a Norman or a Saxon, and after that a Frenchman or an Englishman as might be.

The mass of the people were serfs, labouring on the land, without effort to change. They were full of strange fear, a fear of death, and of a curious excitement, expecting something wonderful to happen. The dark forests, the cold winters with flashing northern lights, the storms, the sudden plagues, the famines, the wild beasts, the seething of a changing world, all helped to fill men in those days with a dread of life, and a vision of something more beautiful, delightful, or more marvellous, more exciting. The clergy came and taught them of the life after death, Heaven which was so lovely to a sordid, wretched, frightened serf, and Hell which was so awful. In those days men believed passionately in Heaven and the angels, they longed for the grandeur of the angelic city, the living in the brightness, speaking beautifully with the noble and splendid angels, wearing delicate white clothes and looking on the face of God. They believed just as strongly in the Devil. Angels hovered among them as they toiled in fields or forests, devils tempted them from the bushes or out of the darkness of night, monstrous and wonderful things were semi-hidden everywhere.

It was the great Church which offered the supernatural

terrors and beauty and hope and marvels to men whose soiled, heavy, imprisoned lives were not satisfying to them. Still, in places, peasants worshipped the dreadful old gods of fear, sacrificing to trees and springs of water. But after so much fighting and gruesomeness, in the midst of so much hopelessness, the thought of Almighty Jesus and of Heaven was almost unspeakably wonderful to men. At the same time, they still loved their own wild, fierce, brutal ways. So that with one half of themselves they turned with ecstasy to the teachers of Heaven and love, the priests of the Church. With the other half, they still wanted the satisfaction of violence and lust, the bloody excitement of fighting and killing, and superstitious sacrifice.

There were only two great powers above the people— the barons and the clergy. The barons, seated in their castles, meant serfdom and war and the excitement of adventure. The clergy, with their Christian teaching, meant mystery, submissiveness, and humble labour, with the great glamour of an after-life beyond.

But to make war costs money, and the barons were always short of money. So we have the Jewish money-lender, a very important figure in those days, when money-lending was forbidden to Christians. And besides the money-lender the merchant rose up in the towns, under the protection of the barons. For the merchants paid heavily for the barons' shelter and protection.

Lastly, among the clergy themselves, were the monks. The people of that day had two kinds of heroes : first, the great fighter who made himself renowned on earth ; secondly, the great saint, who would have power in heaven. Men who were soldiers would suddenly put off their armour to enter a monastery, to find the eternal salvation. And men who were soldiers mocked at the folded hands and bowed, shaven heads of the monks, who, they said, were neither men, women, nor good cattle. Then again, in time of danger, monks would put on armour under their

habits, and sally forth to fight, ferocious as any men-at-
arms. Thus all Europe swayed between two passions—
the passion of fighting and violence, and the passion for
blissful holiness.

So we have the life : fierce castles on the rocks, great
monasteries by the streams and ponds : and between the
two, the villages of miserable huts, with a parish priest
and perhaps a church or chapel, and a people full of fear,
misery, superstition, delight, and excitement.

It was necessary for the Church to become more powerful,
for the Church was the great civilising influence, teaching
men the arts of peace and production. And yet in the
hearts of men was an absolute necessity for fighting and
adventure. How were the two to go together ? The
Church would have to satisfy the fighting instinct in
her people, otherwise she would never hold them, would
never succeed in quieting them and bringing them to
order.

Mahomet had begun to preach in Arabia in 609. His
followers had soon grown powerful, had overrun Asia
Minor and were attacking Constantinople. They, of
course, seized Jerusalem and the holy places in the far
East. Now the Christians had made pilgrimages to Jerusalem from early times. This making of pilgrimages was
a pagan custom. The old Greeks would travel far to a
sacred shrine or temple where they wished to make a vow
or a supplication. So the Christians went to Jerusalem.

After the Arabs took the Holy Land, they still allowed
the Christian Patriarch to hold the Holy Sepulchre. For
the Arabs allowed that Jesus was a prophet, but a much
smaller prophet than Mahomet. So vast numbers of
people came from Europe to Jerusalem, each one paying
a certain fee which enriched the Mohammedans. They
came in comparative safety, particularly in Charlemagne's
days, for Charlemagne was a friend of the great Caliph or
Prince Haroun al Raschid ; moreover as yet the Mohammedans felt no holy hatred of Christianity. Every spring

whole caravans of Christians, princes, bishops, poor people, travelled across Europe and Asia to Jerusalem.

But in the year 1000 the Turks began to move out of Asia against the Arab Mohammedans. About 1070 they captured Asia Minor, and Jerusalem fell into their hands. The Turks became Mohammedans, but they by no means treated the Christians as the more civilised wise caliphs had done. They fell upon the Christian caravans, robbed and tormented them. Every step was danger and misery. At last some wretched pilgrims returned wasted and spent, to tell of their sufferings at the hands of the Turks. Great numbers never returned at all.

About 1090 a hermit of France, called Peter, reached Constantinople on his return from the Sepulchre. He was a battered pilgrim, a monk. He had been a gentleman. He and the Patriarch of Constantinople wept together over the sufferings and shame of the Christians, whose most holy places must lie in the hands of cruel heathens. The Patriarch could get no help from the weak, vicious emperors of Constantinople.

'I will rouse the martial nations of Europe in your behalf,' cried Peter. The astonished Patriarch gave him letters of credit, and Peter hastened west. He kissed the feet of the Pope in Rome, and proclaimed his mission. He was a mad fanatic, but wonderful as a preacher and an inspirer of the people. Pope Urban ii. saw that it would be wise to let him rouse Christendom to one great united act, and he gave Peter his blessing, and encouraged him to proclaim the deliverance of the Holy Land.

Peter the Hermit was a small, insignificant-looking man, but his soul flamed, his eyes were flashing, he was wonderful in exhortation. Riding on an ass, he carried a heavy crucifix before him. His head and feet were bare, he wore a coarse dark garment, his body was thin and worn with fasting and vehemence. And so he traversed Italy, then France, then Germany, preaching to great crowds in the churches, in market-places, by the roadside, telling the

sufferings of the pilgrims, wailing the shame to Jesus that
the sacred Sepulchre was defiled by the Turks, calling to
Christ and the Mother of God, as if he saw them in the
air above him, weeping and crying to them to be with this
people, to lighten their steps. He went into cottages, or
castles, or palaces alike, and whether it was a poor man
eating his grey porridge, or a baron before his venison and
wine, he cried on the inmates of the house to gird their
loins and prepare for the holy expedition. And peasant
or baron, farmer or bishop, they all listened alike, and
groaned and wept as if they saw Jesus in trouble, and
vowed themselves to this service of the dear God. For
in those days men felt Jesus as if He were suffering and
beautiful amongst them, they defended Him as if He were
a delicate, most wonderful heart's-brother. And all men
shared this feeling—serfs, barons, kings, bishops : when it
came to the wonderful, sweet, delicate Jesus and His tender
Mother, all hearts burned alike, all men were filled with
one great hot yearning. And this passion for Jesus united
men and made them one, across all the difference of serfdom and tyranny. They were united in one passion,
slave and lord alike, their hearts beat the same. It has
never been so again, since the strange passionate days of
the early Middle Ages.

Pope Gregory VII., the great Hildebrand, had already
begun to arm Europe against the Mohammedans : but it
was Urban the Second who was the great maker of the
movement. He called a council of two hundred bishops
of Italy, France, Burgundy, Suabia, and Bavaria ; four
thousand of the clergy, and thirty thousand of the laity
attended the vast meeting, which was held on the plain
outside Placentia. The ambassadors from Constantinople
told the sad tale of the East, the shame that lay on Bethlehem and Calvary, the tale of the misery and suffering of
the eastern Christians, till this vast assembly, thousands
of men, burst into tears and wept. The most eager
declared their willingness to march at once to rescue God

and His servants. But Pope Urban knew that a short delay would gather greater hosts and stir the feeling deeper. Meanwhile in every parish the clergy preached the mission. Another great meeting was arranged at Clermont, in Aquitaine. When Urban mounted the high scaffold in the market-place, masses of people had gathered to hear him. And as he spoke and urged and persuaded them, suddenly one great cry went up from the hosts. Deus vult ! Deus vult ! cried the clergy, in pure Latin. Diex el volt ! Diex el volt ! cried the poorer people from the north. Deus lo volt ! Deus lo volt ! cried the people from the south. But it was all one cry, and had one meaning—' God wills it ! God wishes it ! '

' It is indeed the will of God,' replied the Pope ; ' and let this memorable word, surely inspired by the Holy Ghost, be ever your battle cry, you champions of Christ. Christ's cross is the symbol of your salvation—wear it, a red, a bloody cross, on breast or shoulder, as an eternal mark of your irrevocable pledge.'

The greatest excitement spread over Europe. People were mad to release the holy places of the Saviour, to succour God and to behold the towers of Jerusalem the Golden, to know the wonders of Jordan, to touch the olive-trees for themselves, where Jesus had wept, to see His lilies. All Europe also had heard of the marvellous palaces of the caliphs, of the gold and jasper and emeralds of the magical Arabians, of sweet groves of cinnamon, and of the lovely dark-eyed women of the East. So adventurous souls were fired. They wanted to capture these marvellous palaces, to seize these jewels and this gold, to taste the spices, to know the soft-eyed women. Sure of great treasure from the East, as well as of everlasting glory in heaven, princes mortgaged their estates, barons their castles, peasants sold their cattle and implements. Horses and armour and weapons became enormously expensive, cows, land, furniture very cheap. Every man except merchants, clergy, Jews, wanted to go. Every man must provide himself with staff, and wallet for food. Each must sew on the shoulder of his garment the red cross. The rich sewed scarlet silk with gold thread and gems, the poor stitched on coarse red flannel. Some men branded their naked shoulders with hot irons.

The 15th August, 1096, was fixed for the day of departure. But early in the spring sixty thousand people of the poorer classes, men, women, youths, girls, were gathered in the east of France and in Lorraine, clamouring to be led by Peter the Hermit, at once to set off. In front eight horsemen led fifteen thousand foot pilgrims. The others followed in vast detachments. Behind these again came fifteen thousand German peasants, led by the monk Godescal. And away behind these came many thousands of the worst, most villainous people in Europe, hanging round for robbery and crime. All thoughtful men knew that such an expedition was wickedly foolish. Some counts and gentlemen, with three thousand horse, attended the multitude for its salvation. But in the very front of the mad host were carried a goose and a goat, emblems which were supposed to be possessed with the Holy Spirit. So the mad, raging, shameless mob trailed across Europe.

Peter led the way along the Moselle and Rhine. The first thing to do was to massacre the Jews. At Verdun, Treves, Metz, Spires, Worms, many thousands of these unhappy people were slaughtered and pillaged for having crucified Jesus. In these great border towns the Jews had prosperous trading quarters. These were wiped out. So the terrible hosts moved on, devouring the land, to the Danube. There they had to turn south, through Hungary and Bulgaria, making for Constantinople. The Hungarians, Huns and Magyars had not much food, save their herds, for still they grew little corn, and depended on milk and flesh. Therefore in the vast reedy plains there was small supply for the hosts. The Crusaders demanded provisions, seized the scanty stocks, and speedily devoured them. The Hungarians, newly Christianised but still pagan by blood, in anger mounted their swift little horses, and led by their king darted round the moving hosts, showering them with arrows. The Bulgarians also attacked the vast mob. There was some ugly murdering and fighting. About a third of the defenceless Crusaders, with Peter the Hermit, escaped to the mountains of Thrace. The rest perished, strewing their bones down the Balkan Peninsula.

The forces of the Greek emperor led the refugees to Constantinople, and settled them there to await their real leaders, the more noble Crusaders. But the mob of pilgrims so shamelessly robbed and broke into the houses of Constantinople, that Alexius the Emperor tempted them over to the Asiatic side of the Bosphorus. There, like a herd of savages, they rushed towards the Turks who occupied the way to Palestine. The Sultan tempted them on. In a plain of Nicaea they were overwhelmed by Turkish arrows, and a pyramid of bones stood to show to the later Crusaders, the nobler and more regular host, the place of this defeat. Three hundred thousand of this first mob had perished before the true Crusaders were ready to start : and nothing at all had been done against the Turk.

The band of the true Crusaders contained many great lords. Godfrey of Bouillon, Duke of Lorraine, was one of the greatest : then came Hugh, Count of Vermandois ; Robert, Duke of Normandy, brother of William Rufus— he had pawned Normandy for about £25,000, in order to be able to go ; Robert, Count of Flanders ; Stephen, Count of Chartres ; these four were the chief leaders of the Norman, British, and North French pilgrims : the Southern French were led by the Bishop of Puy and Raymond, Duke of Toulouse ; Bohemond, son of Robert Guiscard, led ten thousand horse and twenty thousand foot from South Italy, his nephew Tancred being his partner, a very famous and perfect knight ; there were innumerable other nobles, too many to mention. The wives and sisters of

the gentry wished to go with them. They converted their
possessions into bars of gold and silver, and, mounted on
horseback, gathered together. Princes and barons took
with them hounds and hawks to amuse their leisure. The
hosts were too many to go together, they would never
find food, so they agreed to take separate routes, and meet
near Constantinople.

Godfrey of Bouillon, Duke of Lorraine, with his Germans
and North French, came by the Danube and down Bulgaria to Constantinople. Having listened to the account
of the crimes and the miseries of his forerunners, Godfrey
made a treaty of peace with the King of the Hungarians.
He arrived in the eastern capital without any bloodshed.
Raymond of Toulouse with his Provençals came by Turin
and Venice, round the head of the Adriatic, and down
through Dalmatia, forty days' wretched march through
perpetual fog and half-hostile mountain natives, having
little food to eat and no peace, till he too arrived at Constantinople. The Normans, French, and British under
Robert of Normandy and Hugh of Vermandois marched
splendidly over the Alps, along the Roman roads to Rome,
feasted and welcomed in all the Italian towns. Their
ranks were thinned by desertion, for the northerners could
not withstand the temptation of remaining in the beautiful
Italian cities. After a great display in Rome, this host
passed on to Brindisi, where it had to wait till spring for
a crossing, and did not reach Constantinople till the early
summer of 1097.

Meanwhile the fourth host, the Normans of Sicily with
the South Italians, under Bohemond and Tancred, kept
near the sea, for they were a well-armed host and well
attended with ships. The inhabitants of these old lands
were Greek subjects of the Emperor, but they did not like
this crusading invasion. Bohemond was fierce. He
stormed the castles that interfered with his progress, and
pillaged the lands of such offenders.

Poor Alexius, who had pleaded for help from the Roman

Christendom against the Turks, now had tidings of the approach of host after host of terrible and ruinous friends who devoured the land. Twenty-four knights in golden armour rode in advance into Constantinople to announce the coming of Hugh of Vermandois, commanding the Emperor to revere the general of the Latin Christians, the brother of the King of Kings, Philip of France. Alexius was astonished and indignant at this announcement, for to his imagination the King of France was a barbarian, not much more important to him than an African chief to us. He waited. There was no preventing the advancing armed bands of northerners from ravaging the lovely Greek estates. Proud and insolent arrived Count Hugh, so unbearable that at last the Emperor had him imprisoned, before his forces had come up. Godfrey of Bouillon, the best and strongest leader, came down after his wretched, weary journey through the Balkan Peninsula to hear such news. He was very angry, and fell on the suburbs of the glittering city of Constantinople. Poor Alexius was at his wits' end, finding the Christians far worse than the Turks. He was accused by the Crusaders of intending to starve and drown their hosts.

But peace was made, and at last the Emperor persuaded Godfrey to allow his army to be conveyed over to the Asiatic side of the Bosphorus. This was done, and the ships immediately returned to Constantinople, so that no Crusaders could come back. Then the army of Hugh was transported. As fast as one army arrived, the Emperor had it conveyed across, so that it should never join forces with the next comers in the great capital. He dreaded lest they should seize and sack the finest and wealthiest city in the world, his beloved Constantinople. The leaders remained his guests in Constantinople, while their armies or hosts were on the Asiatic side of the water.

One after the other, the great princes were presented at court. Bohemond and Raymond of Toulouse on their arrival urged Godfrey to unite with them and attack Constantinople. Godfrey refused. He had come as a Crusader—not as a marauder. So the poor Emperor trusted to Godfrey, even adopting him as his son. And in this way relations were more or less friendly with the Greek court, Alexius doing his best to conciliate the fierce chiefs. Bohemond, whom the Greeks dreaded, was lodged in a splendid palace, and served like an emperor. One day, as he passed through a gallery, a door left carelessly open showed an interior where gold and silver, gems, silk, and curious furniture were piled in disorder in great heaps. 'What conquests,' said greedy Norman Bohemond, 'might not be achieved by the possession of such a treasure.' 'It is yours,' said the Greek attendant. And Bohemond was greedy-spirited enough to accept it, and the Greeks now felt he had submitted to them. Robert of Normandy, Stephen of Chartres, Raymond of Toulouse, one after another they bowed before the pompous and resplendent throne of the Byzantines.

They all marvelled at the splendours of the court of Constantinople, looking with wonder on such things as they, from their rough northern castles, could not even imagine. They were like the barbarians at Rome. But they hated having to do homage to the eastern Emperor. It was necessary, for they could not cross the Bosphorus without his ships, and they needed his support and guidance through Asia Minor, where his empire extended. So they bowed the knee before him as he sat on his high golden throne. But they hoped in their hearts that, when once in Asia, they could turn their swords against him.

Anna Comnena, daughter of the Emperor, a young, clever princess, wrote her memoirs in which we may still read her account of the visit of these Crusaders to her father's capital. She did not like the counts and nobles of the north. She thought them the merest barbarians, insolent, overbearing, vulgar, gaping greedily at the treasures of the palace. Their rude manners disgusted the delicate little lady, their very names, so uncouth, offended her Greek tongue. Some, she allows, were handsome, but all were uncivilised. She liked Raymond of Toulouse best, and hated Bohemond of Sicily. And she writes as if all these great chiefs of the north were but paid soldiers whom her father had hired.

But she is thankful when at last they are all transported over the Bosphorus, for she is staggered by their numbers. All Europe was loosened from its foundation, she says, and hurled against Asia. More than the stars in heaven or the sands of the shore these people came, and they passed like devouring locusts.

Indeed the hosts were countless. Most came from France, but all countries sent their bands. Even there were naked savages from Ireland and Scotland, for it was forbidden to prevent even the poorest Christian from making this holy excursion. It is impossible to say how many died of disease in the hot southern countries, how many perished from thirst and hunger in Syria. For the Greeks in the provinces of Asia Minor were unfriendly, the thoughtless masses devoured their provisions at once, and famine set in. It is said in their anguish of hunger they even roasted and ate their prisoners. Spies who found their way into Bohemond's kitchen were shown human bodies, bodies of Turks or Saracens, turning on the spit. But this was probably a trick of Bohemond's to make his name more feared. All the while the enemy hung round, cutting off all stragglers, making sudden attacks on unready bands. All the while the European soldiery had to protect the unarmed masses.

The great hosts divided. Nicaea, the Sultan's capital near the sea of Marmora, was besieged and at last taken. Another party moved on. When they were far from the sea and fainting with heat they were attacked by the Turkish host, swift darting horsemen loosing their arrows. Bohemond, Tancred, and Robert of Normandy held the fight, and just as all seemed lost, the rest of the sacred army, under Godfrey and Raymond, sixty thousand horse, came up from Nicaea, and a great battle was fought. Four thousand Christians were pierced with Turkish arrows. But as evening approached the swiftness of Asiatic horsemen yielded to the slow but invincible iron strength of the Franks, and Soliman's forces were routed, his camp with all its treasures seized.

Both the Turks and the northerners felt supreme contempt for the unwarlike Greeks and the soft people of Asia Minor. But in each other they met a worthy adversary. Now at last the Turks learned to respect the invincible slow power of the Franks, for as such they named all the Crusaders, since indeed the greater part of the knights were of Germanic, Norman or Frankish origin. And at last the Crusaders found themselves faced with dauntless, skilful soldiers in the Turks.

The Crusaders crossed Lower Asia, through a land deserted and wasted by the retreating enemy. In the desert places they suffered from thirst, and gave silver for a draught of water. When they came to a river, low in its banks, multitudes rushed, pressing each other, treading each other to death down the steep slopes, pushing many victims into the water. Then they wearily climbed the steep, slippery sides of Mount Taurus. Godfrey of Bouillon had been torn by a bear, and was carried in a litter. Raymond of Toulouse was borne along, grievously sick. Winter was coming on.

In October 1097 they began the great siege of Antioch. Though all scattered bands were called in, still the Crusaders were not sufficiently numerous to surround the city, which still retained much of its Roman greatness. They knew they could not take the walls by force. They knew they could not starve the town into submission. February arrived, 1098, and no progress had been made. The Crusaders were dying off by the thousand. They were utterly starving.

It was agreed that whichever chief captured the city should possess it. Bohemond was most ambitious, he

madly desired the prize, for it was a very great one.   He
defeated an attacking force of the Moslems. Then he
sought all manner of means of success.   The native population of Antioch was Christian, had been Christian since
Roman days.   These native Christians had had the
Mohammedan religion forced on them, but were ready to
turn Christian again as soon as possible. Bohemond con-
trived that one of them, a Syrian renegade who commanded
three towers, should admit him and his bands into the city.
Early one June night scaling-ladders were thrown down
from the walls, Bohemond and Duke Robert, with their
armies rushed silently up, assembled, and seized the town.
In the morning the Crusaders saw Bohemond's flag flying
over the city. The poor perishing Crusaders felt they
were saved.

But Antioch was a trap.   The citadel still held out, and
there was seen arriving a huge army under the Emir
Kerboga, multitudes of dark warriors advancing over the
plains. The Christians felt that they were lost. Famine
or slaughter seemed the only alternative. Many fled from
the city in despair. The rest of the Crusaders shut the
gates and manned the walls, prepared to stand siege and
starve.

Then a miracle happened. Peter Bartholomew, a
cunning Provençal priest, announced that the Holy Lance
which pierced the side of Jesus on the Cross had been
buried under the altar of St. Peter's church in Antioch.
St. Andrew had thrice appeared to him in a dream, and
commanded him to bring forth the relic. In great excitement the digging commenced. The lance was found.
Bohemond's party plainly declared that it had been
hidden there for the purpose by the priest and the Provençals.   But this had no effect on the great body of the
Crusaders. They believed.

Five-and-twenty days the Christians besieged in the city
had spent on the verge of destruction, for the emir camped
against them offered only the choice of slavery or death.

They were but a handful now compared with the hosts
that had set out. There in the far East they prepared to
lay their bones. But on the twenty-fifth day the lance
was discovered—a Saracen lance-head. Wrapped in a
veil of silk and gold it was held up to the Crusaders. A
great shout of inflamed joy and hope went up from the
whole city. Prayers were offered. Then the soldiers
were sent to their quarters, bidden to eat the last of their
food freely, and to give all provender to the horses, and
to be ready at dawn.

By the first light of day the men assembled. When all
were ready the gates were thrown open, the battle array
marched forth and was marshalled on the plain outside.
A procession of monks chanted the psalm : ' Let the Lord
arise, and let His enemies be scattered.' And then the
Christian Crusaders, mad with religious excitement, broke
on the startled Turks. A tremendous victory was won.
It is said that the enemy's army had six hundred thousand
men. This vast, clumsy host was broken, it fled in panic.
Great treasures were captured. It seemed indeed a miracle.
No wonder that the Crusaders believed they had seen
angels and martyrs of God come down and fight with
them, flashing and glistening in their midst, angels with
bright swords thrusting and slaying the dusky Turks.

For the Crusaders were now much diminished. Thousands had died of pestilence and famine during this dreadful siege. In October 1097, sixty thousand crusading
horse had been reviewed before the city : in June 1098
but two thousand remained, and scarce two hundred
could be mustered for battle. Godfrey of Bouillon,
Bohemond, and Tancred had alone kept heart. Yet even
Godfrey had had to borrow a horse for the day of battle.
He owned none, and could buy none.

The victory won, Bohemond demanded the city as his
own. Raymond said it belonged to the Greek Emperor
from whom it had been captured by the Turks. But
Bohemond insisted, and he had his way. He remained

in his city, or county—for he would claim the surrounding land—with a small force of soldiers. The rest rode on towards Jerusalem, a much diminished host, following the coast southwards. Hugh of Vermandois and Stephen of Chartres had already turned back home to Europe. They had had enough.

When the Crusaders came to the seaport of Tripoli, however, not very far from Damascus, Raymond halted and settled down with his forces. It was a pleasant land. He wanted to found a state for himself, a rival to Antioch. Baldwin, brother of Godfrey, had established himself in Edessa. So little did these great leaders care any more for the crusade, so greedy were they for land. They felt they were out on a great colonising adventure, that the East should be made a sort of European colony, themselves as rulers.

The remaining Crusaders, weary of all this, now demanded to be led straight to Jerusalem. They had heard of the decline of the Turkish Empire which they were invading. The Arabs had for thirty years been ousted from Asia Minor by the Turks. Therefore the Caliph of Egypt now watched with joy the crumbling of the power of the Turkish sultans. He wanted his own lands back. While the Crusaders were in Syria he sent his Arab armies against the Turks of Jerusalem, and captured the Holy City. The town was now held, not very strongly, by the Fatimite Arabs from Egypt. The Court of Cairo, after the capture of Antioch, sent ambassadors with robes of silk, and precious vases, and purses of gold and silver to Godfrey and Bohemond, explaining that Jerusalem belonged by right to the Arabs, and that a treaty should be arranged such as had held good in Charlemagne's days, whereby pilgrims might visit the holy places, by paying tribute.

But Godfrey would have none of this. He proudly declared that Christians would ask no permission to visit Jerusalem, and that it was only by a timely surrender of the city that the Caliph could avert an immediate attack. Yet the winter wasted away. Weary to death, the Crusaders scattered to enjoy themselves in the sweet, luxurious cities of Syria. They were well supplied with food, the emirs paid rich tribute to them. For the Turks were disunited and weakened, they gave presents to their enemies so that they need not fight them.

At last, almost a small band now, led by Godfrey, the Crusaders marched from Caesarea, and in June 1099 they saw Jerusalem on her hills. Then the travel-worn heroes cried aloud, and wept hot tears, seeing the Holy City they had suffered so much to win, the city of God.

Godfrey planted his standard on the first swell of Mount Calvary ; to the left lay Tancred and Duke Robert ; Count Raymond, who had come along, pitched his quarters between the Citadel and Mount Sion. On the fifth day, they made a tremendous assault, but were driven back by the skilful Arabs with much slaughter and shame. So they had to sit down to a siege. They suffered again bitterly from lack of food and water, but chiefly for want of water, for the hills of Jerusalem are dry and stony. And they could find no timber to make the engines of assault.

At last, however, the movable towers were constructed. These high wooden towers were wheeled close to the walls, and from their summits the crusading soldiers fired arrows down upon the defenders of the ramparts, driving them off. Then a wooden drawbridge was lowered from the high wooden turret of the siege-engine, on to the wall, and on a Friday, July 15, 1099, at three o'clock in the afternoon, Godfrey of Bouillon stood victorious on the walls of Jerusalem. And thus, four hundred and sixty years after the great Arab Omar had captured the city, was Jerusalem set free once more from the Mohammedan yoke.

A terrible massacre took place. Tancred alone showed some pity. For three days the Crusaders savagely slaughtered the Moslems, men, women, and children. It is said the Christians waded up to their ankles in blood. The

Jews were burnt in their synagogue. Seventy thousand Mohammedans were put to the sword. After a week or two the infection of masses of dead bodies produced a pestilence.

Bareheaded and barefoot, in a humble posture, when the city was quieted the conquerors ascended the hill of Calvary walking in slow procession, to the loud singing of anthems by the priests. They kissed the stone which had covered the grave of Jesus, weeping burning tears of joy and penitence.

Godfrey of Bouillon became ruler of Jerusalem, with the title of Defender of the Holy Sepulchre. In Europe, Pope Urban had died eight days after the capture of the city. He never heard of the event. So ended the First Crusade, wonderful as the first act of united Christendom, the first great movement of waking Europe.

Godfrey's successor, Baldwin, became King of Jerusalem. Far away there in the East grew up a number of Latin states. Bohemond, followed by Tancred, governed Antioch as if he were king there, Raymond ruled Tripoli in Asia. The Military Orders rose up, and commanded the cities and seaports of Acre, Tyre, Jaffa, Ascalon.

The Military Orders were associations of sacred knights. The first, the Hospitallers, had been begun to maintain a hospital in Jerusalem and to protect pilgrims. The second, the Templars, which afterwards became so very powerful, was begun in 1119, when a band of eight knights united to defend the Temple and the way to Jerusalem. The knights were fighting monks, monk-knights who had sworn to dedicate their lives to conquering the enemies of God. They were to remain chaste and celibate, they had rules of prayer like monks. All over Christendom they had houses, monasteries almost, where men entered and vowed their lives to God, and, after a certain probation, were clothed in the armour with the sacred red cross on the breast, and sent forth in the service of Christ.

Thus from 1100 to 1200 A.D. a steady stream of

powerful warriors flowed out to the East, to guard the holy places and defend the Latin states.

It was partly owing to these Latin states of the East that the great eastern trade of Venice and Genoa and Sicily grew so rich and important. From the Syrian sea-coast, through the Middle Ages ship after ship sailed away for the European ports of Venice, Pisa, Genoa, laden with oriental produce ; whilst ship after ship spread her sails from Europe carrying goods to Tripoli, Tyre, Acre, Jaffa, Antioch. For in these eastern cities dwelt European knights and nobles and peoples, settled there and ruling the land and enjoying life, like the English now in India. These Franks, as the Moslems called them, lived and jousted and fought and traded in the East for nearly two hundred years, conquerors possessing the land. Fleets of ships sailed straight for their ports from the ports of Italy, and thus Constantinople, which had been the great port, the only port of the East, gradually declined, being left aside.

There were many crusades, but none like the first. Never again did the same passion sweep Europe. In 1101 a vast host set out to rescue Bohemond, who had been captured by the Turks, and deprived of his Frankish principality of Antioch. This crusade intended also to take Bagdad. But it failed in every respect.

About 1127 the Turkish House of Seljuk, which had been crumbling when it was attacked by the first Crusaders, yielded in the East to the succeeding House of Zenghi. In 1144 Zenghi attacked the Christians of the East, and his rising power threatened the Holy Land. A new crusade was preached by St. Bernard, Abbot of Clairvaux in France, one of the greatest monks the world has seen. Louis VII. of France and the Emperor Conrad III. set off in 1147. They reached Damascus, which the Turks held, and attacked it, but were driven off. This crusade also utterly failed.

In 1187 Jerusalem fell again. The great Sultan Saladin

had added Egypt to his Asiatic possessions. He fell on Syria and defeated the Christians. Just as the first Crusaders, in wild religious enthusiasm, had conquered Palestine owing to the indifference and careless weakness of the Mohammedans, so the fiery, enthusiastic Mohammedans now reconquered it, with all the enthusiasm of a holy war, from the indifferent, careless Franks, who were selfish, stupid, and quarrelsome out there in the East.

A third crusade was organised to save the Holy City. Frederick Barbarossa set out, but was drowned in 1189, and only a remnant of his army reached Antioch. Richard of England, called Cœur de Lion, and Philip Augustus of France, were under vow to go. They set off in 1190. Richard went by sea, wintering in Sicily. In the spring he set out for Acre, conquering Cyprus by the way. The Christians had been besieging Acre for two years, when the French and English fleets sailed up.

Richard was a great leader, a great man : not an Englishman, for he could never speak English : a Frenchman, an Aquitainian, writing and singing his poems in the language of Southern France : a tall, rash man, fair, handsome, brave, a great leader, a terror to the Turks. But he and Philip could never agree. In 1191 Richard took Acre. Philip, declaring his health was broken, returned to France.

Acre had capitulated to Richard, and he held two thousand captives as hostage, till the ransom should be paid according to Saladin's promises. Saladin failed to pay, Richard massacred the hostages, and marched to Ascalon. But as he moved into the interior, away from his ships and supplies, he became helpless in a barren land, he could do nothing, masterly leader though he was. He pressed on. In the spring of 1192 he was within sight of Jerusalem. His comrades went up the hill to see in the distance the towers of the city. But Richard would not go up, he would not look. For he knew he could get no farther. He returned to the coast in great bitterness.

He gave Cyprus to Guy, King of Jerusalem. Guy reconquered Acre, but Jerusalem was lost to Christendom.

In 1202 another crusade, a Crusade of Barons, set out. It was to go by sea this time, sailing from Venice. In 1203 the fleet reached Constantinople. The Venetians had a quarrel with the Byzantines, and had come on purpose to take the city. The Crusaders besieged Constantinople. This wonderful city, so long inviolate, fell after thirteen days' siege, and the Venetians and the Crusaders remained in occupation pretending it was too late to proceed east. The Byzantines murdered their emperor, and turning against the Latins, drove them out. In 1204 the city was again taken by the Venetians and the Crusaders, assaulted, stormed, taken, sacked and gutted. Innumerable treasures were destroyed, innumerable lovely statues from old Greece melted down to make bronze money. Then, imitating Godfrey or Bohemond or Guy in the far East, Baldwin of Flanders made himself Emperor of Constantinople, Boniface of Montferrat became King of Thessalonica, other counts and barons became lords of the Morea, of Attica, Boeotia, and parts of Asia Minor. There was a Duke of Athens and a Prince of Achaia—all barons from Italy or the North, most of them Germanic nobles. But Venice was the great gainer. Venice now became mistress of the eastern seas, which Constantinople had been for hundreds of years.

This crusade, called the Fourth, was just a splendid, if rather unholy adventure : a marauding conquest and annexation of the near East, Eastern Europe, by barons from the West and North.

In 1228, as we know, Frederick II. marched to Palestine and made a satisfactory treaty with the Sultan of Cairo, obtaining Jerusalem, Bethlehem, and Nazareth — the three places of pilgrimage. He crowned himself King of Jerusalem. But this was no conquest. It was not even real possession, but rather an occupation by permission.

In 1244 Jerusalem was again lost, and the Latin kingdom

of the East was practically destroyed altogether. Louis IX. of France led an expedition in 1248 against the Sultan of Egypt. He took Damietta, and advanced into the Delta of the Nile. The Saracens attacked his army, Louis was captured, and his host surrendered. With the exception of the king and the chief lords, the army was massacred to a man. A great sum was paid for Louis' ransom, Damietta given up. Then the king went to the Holy Land, trying to strengthen the few remaining Christian positions there, and performing pious works. He returned to France after three years, having done nothing and lost an army.

These crusades to the East were as ruinous for France as the excursions of the German emperors to Italy. But men had to fight somewhere, and perhaps it was better to fight the Moslem abroad than the Christian at home. After the Crusades, Europe never acted again in union. Men ceased to be Christians first and foremost. Nationality now began to count.

XI. Italy after the Hohenstaufens

The great struggle between Pope and Emperor ended with the Hohenstaufens. The two great powers left each other so weak that kings, nations, cities, small republics rose to independence, raising their heads from the ruin of the great ones. The popes no longer hoped to govern Europe from Rome; their large idea collapsed or dwindled. The emperors no longer hoped to rule Italy and the popes, and thus sway Europe. They came to depend on their own hereditary dominions, just as the popes became merely Italian, less and less European.

The greatest emperors of the Hohenstaufen family were the two Fredericks, Frederick Barbarossa, the great fighter, and Frederick the Second, called in his young days the Wonder of the World, and towards the end of his life, when the hatred between him and the Pope's party became so deadly, called the Beast of Europe.

The Hohenstaufens came from the old castle of Wibelin in Germany. They had a great rival family in Germany, called the House of Welf. When the popes fought so terribly with Barbarossa and Frederick ii., they made friends with the rivals of the Hohenstaufens in Germany. While ever the fighting went on, the dukes of the House of Welf sent down to Italy many knights and fierce soldiers to help the popes, so that Italy was full of fierce Germans, who could speak no Italian. These ferocious German soldiers would seize an Italian peasant, and demand: 'Which are you, Welf or Wibelin?' This meant, are you of the Pope's party, or of the Emperor's?

The poor peasant must decide. He came to know the words Welf and Wibelin, to his sorrow. But he could not pronounce them. He said Guelph and Ghibelin. Every man in Italy must be either a Guelph or a Ghibelin.

The Guelphs were staunch for the popes. But when Frederick II. died, the Ghibelins were much weakened. The brave Manfred, illegitimate son of Frederick, assumed the crown of Sicily and Naples, Frederick's fairest kingdom. Pope Urban at once declared Manfred an usurper. The Ghibelins, Manfred's party, seized power in Rome, and drove out Urban. Urban was a Frenchman, son of a cobbler of Troyes, for in those days a man might rise to the highest position from the very lowest, if he entered the Church. The Pope now badly needed help. He turned to his native France, and asked Charles of Anjou to come and take the crown of Sicily from the usurper Manfred. Charles was brother to the saintly, crusading Louis IX. of France.

Manfred was excommunicated; and now began the disastrous occupation of Italy by the French. For hundreds of years the Germans of the Empire had swamped Italy: now it was the turn of the French, the great kingly power, to occupy and destroy that land.

Frederick II. and Manfred were so Italian that they seemed natives of Italy. The French were detestable foreigners. So that those who loved Italy as a whole, who wanted Italy to be settled in peace, a united country, these men were Ghibelins. But those who wanted their own separate little independence, and hated the thought of a united Italy, these were on the Pope's side. Independent, jealous cities were with the Pope, the south of Italy and some northern princes were with Manfred.

Charles of Anjou marched south with his army of French, Swiss, and Lombard Italians. In 1266 Manfred, with an army of dark southerners, and Saracens, Moors from Sicily, marched north and met him. In the hot battle Manfred was slain, his army defeated. He was one of the bravest heroes, and the most gracious man of his day. But since he was excommunicated, Anjou would not even allow him a sacred burial, but had him put in a pit by the roadside, at the head of the bridge of Benevento. Great shame was cried on this. Even the soldiers in Charles's own army put each one a stone in his pouch, and as they marched past the pit, to cross the bridge, each threw his stone upon the grave, so that a large memorial mound was raised. This made the new Pope, Clement iv., very angry. He had the body dug out and buried in an unknown spot in the wastes. So far did the hatred of the popes pursue the Hohenstaufen blood.

In 1268 the last young Hohenstaufen, Conradin, was beheaded. Charles of Anjou now took possession of Sicily and Naples, occupying his new kingdom with his brutal French soldiers. This beautiful garden of Europe, this sunny, exquisite, most civilised realm, with its prosperous people and its gay, fair cities, its great schools, its famous universities where Saracen physicians taught their skill to all Europe, was now to be wasted by callous French troops.

Charles, a bullying prince, keeping fast friends with the Pope, tried to spread his power over Italy as Frederick ii. had done. His Provençal nobles and governors, however, were cruel and rapacious, despising the Italians and tormenting them. Even Clement had to remonstrate with these evil men.

But a revenge was preparing. The South hated the French occupation. Sicily made ready for rebellion. On Easter Tuesday, 1282, the people of Palermo had gone out of the city to a church in the meadows some half-mile away. There they danced and made festival. A party of French horse came up, and the foreign soldiers, dismounting, crowded forward to get their share in the sport. They knocked aside the Sicilian young men, and took hold of the young women to dance with them. One man insulted a bride, who was wearing her crown. The bridegroom, whom the French soldier had knocked away, rushed forward in fury and stabbed the offender. Immediately a cry went up 'Death to the French.' The stored-up hate and rage of the last ten years was let loose. The Sicilians sprang like wild cats at the soldiers, and knifed them all. Not one Frenchman was left alive. Then the holiday-makers looked at the corpses lying among the sunny flowers.

The news spread like wildfire in Palermo. Immediately the Sicilians rushed from their houses, gathered, and flew with their knives upon the French. Before evening, two thousand of the detested foreigners were killed, and their bodies flung into a pit outside the city.

This event was called the Sicilian Vespers. It caused the wildest excitement in Europe. Sicily rose and cast out the French. A Spanish prince of Aragon was invited to take the crown. Meanwhile the House of Anjou still held Naples and the mainland. So began the utter ruin of the fair southern civilisation of Sicily and Naples.

But as the south died, sank down towards squalor, the north of Italy rose towards brilliance. With the French the Guelphs had triumphed. The Pope was the chief power in Italy, though his power was very limited. The cities and dukedoms of the north had now a chance to do as they liked.

We know that after the Roman power had been destroyed and Italy made a desert waste in the fifth and sixth centuries, the surviving Italian nobles and patricians were terribly impoverished. They left their estates and their open villas in the country and retired with some following into the walled cities, where they might keep their lives if not their fortunes. The country was left to roving bands of marauders and barbarians. The cities shut their gates tight and defended themselves.

In these isolated cities the noblemen were no longer lords, they were only burghers or citizens with the rest, for their estates were lost. Still, they were looked up to.

A city must be governed. So the citizens chose these
gentlemen to be their magistrates, and to sit in the Commune or Council. And thus in the howling desert of
Italy these walled cities stood like islands, with some law
and order, and some busy work, and some prosperity
flourishing within their safe confines. These little detached
cities were alone, they governed themselves, they managed
their own affairs.

Various trades were started within the various towns,
and these prospered. Many of the noble families had
saved some wealth. With this they set up industries,
like weaving or tanning or glass-making, and so they
became rich commercial citizens, leaders in the munici-
pality, carrying on busy trade between towns in the
intervals of quiet.

Now these cities, safe and busy and independent within
their walls, were very proud, and clung fast to their own
separate independence. They were never safe, however,
from attack. They might be besieged, taken, and sacked
at any moment. Their corn and wine land outside the
walls might be devastated. So some citizens thought
that if they swore allegiance to the Emperor, they might
remain free, and just by paying tribute or giving military
help, they might have peace and all cities might be kept
at rest. For the growing towns were very jealous of one
another, they made murderous attacks on one another.
They were never safe from each other.

Those citizens who felt that all might be united in prosperity by swearing allegiance to one strong emperor, who
as overlord would protect all without interfering in the
private government of any, these were the Ghibelin party
in the towns. Those who did not want to be united with
anybody in any way were the Guelphs. They stuck to the
Pope, because they knew he could never really master
them. So that the two parties or factions, Guelph and
Ghibelin, divided all Italy, particularly the north. Some
of the great families in Rome, Florence, Milan, Parma,

were Guelph, some were Ghibelin, and the fights of these families and their followers sometimes made the streets of their towns run blood.

But the cities were staunch for independence. They had their own armies, their own standards, their own battle-cry. It was the cities of the Lombard League that defeated Barbarossa. And when Manfred sent an army against Florence, the great Guelph city of Tuscany, the Florentines marched out, surrounding their famous *caroccio*. The *caroccio* was a strange chariot or ark on wheels, bearing the standard, and representing the city. It was surrounded by a picked company of citizens, called the Company of Death. Before the *caroccio* was surrendered each of these citizens would be dead. Manfred's army, however, for the first time in history captured the *caroccio* of Florence. The lovely Tuscan city was in the hands of the enemy Ghibelins. Fortunately it was not, as was usually the case, sacked and destroyed. And soon after the death of Manfred it was free again in its own separation and fierce independence.

Florence was a fine city, well developed under her famous citizens. In 1266 the trades and traders of the town united themselves in seven great guilds or *Arti*. Each guild governed its own trade and its own workers. The rules were strict, and no man was allowed to break them. The heads of the guilds were rich, famous citizens, and as a rule members of the Commune or Council which governed the city. So now we have new republics born, governed by a number of rich and influential citizens, depending almost entirely on trade.

One of the great guilds of Florence was the Calimala, or Cloth-dressers' Guild. From England, France, Flanders, cloth was sent to Florence to be dressed and dyed. It came in ships up the Arno, or on the backs of pack-mules, large bales of dirty, greyish, greasy stuff. In the hands of the Florentines it went through many processes, and was sent out again smooth and supple, dyed in lovely tints.

The secrets of the processes were preserved by the Calimala from all the world.

Every roll of cloth was stamped with the mark of the Guild, and this was guarantee enough. There would be no false statement of length or breadth, no flaw in the pieces, the dyes would be fast. If one of the workers or packers attempted fraud or even slovenliness, he was fined. If he did not pay the fine he was expelled by the consuls of the Guild. And then, no more work for him in Florence.

The Guild became rich. It had strong protectors. In all the great cities of Europe Calimala consuls were established, to guard the rights of their merchants, and to control the trade of finished cloth : for everywhere, in all countries, men wanted the cloth dressed by the Florentine Guild.

The great citizens, heads of the Guild, became important as princes. Their consuls were received like ambassadors. Kings treated with the rich citizens, asking for loans of money or guarantees of security. And thus the Florentine merchants were in a position to control peace and war, for they might grant the loan by means of which the war could be carried on, or they might refuse it. Kings were almost at their mercy, for the prosecution of war is dependent on the proceeds of the arts of peace. So trade dealt its first great blow against kings and barons. And so the great banking interest began to show its power in the world.

At home, the merchants lived in a stately manner. They built noble palaces. And yet, in Florence at least, they were careful not to pretend to be princes. They were friendly and familiar with the citizens. All the splendour they made they professed to make for the city, not for their own persons. And the citizens were glad. They were passionately proud of their city. They wished their greatest burghers to have the handsomest palaces in the world, the finest fame. For the city—all was for the fame of the city.

And thus arose the perfect palaces of Florence, Venice,

Genoa, the wonderful cathedrals of Rome and Milan and Pisa. These lovely buildings must be perfected with sculpture, statues, and frescoes on the walls. And so began that marvellous time of Italian painting, when the finest pictures in the world were produced. Then men felt their hearts bursting with splendour. Poets wrote great poems, famous for ever : the people gaily sang the songs and poems of their city, filling the streets with liveliness. The populace were proud of all glorious and lovely things that arose around them, proud of the pictures, the poems, the brilliant learning of the universities, the noble statues and buildings. It was not that they wanted possessions for themselves. Their delight was in knowing that splendid creations were brought forth within their cities. If this were so, the citizens were glad to be poor and see others rich. They knew that they themselves could not produce the beauties and the glories, however rich they might be.

Florence was a Guelph city. Yet it had a large Ghibelin party, many of its famous citizens were Ghibelins, who wished a strong emperor might come to take the allegiance of all cities and make the land whole. In Florence the two factions quarrelled and fought bitterly, each exiling the leading opponents when opportunity arrived. But this struggle only strengthened the nerves and tempers of the Florentines.

In 1284 Florence, but particularly the Guelph party, had a great rejoicing over another's misfortune. At the mouth of the Arno lay the city of Pisa, the great mediæval seaport. All the sea-trade of Florence must pass through the fingers of Pisa. And Pisa was a staunch Ghibelin city ; she made Florence feel the penalty. Therefore loud was the rejoicing in Florence when news came that Pisa had met her great sea-rival Genoa in battle on the waves, and that the Pisan fleet was terribly beaten, many ships sunk or taken, most of her best sailors gone for ever.

Pisa never recovered. She had had a great trade with

the Crusaders' cities in the East—Tyre, Jaffa, Acre; the Levant trade, it was called. She had rivalled Genoa and Venice as the greatest sea-force in the Mediterranean. She had rivalled Florence as a land power in Italy. And now she fell, never to rise again. To-day Pisa is a half-dead city, beautiful, rather forlorn, with her great cathedral, and the baptistery and the leaning tower, so silent and gold-coloured on the grassy square in a corner of the town, showing the glory of the Middle Ages, while the little tram-cars run to their terminus within the enclosure. But Florence, when Pisa fell, became the undoubted centre of all that great stream of traffic that flowed in those days along the Arno Valley—Florence, the queen of Tuscany, the flower of Italy.

Meanwhile the outer world was not quiet. The last of her great popes was to bring down the Church of Rome to ignominy. We know of three most famous popes : first, Gregory i., called Gregory the Great, who from 590 to 604 saved Rome and succoured the people in the distress of barbarian invasions, and who sent forth missionaries to Britain ; then Hildebrand, called Gregory vii., who conceived the great idea that the Pope should rule Europe, who brought the Emperor Henry iv. to his knees at Canossa and who died sorrowful ; and then the great Innocent iii., who from 1198 to 1216 ruled the papacy in her most magnificent days, from his seat in Rome dictating like a president of the European states all that should be done by the rulers of Christendom. This was in the days when Barbarossa was dead, and when Frederick ii. was still too young to reign. And even then Innocent had to scheme hard to keep his authority, and too often he sadly failed. Luckily he died before he saw the sad havoc his young charge Frederick would make with the papacy.

Now, in 1294 Boniface viii. was elected Supreme Pontiff. He was a fine-looking, handsome man, of good Italian family, skilled in law, clever, confident, and arrogant. He thought he could do as Innocent had done, in the days

before the terrible Frederick.   Therefore he began to interfere in Europe.   But he had not any longer just one
single opponent to face, in the person of the Emperor.
He had all the young nations, with their kings just growing strong.

Men were becoming less interested in heaven, and much
less afraid of hell.   Kings did not mind a great deal if the
Pope threatened to excommunicate them and condemn
their souls to eternal torture.   They wanted to establish
themselves and their own kingdoms on earth, and were
not to be interfered with by threats from a pope.

So Boniface's efforts at commanding kings led to disaster.
These were as tired of supreme spiritual rule as they were
of supreme imperial rule.   Nations and cities wanted to
act for themselves, without interference of any so-called
higher power.   When Boniface bade Prince Frederick of
Aragon to leave Sicily, after the Sicilian Vespers, Frederick
refused.   When the Pope excommunicated the prince, the
Spaniard ignored the event, and had himself crowned in
Palermo.   When Boniface issued a Bull preventing kings
or princes from levying taxes on the clergy and on the
lands of the Church, the Archbishop of Canterbury
obediently forbade the English priests and bishops to pay
their taxes to the tax-gatherers of Edward I.   Edward I.
immediately outlawed all his clergy, and the clergy,
afraid, paid their taxes but called them voluntary gifts.

France, however, was the great kingly power of the
Middle Ages, and it was with France that the real tussle
took place.   Philip IV. of France, in defiance of the Pope's
Bull, forbade any money to go out of France to the papal
revenues.   The quarrel became most bitter.   Philip taxed
his French clergy heavily.   His bishops complained.   The
Pope stepped in to defend them.   But Philip seized the
papal legate and put him in prison, charged him with
treason for having spoken words against the king.   Then
the Pope's next Bull—called the Greater Bull—was
publicly burned by the hangman in Paris.   Immediately

after this Philip was defeated by the Flemings at Courtrai, and people said it was a judgment on him. The Pope made friends with the Emperor Albert, and Albert made public declaration that he received his power at the hands of the Pope. This was a triumph for Boniface. In return Philip summoned the French Council, called the Estates General, and Boniface was accused of heresy, wizardry, and foul crime. Then Philip announced that he could no longer regard Boniface as Pope, and appealed to a General Council of the Church. At last, in September 1303, Boniface excommunicated Philip. He released all the subjects of the French king from their allegiance, and put that monarch outside the pale of Christianity.

It was now the time for the last blow. Philip sent his general, William of Nogaret, and the Roman noble Sciarra Colonna to Tuscany, well supplied with money, to raise forces against the Pope. It happened that Boniface, who was now an old man, had retired to his little native town of Anagni, to escape the summer heats of Rome. On September 8 cries and clatter of hoofs were heard in the sleepy little town of Anagni. The inhabitants looked out in astonishment. It was William of Nogaret and Sciarra Colonna, who had entered the gates with three hundred men, and ensigns and standards of the King of France flying gaily as they shouted ' Death to Pope Boniface ! Long live the King of France ! '

The townsfolk gaped in amazement and did not stir. The band of troops clattered up to the sunny papal palace. There were no soldiers to defend it ; Pope and cardinals were helpless. The cardinals gave themselves up for lost. But the Pope was a brave man. ' Since,' he said, ' like Jesus Christ, I am willing to be taken, and needs must die by treachery, at least let me die as Pope.' He bade his attendants robe him in the mantle of St. Peter, with the crown of Constantine on his head, and the keys and cross in his hand ; he seated himself on the papal chair.

He sat whilst Nogaret thundered at the doors. He sat as he heard the iron-mailed feet tread the corridors. Then the French and Italian enemy came into presence. Boniface sat unmoving. He was old, stout, but still a handsome figure. Nogaret demanded that he should at once abdicate from the papacy. He constantly refused. He was seized, dragged from the throne, taken prisoner, and threatened with instant death if he did not at once agree to abdicate. Still he refused. So he was kept confined until he should submit.

On the third day the people of Anagni, ashamed at last of this treatment of their old, proud Pope, rose and drove forth the mere handful of the enemy. Boniface was free, but the shock had been too great for a man of seventy-nine. Escorted by the Orsini family, who were bitter enemies of the rival Roman House of Colonna, Boniface returned to Rome and entered it amidst the cheers of the people. But his time was nearly over. It is said his mind gave way, and that he gnawed at himself as if he were mad. In three weeks he died—the last great pope of the Middle Ages had passed away. The papacy never again rose to European power. Monarchy was now triumphant, kings were the greatest men in the world.

The next important pope was elected in France. He was Bertrand de Goth, Archbishop of Bordeaux, which city then belonged to England. But Bertrand was a Frenchman, and unwilling in any way to offend the French king. He did not depart for Rome, as every pope had done. New cardinals were created, all Frenchmen, and the papal court was set up in the Archbishop's palace in Bordeaux.

In 1309, however, the Pope and his cardinals removed to Avignon, an old town in Provence, on the Rhone. There the papal court would still remain under the protection of the French king. Once again Provence knew the gay splendours it had seen in Roman days, when it was the brilliant Province. The town was ancient, sunny, delightful, full of memories of the great past. It had an excellent climate, much better than that of Rome, and the towns-folk were quiet and pleasant, not like the turbulent citizens of Rome, who were constantly rising in dangerous rage against their popes. The valley of the Rhone was delight-ful, beautiful to look at, pleasant to ride through, excellent for sport. It was full of the memories of old Roman greatness, but memories all mellow and sweet, not bloody.

The popes now became like the Gallic bishops in the Frankish days. They did not trouble deeply about any-thing. In their great palace on the Rhone they spent days of festival, they took their pleasure on the river and in the shady woods. The cardinals established themselves in palaces in the city, and the old streets were brilliant with gay processions as these prelates, vivid in their scarlet, rode laughingly towards the Pope's palace, followed by a retinue of gentlemen and ladies. Now for the first time ladies were invited to the papal feasts. Poets sang to the harp, fools and buffoons made merriment, the wine cir-culated, the handsome halls rang with mirth. Then musicians struck up for the glittering dance. But in time the Avignon popes suffered from lack of money, for the revenues did not come in to the papal treasury in France as they had in Rome.

For seventy years, from 1305 to 1376, the popes resided in France. This period is called the Babylonish Captivity, when the Church was supposed to be in captivity in France as the Jews had been captive in Babylon. But though France was the greatest power in Europe at that time, before the great struggle of the Hundred Years War, yet the popes were not altogether slavish, not really under the thumb of the French King. None the less the reverence for the papacy withered in all countries in Europe during the Captivity. Men began even to despise the great head of the Church, whom before they had regarded as being very near to God Himself, very powerful.

XII. The End of the Age of Faith

Just as men grew restless under supreme authority of an emperor, so they rebelled against the authority of the Pope. The popes wished to keep supreme religious command over all Christians. The only way to do this was to make the people believe that the Pope stood much nearer to God than they did, and that he received holy secrets and commands straight from heaven. To keep up this belief, there must be much mystery and strangeness in religion. It would not do for people to know everything. The priests must keep the great secrets, they must stand between God and the masses. And this was the way in which the Catholic Church ruled Christendom. The Bible was a mysterious holy book which the common people never saw, and which they could never read if they did see it, for it was written in Latin. Sometimes the priests read them little pieces : about the heavens opening, or about the stones rolling back from the Sepulchre as Jesus rose from the dead. And it seemed terrible and wonderful. It seemed to the people as if the priests knew great, deep mysteries, of which only a fragment was revealed to ordinary men. The ordinary Christians read nothing and knew nothing by themselves. Everything was told to them by the priests. And so, as when we tell tales to children, they heard vivid and marvellous stories of miracles and wonders, terrible accounts of the devil and the horrors of hell, lovely descriptions of heaven. All was real and actual to them. They really believed that devils lurked in houses, or possessed the souls of neighbours or friends.

They really believed that the priests and saints could speak
to these devils.   They could almost see the devils cringing
as a priest approached making the sign of the cross, they
could almost hear the imps whimpering with pain if they
were touched with a drop of holy water.   As nowadays
children sometimes believe in fairies, and imagine they see
them, so in the early days all men and women really believed in devils and angels.   And if the ordinary priest, with
his mysterious knowledge and his magical Latin, had such
power over devils, how much more had the Pope ?   The
Pope was master of Satan himself.   Archangels talked with
the Pope.   He was lord of Christendom, he held the keys
of heaven and hell.   If the Pope excommunicated a man,
that man was condemned to burn for ever in fire and brim-
stone, tortured by legions of imps.   So all men believed
quite simply.   Hence the great power of the popes.   And
hence we call the Middle Ages the Age of Faith.

After the Age of Faith dawned the Age of Reason.   Very
early, students and thoughtful priests began to study the
New Testament.   They found nothing about the grandeur
of a pope or the rich splendour of bishops, nothing about
the power of priests.   They only saw the plain lesson,
that Christians must give their goods to the poor, think
nothing of the pleasures of the body, and everything of
saving the soul.

Before 1200 some people in the south of France, that
old, cultured land, got hold of a translation of the Bible,
and began to form their own opinion from it.   They
believed in poverty, they would not marry, they fasted
and denied the body.   The rich luxury of the bishops was
denounced.

These new people were called ' the Poor Men of Lyons.'
The Pope saw that if such sects increased the whole power
of the Church would collapse.   So the Poor Men of Lyons
were bitterly persecuted.   A crusade was preached against
them, by the Pope's orders.   In 1209 Simon de Montfort,
Earl of Leicester, set out against them.   The ' Poor Men '

were massacred in hundreds, the old towns of the Languedoc destroyed. Only Toulouse, the old Gothic capital,
at this time headquarters of the new people, held out against
the besieging armies, and Simon de Montfort was killed
by a stone thrown from an engine which was worked by
women on the walls of the city.

After this crusade the Court of the Inquisition was
established, to examine and punish men guilty of heresy
—that is, guilty of false beliefs. In 1233 the learned
Spanish monks of the new order of Dominicans were made
Papal Inquisitors, the Court of Inquisition was in their
hands. They punished witches, wizards, heretics, burning
them at the stake. For the Ages of Faith were ages also
of deplorable cruelty.

At the same time another great religious movement
began. St. Francis of Assisi, a young Italian of well-to-do
family, frail in health but passionate in soul, suddenly
realised in his own way what the Christian life meant.
He gave away all his goods, and said he would own
nothing. He declared he was wedded to Our Lady
Poverty. He was very happy in his new discovery.
Whilst Italy was torn between struggling emperor and
pope, Francis went about joyously telling all men how
sweet and delightful it was to live for love alone, to own
nothing, to be defenceless and helpless, but always to love
and to help and to rejoice, looking forward to the life with
Jesus.

Many men were attracted by St. Francis' way of life.
They left everything and came with him, as the disciples
had followed Christ. Then St. Clare, who loved Francis,
gathered the women about her. And soon there were
many Franciscans, men and women.

Pope Innocent III., the greatest of all the popes, had,
like his predecessors, preached the Crusade in which the
Poor Men of Lyons were massacred. But Innocent loved
Francis, and gave him the right to establish the great
Franciscan Order, that order of wandering friars after-

wards so famous in Europe, and such a great help to the
Church.

The Franciscans were not like other monks. They did
not shut themselves up. Their duty was to wander the
earth, teaching, helping, loving all men—possessing nothing
themselves, and giving love to all men. The older monks
were dark, loveless men, who never looked at the earth.
The great St. Bernard once sailed down the beautiful
Lake of Lucerne without even glancing around him, his
mind was so bent on his own affairs. But Francis taught
differently. He loved the sky and the grass and all living
things. He once stood and preached a sweet sermon to
the birds that fluttered round him, calling them, ' my little
sisters, the birds.'

The Dominicans also wandered about teaching. But
they were learned monks, and they taught strict morality
and obedience. The Franciscans taught joyousness and
sweet love. They taught hope. They told men that the
reign of love was at hand.

All over Europe began a great ferment in the souls of men,
towards the end of the thirteenth century. The fearful
struggles of the emperors were over, the crusades were
more or less finished. A strangeness seemed to hang in the
air. Men felt that something was going to happen.
There was a feeling of fear, of calamity ; and at the same
time a feeling of frightened hope or expectation. Something terrible and wonderful was going to take place.
The little poems of the Middle Ages constantly chime—
' The fear of death oppresses me.'

Out of the ruin and chaos which followed the death of
Innocent III. and Frederick II., strange thoughts arose.
Men came forward declaring themselves prophets. They
told curious and terrible things, and people were filled with
dread. In 1254 a book was published called ' *Introduction
to the Everlasting Gospel*,' supposed to contain the teaching
of a famous seer or prophet, the Abbot Joachim, who had
died at Naples in 1202. In this book it said that Judaism

was the revelation of the Father : Christianity was the revelation of the Son : now men must prepare for the revelation of the Holy Ghost.

Wild ideas spread everywhere. Men began to expect the reign of the Holy Ghost. They said that before Jesus was born the Father had reigned : after this, until their own day, the Son had reigned ; now the Holy Ghost would reign. In the *Everlasting Gospel* it was stated that when the Holy Ghost began to reign the papacy and the priesthood would cease to exist. There would be no more Church to govern the souls of men. So the popes condemned the *Everlasting Gospel* as wicked, heretical, false doctrine. None the less it had a great power over the minds of men.

In 1260 Gerard Sagarelli, a workman of Parma, sat in the market-place of his town and flung away all he had among the crowd. Then he stripped himself naked, had himself wrapped in swaddling bands and laid in a cradle. After this he declared himself born again, an apostle sent from God. He started a new Order, the Order of Apostles. He went about, wild and strange, preaching mad doctrines. People flocked to him from North Italy. But he was burned in Parma as a heretic, in 1300, by the Dominican Inquisition.

One of his disciples was called Dolcino of Novara. He said men should hold no earthly possession, no earthly connection. Wife should leave husband, a father should leave his children, nothing human should stand in the way of the perfect union of the soul with the Holy Ghost. These men prayed no more to Jesus. They felt the Holy Ghost coming upon them, filling them with strange bliss, and with sheer perfection.

Several thousands of people retired to a lovely valley in the Alps, the Val di Sesia, in Piedmont. There they lived half naked, fasting, praying, hoping for the Holy Ghost to come upon them, prophesying and seeing visions when they felt themselves at last filled with the Spirit. They did no work, but depended on the frightened, awe-stricken peasants to bring them food. This manner of life sent many demented, and they were all beside themselves.

In 1305 they were excommunicated and threatened with the Inquisition. The governor of the nearest town, and the Bishop of Vercelli, with armed forces marched against them. These apostles of the Holy Ghost, mad with unnatural excitement, retired to a steep hill. There with frenzy they hurled and rolled stones and masses of rock upon the attacking force, holding them back. Then they fled up steep precipices, where armies could not follow them.

They were now really mad, no longer human beings. No peasants would come near them with food, they were always starving. They came down on villages and lonely houses, robbing, plundering, devouring food like wild beasts. Their eyes glared with strange light. If any one opposed them, they rushed with terrifying looks and stabbed him and slashed him with knives. Then they disappeared again up the secret paths of their precipices, gathering together to call on the Holy Ghost to fill them with power and fury.

At last in 1307 their fastness on Mount Zerbal was stormed. The apostles with their wild, waving hair and mad eyes were slaughtered or scattered, some were captured. Women were there, shrieking and fighting like wolves : for each apostle had a chosen heavenly sister. Both the apostle Dolcino and his heavenly sister were taken. The woman was slowly burned before Dolcino's eyes, and then his flesh was torn bit by bit with red-hot pincers. But he never murmured.

After the Apostles, a great sect formed after the Franciscan idea, called the Fraticelli, was pursued and destroyed by the Church.

In 1320 the shepherds and peasantry of France were strangely stirred. At first little groups of ignorant peasants were remarked wandering barefoot and begging.

No one took much notice. Then the groups became more numerous. Every day bands of barefooted men were passing through the streets of towns and villages, crying aloud for alms and gifts, and declaring that they were going to win back the Holy Places. Then swarms filled the land. No one knew what inspired them, nor whence they came. Band after band gradually flocked together, all possessed as it seemed by the same madness. The educated people looked on in terror as these ragged crowds drew together, masses of ignorant people who had left all work, abandoned everything, and were moving they knew not whither. They were named the Pastoureaux, or Shepherds.

The swarms grew into a great army. They turned to Paris, and by their very masses burst into the city. Then they went through the streets, breaking down the doors of prisons, breaking into houses and shops, taking what they wanted. After this, moved by some herd instinct, they departed southwards, towards Palestine, they said.

As they went they massacred all Jews they came across, recognising them by their distinctive dress. They broke into the castles of nobles, into rich houses, into the houses of priests and bishops, taking whatever they wanted, and saying it was for a holy mission. More bands joined them from every side. The great, blind, dirty host rolled down the valley of the Rhone.

But when they came to the coast they were stopped from entering Italy by the governor of Carcassonne. The Pastoureaux turned and began to spread over the country-side, and over low, swampy districts. They were in such masses that no one dared attack them. Watchful armies waited to prevent their streaming forth. As the weeks went by starvation and exposure brought on deadly fevers. The sickening Pastoureaux died like flies.

At last so many had died that the armies dared attack them. They were slaughtered and captured and sub-dued, and then the remainder were taken back to work.

This rising of the Pastoureaux was something like the risings of the Gallo-Roman slaves and peasants in the days before the Franks, and similar to other terrible peasant risings which have taken place in France. It seems as if the French poor were liable to these attacks of unaccountable uneasiness.

All these later movements and madnesses, however, took place whilst the popes were in Avignon, during the period called the Babylonish Captivity. Men hoped for better things when the papal court returned to Rome.

But it was not to be so. Gregory XI. returned to Rome in 1376. When he died in 1378, the populace of Rome cried loudly for an Italian pope, so a Neapolitan archbishop became Urban VI. Urban was severe, strict, and conscientious. He was very stern with the dissolute cardinals. Therefore many, and the French cardinals in particular, began to cry out against this Italian pope, and to declare he was not properly elected. They went so far, that in September 1378 the French cardinals elected Robert of Geneva to be Clement VII.

Thus there were two popes. Urban held his court at Rome, Clement at Avignon. There were two sets of cardinals, two governments for one church. This divided all Europe. And this division is called The Great Schism.

Each pope called on all nations to obey him. France, Scotland, Castile, Aragon, Naples, followed the French pope; England, Germany, Scandinavia, Poland and Portugal followed the Italian pope. Then began a great commotion. Both popes loudly declared themselves to be the one and only pope. Then they began to revile each other in letters and public proclamations. Then they excommunicated each other. And at last it went so far, that each preached a crusade against the other. The priests of one half of Christendom preached a crusade against the priests of the other half.

Such a situation was madness. The crusade was never begun, for neither pope had any money. Each court incurred the usual expenses, with not half the income to meet these expenses. So both the popes tried squeezing the countries that remained faithful to them. But none of the countries was willing to be squeezed. There was no money for the popes.

They had recourse to other methods. The sale of indulgences began. On little scraps of parchment were written pardons for such and such sins. Priests and friars filled their wallets with these scraps of parchment, which were sent by pack-load to every bishopric, and set off to preach indulgences. Standing in some open place, or even in a church, they would preach to men and women how the Pope had power to pardon all sins : how he had written out on parchment such pardons ; and now all good Christians were called upon to purchase a pardon which would wipe out for ever from the Judgment Book any sin that had been committed. Small sins cost small sums, greater sins cost greater sums.

When Urban died a new Italian pope was elected, Boniface IX. When Clement died, a Spaniard, Peter de Luna, was elected Benedict XIII. But France did not like a Spanish pope at Avignon, so he was blockaded in his palace by Marshal Boucicault and starved into surrender. He was kept in prison for five years by the French before he escaped.

The Schism was now becoming a real nuisance. All churchmen wished to end it. A great Council of the Church was called at Pisa in 1409, and though it decided nothing, yet now a new ecclesiastical power arose, a power greater than the Pope himself. This was the council of all great churchmen, called the Great Council. The Great Council claimed the power even to depose a pope. It was therefore much dreaded by the later popes, who were kept a little in check by their fear.

Meanwhile new heresies had arisen. About 1380 John Wycliffe translated the Bible into English and began to teach the real meaning of the Scriptures. He denounced

the wickedness of the clergy and attacked the authority
of the Pope. Many followers came to him, and they got
the name of Lollards. But the Lollards were moving
spirits in Wat Tyler's rebellion, so the English Government
began to attack them. Wycliffe's bones were burned
at Lutterworth, in Leicestershire, in 1428, and his ashes
scattered on the river, so that the spirit of such a heretic
should never find its body at the Resurrection.

His teachings, however, spread to the Continent. Thousands of English students went to France to hear the great
teacher Abelard. Many wandered on from monastery to
monastery, university to university. So they carried the
Lollard or Wycliffe writings with them, and the new
doctrines spread.

One of the greatest disciples of Wycliffe was the Bohemian, John Huss. Huss was the son of prosperous peasants,
who had given him a good education. He entered the
Church, became a priest. But he was very clever. He
took his Master of Arts degree in 1396, and became a
teacher in the university and a preacher in his town. Soon
he was the most honoured teacher in the university and
the most famous preacher in Prague. The chapel where
he preached was called Bethlehem. There the people
flocked to hear him, for he was a passionate, brave man.
He told his people that Christ was the Head of the Church,
not the Pope, and that it was Christ's teaching they must
follow. He also told them that the sale of indulgences
was a scandalous money-making trick. But this was not
enough to make him a heretic. However, the bishops were
furious.

At this time Europe was making a determined effort to
end the Schism. The two popes had now become three,
Gregory XII., Benedict XIII., and Pope John XXIII. The
Emperor Sigismund demanded that another General
Council should be called. The free imperial city of Con-
stance was chosen for the meeting-place.

In October 1414 the members of the Council began to

arrive. The beautiful little city that stands where the Rhine runs out through low banks from Lake Constance had never seen anything so brilliant as this gathering. Pope John opened the Council in November. But it was not till Christmas Eve that Sigismund arrived. His boats, flickering with gay lights, came sailing across the lake in the wintry darkness. At two hours after midnight the Emperor with his brilliant retinue landed at Constance, and marched to the palace, torches flaming everywhere. On Christmas day Pope John preached in the cathedral to a vast number of townsfolk, nobles, doctors, cardinals, whilst the Emperor read the lessons from the Gospel— 'There went out a decree from Caesar Augustus—'

The Council met for three purposes : to end the Schism, to reform abuses in the Church, to extirpate heresy. For the last purpose, John Huss was summoned to Constance. He received his summons when he was in Prague, and his heart sank. He felt he would never return. His people clamoured round him, saying he should not go. But then the Emperor Sigismund promised a safe-conduct. So Huss began to put his affairs in order. He still felt he would not return.

At last he set off across South Germany, and arrived in Constance. He had received the Emperor's safe-conduct, but was none the less kept fast in prison. In the spring he was brought out for trial for heresy.

They could prove nothing against him. But they wanted to make him say he had erred, and he refused, for he felt he had done only what was right. And so they condemned him to be burned. On 6 July 1415 the noble-minded Huss was burned in the market-place of Constance. The Emperor Sigismund stood looking on, remarking that the safe-conduct which he had given held good only for the journey, he had not meant it to protect the heretic from just condemnation in Constance.

Next year, in May 1416, they burned Jerome of Prague, the follower of Huss, also in Constance. An eye-witness writes : ' Both met their death with a constant mind, and hastened to the fire as if invited to a feast, uttering no sound that could reveal their agony. When they began to burn they sang a hymn, which the flame and the crackling of the fire could scarcely prevent.'

The Council sat on. It kept Pope John prisoner, then charged him with many crimes. He was deposed from the papacy, and ended his days peacefully as a cardinal. The old Pope Gregory xii. resigned, and died in 1417. But the Spaniard, Benedict xiii., refused all persuasion. He insisted that he was still Pope, and fortified himself in his rock-fortress on his own estate. The Council, however, declared he was no longer Pope, and men decided to take no further notice of him. At last, in 1417, the Roman nobleman, Cardinal Colonna, was elected Pope, and became Martin v.

Thus the Schism was ended. But the power of the popes was also finished. They were no longer absolute—they might be deposed by a General Council. They no longer claimed universal power over Europe, but remained in Italy, and took part in Italian politics rather than in European.

The Bohemians, however, were up in arms after the burning of Huss. The Czechs determined not to submit to Sigismund, who had burned their leader so treacherously. Armed with their deadly scythes, or ' flails,' and led by the famous blind general, Ziska, they rose in a revolt which shook Europe. Crusades were preached against them. Henry, Bishop of Winchester, came to take part in the Holy War against the Hussites. For years the fighting went on. Through long practice the peasants became very fierce and expert. They were hard, vindictive veterans. They could give twenty or thirty strokes with their terrible flail in a minute, and each stroke was enough to cut a man down. They hated the Emperor's men and the Pope's men with a perfect hatred, branding their prisoners with a cross upon the forehead. Then the imperialists took to branding a cup on the forehead of any captured Hussite, because the Bohemians demanded to drink of the sacramental wine at the Communion Supper, whereas the Catholics allowed only the bread to the communicant.

Ziska died in 1424. In 1431 Sigismund invaded Bohemia with a great army, but was defeated because his German peasant soldiery sympathised with the Hussites and would not fight for him. So the war dragged on, till at last the Pope invited the Bohemians to send representatives to the Council of Basle, to patch things up. This was done, and in 1434 Sigismund was accepted King of Bohemia, and the Hussites received liberty of worship. They alone, of all the catholic nations, were allowed to partake of the sacred wine, as well as of the wafer, at Communion. It was the first victory against the Church.

In Italy the popes had lost their sacred power. When Urban vi. sent two legates to excommunicate the Tyrant Bernabò Visconti at Milan, Bernabò received the legates and rode with them to the bridge over the river Naviglio. There he took out the papal Bulls of Excommunication, and looking at the legates, asked them whether they preferred to eat or to drink. The legates turned pale, for the river was rushing swiftly below. They looked at the dangerous flood, and at the tough parchment of the papal Bulls. Then they said faintly they preferred to eat. And Bernabò made them eat the Bulls they had brought. What did he care for excommunication !

The Church was not reformed. Popes and cardinals were more rich, lavish, and openly wicked than ever they had been. Reformers rose up in Italy, preaching a purer life. The greatest of these preachers was Savonarola. In 1490 Lorenzo the Magnificent, hearing of the fame of this preaching friar, invited him to Florence to add to the renown of the city. Savonarola came. He was a swarthy, narrow-browed, hulking friar, haggard with fasting so that his great bones showed and his dark eyes burned. His voice was weak, and his movements were clumsy and ugly.

Yet he had a truly magnetic power over the people. They thronged in crowds to hear him. He preached in San Marco in Florence and then in the Duomo, the domed cathedral. He wished to purify the land from the flaunting gay wickedness he saw around him. Using strange, gruesome language, he pictured the horrors that would come on Italy as a judgment for her lusts and vices, all the ghastly plagues and burnings and death. He harshly denounced from his pulpit the Pope, the clergy, and even his patron Lorenzo di Medici.

Lorenzo had a gay and beautiful court in Florence, thronged with the most exceptional people. The Italians of the later Renaissance, having studied Latin and Greek, were fascinated with the beautiful old pagan myths, they became indifferent or careless of Christianity and its severe teaching. They loved beautiful, rich things, and delicious pleasures. Beauty, pleasure, knowledge, skill, these were their aim. So Savonarola, who wished all men to go in sackcloth and ashes, for fear of hell, abused the witty Lorenzo, and tried to work up the citizens against their tyrant, to restore the liberty of Florence. When Lorenzo was dying, in 1492, Savonarola was his confessor. The dark, fanatic monk bent over the dark, subtle Lorenzo, who was so wise in the wisdom of the world and the ages. Lorenzo confessed his sins and affirmed his ' perfect faith.'

' Wilt thou restore Florence to liberty, and to the enjoyment of her popular government as a free commonwealth ? ' sternly said the fanatic friar. Lorenzo turned his dying face away, as if weary at this question, and said no more.

In 1494 Charles VIII. of France invaded Italy and the Medici fled from Florence. Savonarola had been prophesying that tyrants would flee before a deliverer. The people went wild, thinking the prophecy had come true. Savonarola, who was now Prior of the Dominican House of San Marco, swayed all Florence. The city was completely under his spell now the Medici were gone.

A strange change took place. After all the games and sports and carnivals of the Medici days, men became desperately religious. The city looked suddenly grey, for none wore bright clothes any more. Bands of men went about wringing their hands, lamenting their sins, and destroying sinful objects. Bands of children clothed in white patrolled the streets singing hymns, entering the palaces and smashing those statues they thought were immoral, slashing up the lovely pictures. These holy children assumed authority over the citizens, and none dared oppose them. For the followers of Savonarola, called the Weepers or Snivellers, were masters of the town.

Then Jesus Christ was proclaimed King of Florence, and the citizens went round crying loudly ' Viva Cristo ! Viva Cristo ! '—Long live Christ ! When carnival came, the time for wild festivity, a great Bonfire of Vanities was arranged. Savonarola's followers, the Weepers, marched in solemn procession through the streets, and the Innocents, the children, made their rounds of inspection. People brought their silks and ornaments, their books of stories such as the Decameron, and their books of profane poetry, their fans, perfumes, mirrors, statues, statuettes, the classic books supposed to be immoral, and some priceless pictures. Sandro Botticelli, an old, lame man now, threw on the heap in the public square many of his drawings and paintings—and then, to loud chanting, the whole pile of worldly treasures was burned, many exquisite things that could never be replaced.

Meanwhile Savonarola's preaching became more and more wild, the city was going mad in intense religious excitement. Savonarola prophesied in the pulpit, a worn, hectic, strange figure. He listened to an epileptic monk in his convent, asking the poor epileptic, whom he supposed to be inspired, for advice. And then he told the people the real reign of Christ was at hand, that angels came down and told him so.

Alexander vi., the great but wicked Borgia pope, tried

to lure Savonarola to Rome. He did not succeed, so he
suspended the friar from preaching. Savonarola was
silent for a time, but in 1496 he preached his Lent sermons,
denouncing the wickedness of the Pope and clergy, threatening an end, and promising strange, stupendous miracles.
The end of the world was near, the Saviour was to come
to Florence. The Florentines were beside themselves
with excitement, though sane men did not like this return
to the dreadful superstitions of the early Middle Ages.
The governors of the city, seeing their town out of hand
and beside itself, turned against the fanatic friar. Taking
advantage of this, the Pope excommunicated Savonarola,
in 1497. For six months the friar ceased to preach,
remaining in his convent. On Christmas Day he celebrated Mass in San Marco, and in February preached once
more. The populace were drunk with frenzied excitement. The Signory, that is, the Gonfaloniere of Justice
and the Council of Eight Priors, suspended Savonarola
from preaching.

Savonarola now wrote letters to the sovereigns of Europe,
calling for a general council. In Florence he had continually spoken of miracles that were to come. His
opponents, even his followers, demanded the miracle. A
Franciscan monk offered to pass through flames, if Savonarola would do the same. Savonarola was still sensible
enough to see that this was tempting Providence. But
he had gone too far. His friends wildly believed in his
power to perform a miracle : his enemies urged him to
try. He agreed.

Tremendous preparations were made, the stacks ready
to be ignited for the passage through the fire were built in
the great square. On April 7, 1498, thousands of people
assembled in the early morning, waiting to see the miracle.
The nobles and rich had platforms and reserved places.
Slowly, towards midday, the Franciscans approached from
one direction, the Dominicans with Savonarola from
another. The masses could hardly contain themselves.

They were going to see a miracle, a miracle like those recorded in the New Testament.

But then started a long quibbling. The Dominicans raised objections, saying the Franciscan monk's clothing had been charmed by magic against fire, and he must change everything. This was done, and then the Franciscans began to raise objections, saying that Savonarola should not carry the Host in his hand as he passed through the fire, as this would be burning the body of the Lord. Savonarola would not agree. The argument went on before the wildly excited mob. The city authorities prepared to stop the ordeal. Then the bright sky clouded, thunder was heard, and a heavy shower fell, soaking the piles of wood. All was abandoned for the day.

The mob were furious. Next day they attacked San Marco. Savonarola and his two chief supporters, Fra Domenico and Fra Silvestro, the epileptic, were arrested. At the Pope's command Savonarola, worn with excitement, fasting, anxiety, and frenzy, was tortured to make him confess his errors. Perhaps he cried out in his agony that he was no true prophet : how shall we know what he confessed in the secret torture-chamber ? He and his two followers were declared heretics and schismatics, traitors to the state, and condemned to execution.

Three high gibbets were erected in the great square. ' From the Church militant and triumphant I separate thee,' said the Bishop of Vasona as he unfrocked Savonarola. ' From the Church militant, yes ; from the Church triumphant, no ; that is not yours to do,' answered the doomed Prior of San Marco's.

So the three were hanged on the high gibbets, and fires were lighted under the bodies, as they hung in chains, to consume them. The people in the square, looking on the three crosses, were reminded of Calvary. But they did nothing to save their prophet. They hated him now.

Savonarola had tried to reform the abuses and wickedness of the Church, and to make life pure and moral, but he had gone the wrong way about it. Instead of making men understand with all their soul and with all their mind what they were doing, and what was good to do, he had gone back to the old methods. He talked as if he knew magical secrets, as if he had magical powers. He made the people believe he could open heaven and earth. He filled them with a wicked madness of destruction, and an ugly lust for exciting events. He set them craving for supernatural powers and supernatural scenes. They ceased to be human men and women. Under the spell of Savonarola they were like frenzied demons. Truth, beauty, happiness, wisdom, these meant nothing to such fanatics. They wanted magical violence and wonderful horrors. They were greedy for pains and penalties and severities, instead of for pleasures and delights such as the Borgia pope lusted for.

And so Savonarola's great movement was felt only as a shock, horrifying Italy and yet further weakening the old order. Savonarola, the last, almost degenerate representative of the Dark Age of Faith, perished and was detested and despised as a fraud.

XIII. The Renaissance

PERHAPS the most wonderful century in all our Europe's two thousand years is the fifteenth century. Then lived the greatest painters, great poets, great architects, sculptors, scientists and men of learning, such as had not been seen before. Then men were alert and keen, full of enthusiasm, full of imagination, full of life.

This splendid century was most glorious in Italy. But the beginnings of the glory lay in the two centuries preceding. Already in 1250 the noble citizens of Florence were resplendent in their palaces, the guilds were formed, the city was alert and alive, ready for great things. In 1265 was born the first world-famous Florentine, Dante Alighieri.

He was the son of a well-to-do citizen, and he was given the best education the times afforded. In those days the schools were all attached to monasteries. Even in the universities monks were the chief teachers. For in the peace and seclusion of their monastic fortresses the monks had been able for hundreds of years to study all the existing books. In the monastery libraries the books of Europe, all written by hand upon parchment, were carefully stored. Seated in silence at their benches, the monks slowly and beautifully copied the old books, all in the Latin tongue, making new, clean volumes, often beautifully decorated in colours. And as they copied they studied. Then the most learned would teach daily in the school within the peaceful bounds of the monastery, or they would go forth, to lecture in a university, or to teach groups of young people in some palace, or to be the tutors in some rich family.

Dante was first taught by a priest, then he went to one of the schools, then to various masters who instructed him in various subjects. All the time, till he was thirty-five he stayed in Florence, never departing to a university. This was unusual in those days. In the Middle Ages, when a man had heard the teachers and doctors of his own university, say of Oxford, he set off on foot or on horse-back, wearing the grey robe of a student, and travelling peacefully along the wild roads, to another university. So many Englishmen came from the north to Oxford, and from Oxford, after their term, set off southwards for France and Italy. Everybody knew a student by his dress, and respected him for his learning. If he came to a monastery, he would at once be admitted as a guest. Then he would spend a few days in seclusion, discussing learned subjects with the abbot and the more book-loving brothers, would study some book in the library, and then, perhaps having written a Latin poem in praise of the monastery, he would take the road again, and travel till he came to the famous University of Paris, where he would settle down to hear the great teachers. Then on from Paris he would go, down to Italy, walking slowly or riding towards the great universities of Bologna, Padua, Salerno. He needed very little money indeed. Some he could earn by writing letters or doing other clerical work. When he came to a university he was sure of a welcome.

Europe then was not like Europe now. If a man were a Christian, all countries were his, for everywhere was the one Church of which he was a son. If he were at all educated, he spoke Latin, and Latin was the speech of all churchmen, of all Europeans of any standing. What did it matter if a man were English or French or Spanish? He was a European, a member of Christendom. He travelled along the roads where all travelled, and on the full high-road every European was at home. People took no notice of foreigners and foreign tongues, for the civilised countries were always full of outlandish troops, and priests might belong to any nation. So the student leaving Italy would calmly take the great north road, to come home through the Alps to Germany, walking often on foot without any fears. He would make his way to the great monastery of St. Gall, near the Lake of Constance, and there call his greeting to the gate-keeper. Nobody asked if he were English or Irish or German or Italian. He spoke in Latin to the monks and was received as one of themselves. Then in the evening they would gossip and talk. So we know many English and Irish, Spanish and Italian came to St. Gall. Some, even wild Irish, stayed and became monks, some became even parish priests to the German peasants. So there was a great, quiet interchange going on all the time ; Europe was one realm of the Church as it has never been since the fifteenth century, when national boundaries began to make fixed barriers.

Learning was a hard, dry business in the Middle Ages. The four great subjects were theology, astronomy, arithmetic and history. All teaching, of course, went on in Latin. The mediæval schoolmasters divided true learning into two branches : the Trivium or threefold, which consisted of grammar, dialectic or argument, and rhetoric or eloquent speech ; then the Quadrivium or fourfold, which consisted of arithmetic, geometry, music, and astronomy. Many a poor student wept over the clumsy difficulties of the Quadrivium, many a man cracked his brains trying to master the Trivium.

Dante, however, without a great deal of help from masters, became deeply learned in all the seven branches of mediæval science. Alone in his room in Florence he read what books he could buy or borrow. Admitted to the libraries of the city, he studied all that was to be known. He was very happy studying and learning and thinking. It made him feel rich at heart, and cheerful.

He loved to meet with friends or learned monks, to hold deep converse by the hour. This was one of the delights of the Middle Ages, this meeting for serious, enthusiastic talk.

The family of Dante belonged to the Guelph party, and during all his youth the poet was mixed up in the serious party strife of Florence. In 1289 the Ghibelins collected from all the Tuscan cities and met the Florentine Guelphs in the battle of Campaldino. Dante, who was twenty-four years of age at the time, is said to have taken part in the battle. The Guelphs were victorious, and the Ghibelins never lifted their heads again in Florence. This victory over the united troops of the Tuscan cities made Florence finally the Queen of Tuscany.

Whilst he was a young man Dante must have met or known the beautiful Beatrice. We do not know if he ever spoke to her. But all through his after-life he made beautiful her memory. His first poem, the ' Vita Nuova ' or New Life, tells the delicate, touching story of his love. But Dante married and lived happily enough with his family. It was not so much the person, the actual individual, that he loved in Beatrice ; it was his own vision. Beatrice was like a vision to him of the life that might come, when men were pure and spiritual, loving their women with purified love. She was a vision or illusion of the more spiritual, more passionless days to come, even the later days which Europe has known and which Dante would never know. If he had married her, she could not have remained a vision to him. And it was the fair ideal he needed, not the actual woman. So that what he calls his grief, in the loss of Beatrice, is really his wistful joy.

Dante was a member of one of the great guilds, the Guild of Doctors. In 1300 he was one of the Chiefs or Priors of this guild. There were seven guilds : the Judges and notaries, the Calimala, the Money Changers, the Woollen Manufacturers, the Doctors and Druggists, the Silkweavers and Mercers, the Skinners and Furriers. The

Priors were elected for a period of two months' time, during which period they were practically governors of the city.

There was, as usual, bitter party struggle. Dante and the Priors exiled a struggling faction. The more aristocratic exiles appealed to Pope Boniface VIII. Boniface invited the French into Tuscany. In 1301 Charles of Valois entered Florence. In January 1302 Dante left his beloved native city, exiled for ever.

He was now a wanderer, but never homeless. He was a learned, cultured man, and such a man was at home everywhere in Europe at that day. Sympathetic nobles invited him to their homes. They gave him little simple rooms within the thick walls of their great castles, and as he wrote he would look out of his loop-hole window at the wild hills or at the river. Thus he composed his long poem called the 'Divine Comedy,' one of the world's greatest works. From his writing in his lonely rooms he would go down the cold, massive stone stairway to the hall where the family dined, and there he would sit in conversation with the lords and clergy, an honoured if penniless guest. He knew the bitterness of dependence, but still we must believe he was happy, composing his work in peace and having converse with generous men. Particularly he liked to stay in the castle of his friend Can Grande della Scala, at Verona.

At times, also, he departed to the universities, where he was warmly welcomed. There, at Bologna, Padua, Paris, perhaps even at Oxford, Dante heard the doctors, and himself opened a lecture-room, where he lectured in his own way. By this means, no doubt, he obtained some money for his maintenance, from the fees of those men who attended his lectures and could afford to pay.

Dante spent the last three years of his life at Ravenna, that old city, half Italian, half Byzantine, where the last emperors had sheltered themselves behind the marshes when the barbarians invaded Italy. In Ravenna Dante lived with his two sons and his daughter, all guests of his good friend, the nobleman Guido da Polenta. They looked out over the wild, flat country, the old marshes; they went down to the Adriatic sea-shore; they visited the great churches. And in 1321 Dante died, and was buried in the Lady Chapel of the Franciscan Church.

Dante belonged to the close of the great mediæval period, called the Age of Faith. His chief work, the 'Divine Comedy,' tells of his visionary visit to Hell, where the violent, passionate men of the old world of pride and lust are kept in torment; then on to Purgatory, where there is hope; then at last he is conducted by Beatrice into Paradise. It is the vision of the passing away of the old, proud, arrogant violence of the barbaric world, into the hopeful culture such as the Romans knew, on to the spiritual peace and equality of a new Christian world. This new Christian world was beyond Dante's grasp. Paradise is much less vivid to him than the Inferno. What he knew best was the tumultuous, violent passion of the past, that which was punished in Hell. The spiritual happiness is not his. He belongs to the old world.

The next great man of letters was Petrarch. He too was the son of a Florentine, but he was born in 1304 at Arezzo, to which city his father had retired when exiled from Florence by the same decree which exiled Dante. Petrarch also loved study. He was brought up by his mother for some years on a small estate which she owned, upon the Arno near Florence : then the family moved to Pisa ; and then Petrarch's father went with his wife and children to Avignon, where, being a lawyer, he no doubt found plenty to do in connection with the papal court.

When he was fifteen years old, the young Petrarch was sent from Avignon to the University of Montpellier, a university most famous in the Middle Ages for law and medicine. There he was to study law. But instead, he got hold of the old books of Rome; the writers of the Augustan Age fascinated him. Instead of studying law he pored, fascinated, over the magnificent pagan poems of Virgil, or over the pagan treatises of Cicero. These books seemed to him so grand, so full of beautiful images and rich, deep thoughts that they moved him far more than any Christian works could do. For in those days the books of our civilisation were not written, and science had barely awakened.

From Montpellier he went to Bologna. Still he did not get on with law. He began to collect old Latin manuscripts, reading with fascination the pagan writers of great Rome. His father came to visit him at Bologna, and saw that he made little progress in law. Then he examined his son's small but very dear library of old manuscripts, realised that this was what hindered him in law, and straightway had a fire made in the courtyard, where the old books were cast on the flames. The young man wept so bitterly when his father cast on the fire the beloved volumes of Cicero and Virgil that the stern old lawyer fished them out before they had caught.

It was no use going on with law. Yet the young man loved study so much. So he took Holy Orders, became a priest. Then he was happy. He had many dear friends, both in the Church and without. He kept these friends all his life, and it was his joy to meet with them, talk and ride and exchange ideas. He set them all busy hunting the old manuscripts of pagan Rome, and many treasures they saved for us. Petrarch set off from Avignon in 1333, to travel in North Europe. He spent some time in Paris, then went on to Ghent, Liége, and to the great bishops-city of Cologne. He loved meeting many men and having exquisite discourse. But the great adventure was in hunting for old, unknown Latin manuscripts.

He spent a good deal of his life at Avignon, and although he abuses the sinfulness of the papal court, without doubt he was happy in the old town—or near to it. For he moved about ten miles away from the too-lively city of the popes. He took a little house at Vaucluse, with hills and meadows

round about, a small river near by.   Here he made lovely
gardens, sunny and still and rich with foliage and flowers,
where he used to study.   Often he wandered alone among
the hills.   For at this time men's eyes began to open to the
beauty of landscape and wild nature, which had not been
noticed before.   His friends came out to drink wine with
him and talk of the wonders with which life was filled,
wonderful books that they had found, beautiful old Roman
ideas which now for the first time dawned on their minds.

In Avignon Petrarch met the famous Laura, the woman
whom he loved, and to whom he wrote his famous poems,
sonnets which taught even Shakespeare the arts of poetry.
Laura was married and had many children.   Petrarch
was a priest.   And therefore the love was once more
visionary and ideal.   Laura was no doubt more real to
Petrarch than Beatrice to Dante.   Still she was a spirit,
a visionary being rather than a woman of flesh and blood.
Laura died of the Black Death, the Great Pestilence, in
1348.

Much of Petrarch's work, his world-stirring letters, his
treatises, his poems, was written in Latin for the learned
only.   But the poems to Laura were written in pure
Italian.   Dante's great poem, Petrarch's poems, these
were the beginning of real modern literature.   The friends
of Petrarch scolded him for wasting his time, writing in
trivial Italian.   But now we forget all his Latin effusions,
and read only the despised Italian, most beautiful and
most real.

From Avignon Petrarch went in 1341 to King Robert's
court at Naples.   He was received with welcome.
Already his inspired letters and his poetry were making
him a name in all Europe.   In 1341 he was crowned with
the poet's laurel wreath by the Senate, on the Capitol of
Rome.   Kings knew of him and admired him.   He had
a passionate love for Italy, and his burning letters to sovereigns and rulers helped to decide the course of history.
He longed for the union of Italy—just as Dante did.   But

Petrarch stands at the beginning of the modern world, whilst Dante stood at the shadowy end of the old.

Petrarch died in 1374, at his house among the Euganian Hills near Padua, in his own country. He bequeathed his precious library to Venice.

The third great Italian writer of this time was Boccaccio. He was Petrarch's good friend. Boccaccio was also a Florentine, born in 1313. His father was a merchant of Florence. At the age of twenty the young Boccaccio was sent to assist in the counting-house of a merchant in Naples, in order to gain experience in commerce.

But Naples at that time was a bright city. The French House of Anjou still ruled the Neapolitan kingdom. King Robert kept a brilliant, gay little court, almost reminding one of old Hohenstaufen days. The young Boccaccio was introduced to this gay court. Being of a lively, pleasant disposition, he was very happy. For he was also rich, kind, of good Florentine birth, and a true scholar. So King Robert held him an ornament to his court, and Boccaccio was often employed as a diplomatist, transacting affairs of state for Florence.

Boccaccio remained a rich merchant, but he never ceased to love learning and poetry above all things. In Naples he met the lady whom he in his turn made famous, the bright Fiammetta. Like Dante and Petrarch, Boccaccio could not marry the woman he loved, for she was already married. But he did not complain. Many a happy time they had, hunting in the country, or dancing at court; or, at some lovely villa among the hills, reading together; or telling tales under the trees with a company of bright and beautiful men and women; or listening to the singing of poems, or playing games on the grass: all rich and rare and bright women and men, delighting in life.

In 1350 Boccaccio returned to Florence, just after the Great Plague. There he wrote the hundred Italian tales, called the Decameron. The introduction to the Decameron gives a terrible description of the plague in Florence, from which the ladies and gallants withdraw to a secluded villa in the country. But the tales which these ladies and men are supposed to tell are mostly gay and amusing, sometimes sad, touching, but never tragic.

These hundred little novels of the Decameron form the most famous work of Boccaccio. They are written in pleasant, simple Italian which we can read to-day without much difficulty. It is said that these stories gave the form to modern Italian. Certainly they seem much nearer to us than the dark, difficult old Italian of Dante, or the more learned old Italian of Petrarch.

But Boccaccio, like Petrarch, was scolded for not writing always in good solid Latin. The native dialects, as the European tongues were then called, were despised by the learned. And Boccaccio was very learned—his big palace in Florence was thronged with scholars, poets, ladies, gay as well as clever. Boccaccio must have been a delightful man to know : so fine in himself, yet so kind and generous and patient, more lovable than the austere Dante or the scholarly Petrarch.

At this time the Greeks from Constantinople were beginning to visit the new cities of Europe. Constantinople shrank and sank lower, but Venice, Florence, Rome, Milan, were becoming every year more brilliant. At that time very few people in Europe, save in the east, knew anything about Greek. Petrarch had heard all about Homer and Plato, but he could never read them in the original. He bitterly wanted to know Greek. But no one could teach it him, and there were no books to learn it from. The wonderful Greek language was shut off from Europeans. 'I have a Homer,' said Petrarch. 'But Homer is dumb to me, or I am deaf to him.'

But now Greek professors began to appear in Italian towns. One of the first that came to Florence was invited to Boccaccio's house, and maintained there. Boccaccio learned Greek, and established a Greek chair in the university of Florence. And to the ungrateful, fretful, spiteful

Byzantine who came and went and was never satisfied, the kind-hearted Florentine was always gentle and generous, never heeding the petty treacheries of the stranger, never denying him a home. For to have learned Greek was like wealth to Boccaccio. To be able to read Homer, Plato, Herodotus, this was to have a new world opened to one, a new world of the past rich with thoughts.

In these days great visions opened. First the grand Past offered to man visions, beautiful adventures, marvellous thoughts. It was as if the soul and mind had been shut up in a box, in the old narrow way of dogmatic faith, and now was set free into all the air and space and splendour of free, pure thought and deep understanding. No wonder men were excited and glad, no wonder they set off in search of new worlds, new lands on earth. So, secondly, the great sailors crossed the sea, America was discovered, and Southern Africa. Here was a whole world of the future opening ahead, a whole grand world of the past opening behind.

No wonder the period is called the Renaissance, or re-birth. During the dark, violent Middle Ages man was alive, but blind and voracious. In the fourteenth and fifteenth centuries, however, he awoke. The human spirit was then like a butterfly which bursts from the chrysalis into the air. A whole new world lies about it. The narrow, devouring little world of the caterpillar has disappeared, all heaven and all earth flash around.

With the Renaissance the new way of life comes into being. Men do not live just to fight and conquer and capture possessions. They live now in the joy of producing, the joy of making things. So Europe begins to weave and work, instead of fighting or fasting or making crusades. Then the goods produced must be exchanged. Commerce needs good safe roads, safe seas. Peace begins to win her great victories over war.

By the Renaissance we do not mean just the Revival of Learning. We mean a whole new way of life. Men shake

themselves ever more and more free. The greatest institutions, Empire and Papacy, are broken ; men are freed
from the enclosure of these vast forms. Then kings rise
up, to hold millions of people in their hands. But as kings
are rising, so is commerce. Kings are really war-lords,
war-leaders. Commerce needs no king. Thus the power
of kings declines as the power of commerce increases.
And yet there is something even more powerful than commerce, or industry.

At the Re-birth, great kings, dukes, tyrants shine
splendid where emperors and popes have fallen. Popes
are no more than dukes, tyrants like the rulers of other
Italian towns. But side by side with kings and dukes
commerce and industry are slowly, almost invisibly rising,
at last to overshadow all kingly rule. And against the
slowly rising flood of commerce moves the almost invisible power of learning, wisdom, understanding. Emperors
have reigned, and popes ; kings, tyrants, dukes have had
their turn ; commerce has taken full power in the world.
There still remains the last reign of wisdom, of pure understanding, the reign which we have never seen in the world,
but which we must see.

Florence in Boccaccio's day had probably not more than
100,000 inhabitants. London had only 50,000. But the
great cloth industry of Florence brought in more than a
million florins a year. It was very difficult in those days
for Florence to make her payments in other countries :
to pay for wool in England, or undressed cloth in Flanders.
For money was continually changing, and what was valuable one year might become worthless the next. In early
days rich Jews had kept moneys of all kinds. Florence
would pay her coin to a rich Jew, and he would pay her
debt in England, with English coin out of his treasury.
But he charged heavily for the transaction. Then the
agents of the Pope, secretaries of bishops and cardinals,
had been empowered to carry money from one State to
another, and this enriched the papal revenue.

But now rich Florentine merchants established in their counting-houses a department for exchange of moneys. They received coin of all kinds from every country. So they could pay a bill for a man in any country, and charge for doing so. Then they would receive bills of promise instead of coin for payment. Trusting to these bills they would settle accounts for a merchant, and wait until he paid the cash later on. For this delay they charged him a certain percentage. So money was made to breed money. Then the banking merchants began to lend cash to princes or States, large sums, from which they drew good interest. . And so the great banking system of the modern world began.

Of course there was risk in this. When in 1339 Edward III. of England repudiated his debts, there was great distress in Florence, for he owed that city great sums. Many merchants became bankrupt and penniless, and Florence cursed England. In 1348 came the Great Plague, when night and day the inhabitants of Florence died in the streets. Many citizens fled, the city was deserted, work at a standstill. But the plague passed, people returned, in a few years' time all was busy as before.

The control of the city was changing hands. The new banking merchants had been insignificant citizens. Now, they became very rich indeed. Meanwhile the old noble merchants, who had been the governing class in the city, began to wane and sink in importance. For they kept up the old system, and so were outstripped by the new men. These new families became very powerful and famous. The chief of the Florentines were the Medici, the Strozzi, the Albizzi, all bankers, not productive manufacturers or merchants.

The Medici became world-famous. They were not a noble family by origin, only well-to-do citizens. But as their wealth increased their importance grew in Florence. In 1421 Giovanni de' Medici became Gonfaloniere of the city. The Gonfaloniere was the prime citizen, the leader of the Priors of the Guild, the president of the Councils of the State.

Though the great cities of Italy were established upon peace and commerce, they were by no means peaceful. They were liable at all times to attack. And they were ready in their jealousy to fight a rival city. Now any State which must needs act quickly, either in the defensive or offensive, must be under the supreme control of one man: since many minds, though they may be sure, are usually slow. Therefore the chief citizen in Florence was really in supreme command of the State, at least during the city's great days. And a citizen in supreme command was named, after the Greek style, a tyrant. But a tyrant is not in this sense a bully. He is merely a supreme commander of a civilian State, a president who has an almost absolute authority.

So the Medici became tyrants of Florence. They had to defend and fight for their city. But in the fourteenth century a new way of fighting had sprung up. The Florentines were busy, they did not want to be soldiering. Therefore with their power of money they hired special trained bands of soldiers. These condottieri, or Hired Ones, were soldiers of every nation, united under some clever captain. The greatest of these captains was Sir John Hawkwood, who commanded the famous White Company in Italy.

He was the son of a tanner in Essex. He served in the armies of Edward iii., fought no doubt at Crécy and Poitiers, and was knighted. When France and England signed the Peace of Bretigny in 1360, Sir John Hawkwood turned to Italy, hoping for more fighting in that divided land.

The roving bands of soldiers united under him. He trained them perfectly. New methods of fighting were coming into fashion; war was re-born, as well as peace.

Edward iii. had created the professional soldier. Instead of madly hurling themselves at one another, as in the old days, armies now entered into careful and skilful campaign.

Sir John Hawkwood was perhaps the most skilful campaigner of his day. With his White Company he sought always to out-manœuvre the enemy, not to destroy him. He did not want to lose his own carefully trained professionals. So in the wars of the condottieri not many men were killed, though cities triumphed or were defeated.

When the condottieri hired themselves out, they were perfectly faithful to their pledge. But immediately the campaign was over, the connection was finished, they might hire themselves to any other bidder. In 1363 Hawkwood with his company fought for Montferrat against Milan ; in 1364 for Pisa against Florence ; in 1368 he was fighting for the Visconti, Lord of Milan ; in 1373 he was engaged by the Pope against this same Visconti. After this he was chiefly engaged by the Florentines, who appreciated him greatly. He was a kindly, human soldier, who loved the skill and science of the fight. In 1392 he led the Florentine forces and defeated the Visconti, although he had married a daughter of Bernabo Visconti, Tyrant of Milan. He spent the remainder of his life in a beautiful villa outside Florence, and his children were Italian nobles. He died in 1394, and the citizens gave him a splendid funeral.

So the tyrants of the Italian cities fought against one another, without shedding the blood of their citizens. The Visconti, Tyrants of Milan, were cruel and vindictive, though they built some lovely edifices, and under their rule the great cathedral of Milan was begun. But the Medici, the merchant bankers who became Tyrants of Florence, excelled all in peace and in cunning diplomacy.

The first great Medici was Cosimo, who in practice ruled the city till he died in 1464. He was splendid as a king. He kept a gay court, and spent great sums in beautifying the city. He built the Medici Palace, and chiefly assisted the architect Brunelleschi to raise the dome of the cathedral of Florence, one of the first and most famous domes of Europe. Perfect painters, whose works have rejoiced all men in all lands, worked for Cosimo, poets and musicians thronged the courts.

But in 1478 rich citizens, with the connivance of the Pope, conspired to murder the Medici and the Priors. The two young Medici, Giuliano and Lorenzo, were attacked in the cathedral. Giuliano was stabbed, Lorenzo escaped. The populace, who at this time loved the Medici, rose in anger, crying Palle ! Palle ! Palle ! For the arms of the banker Medici were three red balls, three red *palle*.

Lorenzo de' Medici then became Tyrant of Florence. He is called the Magnificent, Lorenzo il Magnifico. He was one of the most splendid men in the Renaissance. Frail in health and ugly to look at, he was yet delightful, witty and gay, yet learned, a lover of poetry and all the arts, yet a clever ruler. He was very simple in his manner, and kept no pomp and ceremony. He always said he was but a citizen, no noble, no aristocrat, even if he were *first* citizen. So he tried in his manner and appearance to be like one of the people themselves.

The citizens loved him for it. And so, because he was loved, he had supreme power, far more perfect in its way than any papal or Visconti power. He kept a most gay and splendid court—which the Florentines loved. They were delighted by Lorenzo's splendours and gaieties. But at the same time the Magnificent left us treasures for which we cannot praise him enough, the clever Tyrant. There are pictures which might not have been produced if he had not splendidly commissioned and supported the painters, lovely works such as those of Botticelli, besides the sculptures, poems, songs, and beautiful architecture of other men.

The three greatest painters of the day were Leonardo da Vinci, Michael Angelo, and Raphael. Leonardo and Michael Angelo were both Florentines. In 1447 the Sforza, a son of a condottieri captain, became Duke and Tyrant of Milan. His son, called Il Moro, or the Moor, because he was so dark, invited Leonardo da Vinci to the

extravagant court of Milan. He gave Leonardo a house
and an irregular supply of money, and in Milan the great
painter produced his famous pictures. Still we can see
the large wall-painting called ' The Last Supper,' though
it is in a dilapidated condition. Leonardo was a tall,
handsome, fair man. He loved science, and perfected the
science of painting. But he loved all scientific pursuits.
Above all he longed to fly. For years he worked with his
smith at marvellous great wings which he hoped would
carry him. His failure to fly was a great sorrow to him.
But Ludovico Sforza, the Duke, remained his friend till
the French invasion.

Michael Angelo was a little younger than Leonardo, but
his morose nature was jealous of the elder man. Michael
Angelo's greatest work was done for the Pope—the marvellous frescoes in the Sistine Chapel of the Vatican.

Raphael was the youngest of the painters, and the
darling of all. He worked incessantly for the Pope, and
beautified the Vatican superbly. He was rich as a lord
with the proceeds of his painting, and was followed by
a gay retinue through the streets of Rome, like any prince.
But he remained kind and lovable, and was much mourned
when he died in 1520, at the age of thirty-seven.

Whilst Italy and Rome were glittering with creative
activity, the last vestige of the old Roman Empire disappeared. Constantinople, which had remained the
beautiful home of the eastern emperors since Constantine's
day, was taken by the Turks in 1453. The Empire in
the East vanished utterly. The Turks took possession
of the home of Constantine, the first Christian city fell
into Mohammedan hands, the first great Christian cathedral, the Hagia Sophia or Church of St. Sophia, became a
mosque of Mohammedan worship.

But the Turks and Mohammedanism had reached their
western limit. In the north the Spaniards roused the old
Gothic spirit, and drove out the Moors. Since the eighth
century the Moors had held a great part of Spain. There

they had a beautiful, fertile civilisation.   The Moors alone
had kept science alive during the Middle Ages; they were
the great teachers of botany, medicine, geography, mathe-
matics.   In Spain their palaces were graceful and delicate,
their gardens lovely; they had a flourishing trade in silk,
a busy, refined population.   But in 1492 their last stronghold, Granada, fell, and all Spain was in the hands of the
Spaniards.

So the great century came to an end.   The west coast
of Africa had been discovered and opened; the Grand
Canary and the Azores were settled; the Cape of Good
Hope was discovered.   In 1492 Columbus discovered
America, in 1497 Vasco da Gama rounded the Cape of
Good Hope and came upon India.   He landed in Calicut
in 1498.   The sea-way to the East was opened.

Thus the world opened out to man.   And even at the
same time the heavens were explored.   Copernicus, the
great astronomer, was born in 1473.   Before his day men
believed, according to Ptolemy's system, that our earth
was the centre of the universe, and that man was at the
centre of creation.   Round the earth were the seven
spheres, or globes of crystal atmosphere, one inside the
other, each one containing a planet, and all revolving in
different directions.   So the planets were supposed to be
carried on their different paths.   Outside of all was a
great outer sphere containing all the stars like many
bright specks in a glass globe.   This great outer sphere
set all the others moving, and in their diverse turning they
made a fine universal music called the music of the spheres.

Copernicus after thirty-six years of study proved that
the theory of the moving spheres was wrong.   He showed
that the earth moves in a path round the sun.   This
roused a great storm of wrath, for it put the Church out
of her proud, central position.   If our earth were not the
centre of the universe, then man, instead of believing
himself undisputed lord of creation, must humble himself
and allow that there may be other worlds with other

lords. So the great mediæval pride of man received its great blow.

After Copernicus, Tycho Brahé, who was born in 1546, built the first observatory for accurately studying the heavens. He also constructed the sextant and quadrant, which have been of such invaluable service to mankind.

In 1564 was born the great Galileo, ' the Italian star-wright.' He invented the telescope, and proclaimed the new theories and discoveries of the heavens to mankind, for which he was imprisoned by the Pope, who found it necessary that the earth should remain the centre of the universe. With Galileo modern astronomy began.

XIV. The Reformation

It was the north, the northern Teutonic race that had defied the Caesars of Old Rome, which was now finally to break the power of the Roman Papacy. The Germanic temperament all through our course of history has reacted against the old social forms, gradually breaking them down and making room for a wider individual liberty. From the south come the impulses that unite men into a oneness : from the north come the strong passions which break up the oneness and shatter the world, but which make in the long run for a freer, more open way of life.

The great men of the New Learning were northerners. It was in the north that men began to use their reason fearlessly in all matters that interested them. It was in the north that the great men passionately desired to be free to understand all that their souls were troubled with.

The first of the northern teachers before the Reformation was the German, John Reuchlin. He studied Hebrew so that he could get at the true meaning of the Old Testament. He tried hard to save the Jewish writings from the flames of the Inquisitors. For he wanted to show the natural, human side of the Old Testament. The priests of the Church had hidden the Bible from the people and had tried to make everything out of Scripture seem marvellous and supernatural and awful. The men of the New Learning wanted to see things naturally, in the light of the true human understanding. For this reason they were called *humanists*, because the human understanding was to them the measure of truth and reality. They did not wish to believe in abnormal or monstrous things, just because men had always believed in these monstrosities. They did not want to consider life awful and supernatural. They wished to see everything in the human light, the light of the deep, real human intelligence, which is the best that man is capable of. Another early German reformer and scholar was Ulrich von Hütten, called the Stormy Petrel of the Reformation, for he was very fiery and passionate. These Germans were very eager to slay old lies, old untruths, to expose old impostures, to destroy the old imposed authority of the Church.

The Oxford reformers were different. They loved the new learning, but they did not want to break with Rome. They wanted more purity in the Church, but peace, not schism. John Colet, son of the Lord Mayor of London, came back from the study of Greek in Italy, in the year 1496. He began to lecture on the Epistles of St. Paul. The New Testament, as we know, exists in its earliest form in Greek. So Colet was able to read the real words, and to connect them with the history of the times, and to understand St. Paul's relations to the great Greek thinkers and to the Roman governors of his own day. So the Epistles became human documents, not just mysterious religious utterances. They belonged to the real history of mankind, to the history of pagan Rome as well as to Christendom.

Colet became Dean of St. Paul's, and used his father's fortune to found St. Paul's School, in 1510. His advice to his students was : 'Keep to the Bible and the Apostles' Creed, and let Churchmen, if they like, dispute about the rest.' Colet had great influence in Oxford, over Sir Thomas More, Grocyn, Linacre, and the great Erasmus —also over Tyndale and Latimer.

Of all the humanists Erasmus of Rotterdam was the most famous. He was called ' the Man by Himself.' He was recognised on both sides of the Alps as the literary chief of Europe, somewhat as Petrarch had been two hundred years before.   Forced into a monastery in Holland when he was young, Erasmus escaped to the university of Paris, and afterwards to Oxford.   He was feeble in health, but he became the greatest scholar of his time, and popes, princes, statesmen and doctors bowed before him.

In his *Handbook for the Christian Soldier*, published in 1503, he showed that each individual was directly responsible to God, apart from any priestly intermediary.   We see the old Teutonic independence breaking out here. But his greatest work was the fresh translation of the New Testament.   He printed the original Greek and his own accurate Latin translation in columns side by side.   This appeared in 1516.   It rapidly travelled all over Europe, and opened men's eyes for the first time to the real story of Christ and the Apostles.   In this true Gospel men could find nothing about a pope or cardinals or any Church of Rome.   This did more than anything to prepare the way for the actual Reformation.

Erasmus himself was a scholar, not a fighter.   He did not want to quarrel with popes or with princes.   He did not want to alter the standing institutions.   He just let men see for themselves.

Martin Luther scorned him, thinking him timid.   But then Luther was a fighter rather than a deep, subtle thinker. Luther was the sturdy son of a peasant, born in Germany in 1483.   In 1501 he entered the University of Erfurt, then most famous for its humanistic studies.   In 1505 he took his Master of Arts degree, and then suddenly entered a monastery, much to his father's disappointment. But though Luther was robust and cheerful by nature, he had many dark hours of struggle with Satan, when the Evil One seemed actually to grip him round the body.

In the time of his monastic life he was a pale, haggard young man, with little joy in life, filled with dread of God, and with anguish on account of sin.   But at last peace came to him.   One day, reading the Epistle to the Romans, the meaning of the text : ' The just shall live by faith,' entered his heart. He knew now why all his confessions and penances had been in vain. He must have perfect faith in the close fellowship of God with himself. He felt that God was with him, and he was filled with joy.

Now the Middle Ages have been called the Age of Faith. But their faith is different. They had a blind belief in the awful and unlimited power of God, and also in a wonderful divine magic which could suddenly set a man amidst the splendour of heaven. But they had no faith in their own being. They had no faith in the pure love that exists between a man and his God, a relationship so near and personal that it is unspeakable. Of this the Middle Ages conceived nothing. They knew nothing of the personal relation between a man and his God, and the faith in this relation. Their faith was all in the magic powers of God, impersonal, superhuman, marvellous. Martin Luther was the first to make religion truly human and near. And when the pure, unspeakable union was established between God and a man's own heart, how could anything or anybody, pope or priest, interfere with it? The new way of religion was an unspeakable joy to men, and a most wonderful rich freedom. The heart was free to be alone with God.

In 1508 Luther was sent as teacher to the new University of Wittenberg, and in 1511 he went on a mission to Rome. Rome was still the centre of the world to him. The first sight of the city filled him with ecstasy. ' I greet thee, thou Holy Rome, thrice holy from the blood of martyrs,' he cried. But he felt very differently when he stayed in the town. Then he saw all the luxury, splendour, and injustice of the Papal Court. He saw how proud the bishops and cardinals were, how they scorned such a nobody as he was. He felt they all held him beneath notice, in Rome. Only God would remember him. In his poor lodging, moreover, he heard many bitter complaints of men who had waited in vain for justice and a hearing at the court, and of men who were spoiled, broken in life by the cruel arrogance of prelates and pope. While all the gorgeous feastings and shows went on, he thought of those who were ruined, whose grievances were hopeless. He turned to the God whose voice spoke to his own heart, and wondered what all this pomp had to do with Him. And he repeated to himself many times, 'The just shall live by faith.' Perhaps some of the *old* faith lingered in Rome, but there was none of the new.

Luther returned rather bitterly to Germany. But he was happy in Wittenberg, especially after he became Professor of Theology and had his own house with his own students. He also was a great preacher, powerful and moving, in his own German tongue.

In 1517 John Tetzel, a Dominican monk, was sent through Central Germany with an indulgence proclaimed by the Medici Pope, Leo x. People were to buy these little sin-pardon tickets, and the proceeds of the sale were supposed to go to the building of the great St. Peter's Cathedral in Rome, which was then in course of erection. But indulgences were already a scandal in North Europe. Erasmus had written against them. Frederick the Wise, Elector of Saxony, forbade Tetzel to enter his dominions. The monk was, however, often enough on the border.

On October 31, 1517, Martin Luther nailed to the door of the Church of Wittenberg an invitation to all to debate with him, either by speech or writing, the question of indulgences. Luther also nailed up his famous ninety-five heads of argument against indulgences, in which he argued that the Pope could not pardon sin, only God could do that : that men who repented could not have any need of an indulgence-ticket, and that men who did not repent could not profit by such a device—and so on.

The ninety-five arguments were printed and spread quickly over Western Europe. All men read them. The German princes were sympathetic, for they had never liked the interference of the papal court. On the other side many faithful churchmen attacked Luther for daring to disapprove of the Pope and to deny the papal authority. A controversy raged. The Pope did not appear to care much. What he did mind, said the Reformers, was that hardly any indulgences were sold.

Luther was summoned to meet the papal legate, Cardinal Cajetan, at the Diet of Augsburg, in October 1518. He went, well prepared to argue the point. The legate refused to hear any argument, and demanded him instantly to take back all he had written. Luther refused, and returned to Wittenberg. Immediately he published an account, telling people exactly what had happened. Throughout all his strife with the papacy he told the world plainly what took place, so that, step by step, the German people followed the situation. Thus there was no sudden flare of enthusiasm as with Savonarola. The Reformation developed gradually and surely in people's minds and hearts, a real conviction, a genuine understanding.

Frederick of Saxony, Luther's prince, was all the way true to the reformer. Leo X. sent a golden rose, perfumed and consecrated, to the Elector, to win his friendship and to get him to bring Luther to write a letter of submission. Luther promised. But then the renowned Professor Eck invited Luther to Leipsic, to a dispute. The famous Leipsic Disputation began on June 27, 1519. Eck wanted to trick Luther into making some statement that would prove him a heretic, so that he might be burned as Huss and Jerome had been. And he succeeded. For when he pressed Luther about the teachings of Huss, Luther plainly said that he could not consider all the teachings of this great man to be false. Now the Church had declared they were. So here was Luther committed, as good as a heretic.

Luther went home pondering what he did believe. And he realised that in truth his beliefs were not really the same as those of the Church. He immediately began to write sermons and treatises, and to publish them, showing people exactly what he believed in his soul. Men read them with eagerness, and Luther was joined by Ulrich von Hütten and by the delicate, cultured young scholar, Philip Melanchthon, who was a much finer scholar than Luther, but who served the strong and undaunted nature of the greater man lovingly and faithfully.

In 1520 the Pope excommunicated Luther. The Elector Frederick refused to have the Bull of Excommunication published in his dominions. On December 10, 1520, in the open space outside the walls of Wittenberg, Luther, in presence of professors, students, and citizens, openly burned the Bull. Thus Luther had cut himself off from the Church.

The Emperor Charles v. had been crowned at Aix-la-Chapelle, in 1520. In 1521 he summoned his first Diet or Council to meet at Worms. Charles was a young, serious man. He hated heretical monks. At the same time he saw that the Church needed reforming, and he did not like powerful popes. Luther might be of some use against the Pope, who was a dangerous rival to the Emperor in Italy.

Luther was summoned to Worms, and a safe-conduct was sent. It was like Huss setting off for Constance. ' My dear brother,' he said to Philip Melanchthon, ' if I do not come back, if my enemies put me to death, you will go on teaching and standing fast to the truth ; if you live my death will matter little.' So he set off, knowing he went probably to meet his death.

On the afternoon of April 17, Luther appeared before the Diet of Worms. He was shown a pile of his own books on a table, and asked if he was prepared to acknowledge the authorship of these works, and to recant his heresies. To the first question he answered yes, to the second, that he needed time. He was given one day. The next day he made his famous speech, before emperor, cardinals, princes, bishops. He said he would recant nothing unless it was proved by the Scriptures to be wrong. ' Here I stand,' he said, ' I cannot do otherwise. God help me. Amen.'

The Emperor and his Spaniards did not like the speech, but the Germans were deeply impressed. They were furious when it was suggested that the safe-conduct should be rescinded, and would not hear of proceeding against Luther as the Council of Constance had proceeded against Huss. On April 27, Luther left Worms with a safe-conduct lasting for twenty days more. At the end of twenty days he was to be seized and burned as a heretic. The German lords had secured him so much safety from the venomous Spaniards and Italians.

On the return journey, Luther's travelling-wagon was attacked and captured and he was carried off, no one knew whither. Wildest rumours flew about. But as a matter of fact his own prince had carried him off to safety, in hiding, in the Castle of Wartburg. Gradually this leaked out.

The imperial ban, called the Edict of Worms, was published on May 25, not until the Elector Frederick had left the city. It declared that the heretic's life was forfeited and ordered all his writings to be burned. After May 14, none were to give him food or shelter, under pain of severe punishment. But the Elector held him in safe keeping, and was not daunted.

While Luther lay hidden in the Wartburg, his teachings became more and more popular, partly because of the excitement of his defiance and disappearance. Monks, priests, and even bishops in Germany began to preach his doctrines. Men declared he had written what they were all thinking. Artists drew pictures to illustrate his works, authors wrote about them. Meantime he was busy at his great work of translating the Bible into German, a magnificent work, one of the proud possessions of Germany to-day, as our English translation is a proud possession to us.

At the same time false, or at least rash prophets rose up from among his own following, men who preached a crusade against monasteries, against pictures and images in churches, seeking to do away with all places of education as well as with places of amusement. Already the movement was beginning to run wild. Luther hastened home from his hiding-place to stop it. On eight successive days he preached to the people, with great earnestness and wisdom, till they recognised their true leader, and abandoned the rash new prophets. For Luther appealed to their deep understanding, the mind and heart as well, not to their excitable passions.

Luther might now have been seized. But the authorities were afraid to enforce the Edict, for fear of civil war. The German rulers told the Pope this when he demanded Luther's instant seizure. So the reformer was safe and free still. In 1524 the Diet of Nuremberg promised to execute the Edict of Worms ' as well as they were able, and as far as was possible.'

There came a reaction against the Reformers, for the new movement was spreading too fast. Duke George of Saxony, the Archduke Ferdinand of Austria, the Duke of Bavaria and the Elector of Brandenburg, urged on by the Pope's legate, met at Ratisbon and decided to take measures to suppress the Lutheran movement. Thus threatened, the reform princes were forced to make a union. Frederick, Elector of Saxony, Philip of Hesse, the Margrave of Brandenburg, and Albert of Brandenburg, head of the Teutonic Knights, joined with the free cities on the Lutheran side. So the two great parties were divided. It was a sad event to Luther, for above all things he did not want war.

Charles was at war with the Pope, so could not take action, and matters stood as they were. After much thought the Diet of Spires decided in 1526 that the Word of God should be preached without disturbance, and that, for the time being, each State should so live, rule, and conduct itself as it hoped to answer for its conduct to God and the Emperor. Thus princes became more independent, and the principle was established : To each State its own religion. Then the Lutheran States and cities began to organise their church and public worship to suit their own beliefs. The services were read in German, Luther's bible and hymns were used, monasteries were suppressed, their buildings used as churches or schools, while monks and nuns were allowed to remain as school-teachers. Then the great blow came, when the Lutherans declared that monks and nuns were allowed to marry, and when Luther, throwing off his vow of chastity, was publicly wedded to Catherine Bora, a former nun.

This put all Europe into a raging ferment. When the Emperor made peace with the Pope, the Diet of Spires of 1529 reversed the decision of 1526. The Lutheran party at once drew up the formal ' Protest ' against the reversion, and henceforth all people of the reformed faith were called ' Protesters ' or ' Protestants.'

In 1530 Charles opened the Diet of Augsburg and asked the Protestants to give to him, their emperor, a written account of all their opinions and difficulties. They therefore drew up the famous Confession of Augsburg, written chiefly by Melanchthon. Luther, still an outlaw, was not present at Augsburg, for he would have been seized. He suffered greatly lest Melanchthon, who was gentle and submissive, should yield too far in his desire to be at one and at peace with the great old Church. Melanchthon, however, kept true to the new faith, and the Protestants would not yield to the Emperor's pressure, so no agreement was come to. The Diet then declared that if the Protestants had not decided to return to the Catholic Church by April 30, 1531, they were to be put down by force.

Then the Protestants had to gather themselves. They met at Schmalkalde, and in spite of Luther's strong feeling against the use of force, they decided to arm themselves in readiness. At this moment, however, the invasions of the Turks in Hungary and Austria, and many other complications in Spain and Italy prevented the Emperor from dealing with the Protestants. For twelve years he had not a leisure moment to bestow on the Reformers, who thus had time to grow very strong in Germany.

Having his hands full, moreover, and detesting as well the Pope and the papal power, Charles preferred to hope for an agreement with his Germans. He was not anxious for war.

So affairs drifted on, till Luther died in 1546. He had lived happily with his family in Wittenberg, and peace had been kept. He saw the new faith spread far and gone deep. Protestantism was already deep in the hearts of the people by the time Luther died. The Reformation was truly a people's movement, and Luther was a great leader of the people. He spoke straight out to every individual man and woman, poor or rich alike. He taught every one to find peace in his own heart. No man was to look outside himself for a master. The master, God, was in his own heart.

This made men free to think and act and live. There was no priest or bishop to overawe and threaten. Quite sure of the presence of God in his heart, a man can never be overawed nor put down. He will bring forth what he believes is true in the sight of his own God, he will live according to his own single faith. And this is very different from living according to the blind faith which is accepted merely on authority.

Protestantism, however, was not yet safe or easy. The very year Luther died, the Emperor began the war in Germany. Charles v. was a Hapsburg. This house has produced many emperors, but very few great men. The Hapsburgs rose to power through marrying princesses and acquiring territory. Charles v. was lord of Austria, Germany, the Netherlands, Spain, and part of Italy. He had been brought up in Flanders, in a court under Spanish influence, for his mother, Joanna, was the daughter of Ferdinand and Isabella of Spain. When he inherited his Austrian dominions he handed them over to his brother

Ferdinand. He cared for Spain most of all; that was his kingdom which he loved.

He was far more Spanish than German. His court was filled with Spaniards, and he was followed by great Spanish armies : for in that day the Spanish infantry was counted invincible. So this Spaniard with his cruel Spanish armies came to possess Germany, to put down the Protestants. In 1547 he defeated the Protestant forces of the Schmalkaldic League.

It was easier, however, to win a battle with his Spaniards than to change the hearts of men. The Germans refused to give up their faith. The Emperor tried to force them into submission with his armies. The German people became so filled with hatred of the vindictive, ruinous, Spanish soldiery, the German princes came so to detest the Spanish emperor and the interfering Italian pope, that all Germans alike united with the Protestants against the imperial forces.

The German princes rose against the Emperor in 1552. Charles escaped over the Brenner Pass into Italy. He made his brother Ferdinand permanent Archduke of Austria, whilst he himself attended to his southern dominions. So Ferdinand of Austria gradually assumed the imperial authority in Germany. He was much more Germanic in sympathy. The Religious Peace of Augsburg was signed in 1555, and the Lutheran Church was legally recognised. Cities and States were free to choose their own form of worship, and in Catholic States Protestants were to be tolerated. But the rulers of all countries still had the power to persecute their subjects, Catholic or Protestant as might be.

So the great Mediæval Church System was broken through, and North Europe started on her modern career of freedom and independence of belief. The Hapsburg emperors remained Catholic, but were usually tolerant by nature. Lutheran Germany went her own way, Bavaria and Catholic Germany dropped a little behind.

And so we see, step by step, great powers are broken down, and step by step individual men and women advance into freedom, freedom to believe as their soul prompts them, freedom to think as their mind sees well, freedom to act as their heart desires : beautiful, flexible freedom of human men and women.

XV. The Grand Monarch

THE early history of France is a history of battles and wars, a history of the struggles of the French king with his great barons, with the English, and with the emperors. Hugh Capet was the first real king of France—the Franks had been kings of the Frankish people. Hugh Capet became Duke of France in 956, and was elected King of France in 987 ; and was war-lord of the central region round Paris.

In Hugh Capet's time Gaul could still be divided roughly into three great divisions. From the Rhine running east and south was the great belt of territory, Eastern France, which was sometimes called Lotharingia. It was the strange strip of land which had fallen to the share of Lothaire, one of the three grandsons of Charlemagne. In Lotharingia lay Luxemburg, Lorraine (which is Lotharingia proper), Lesser Burgundy, Arles, and Provence. In this long region the people were chiefly of true German origin, they spoke the Frankish or Allemannish or Burgundian languages, all German, and they despised the people to the west, particularly those of the great central province, calling them effeminate Galli, or Walli as they pronounced it.

The central region, France proper, occupied Champagne, Normandy, and Anjou on the Loire. The chief towns were Paris, Rheims, Orleans. In this region lived the Normans, and the people who called themselves Francingenae or French. These French were a mixed race of Franks and Gallo-Romans. They spoke the Northern

French called the Langue d'Oïl. And these were the people governed by the Capetian kings of France.

South of the Loire lay the great province of Aquitaine, Gascony lay on the Bay of Biscay and next the Pyrenees, whilst towards the Mediterranean spread the broad county of Toulouse. Aquitaine, Gascony, and Toulouse occupied the old Visigothic kingdom in Gaul. Here the people were much more Roman, much older in civilisation than in France proper. They spoke the delightful old Romance language, called the Langue d'Oc. Hence all this region was often called Languedoc. The Langue d'Oc was the sweet old speech of poets and minstrels, the language of our own Richard Cœur de Lion. Just as the Germanic Lotharingians despised the Francingenae or French, so the French of the Capetian Court despised the southerners, despised particularly the bishops of Aquitaine and Toulouse, calling them women and corrupt weaklings, because they were delicate in dress and speech and manner.

So we see that France was not just one State, it was a collection of States with a little kingdom in the middle. The great dukes of Brittany and Normandy, and the counts of Vermandois and Flanders in the north were independent princes, as were the dukes of Aquitaine and Gascony and Burgundy, the counts of Toulouse and Anjou, towards the south and east. In England the king soon mastered his great barons, and a law was established for the whole land. But for centuries the French king struggled with the great lords of Aquitaine, Burgundy, Brittany, Flanders ; and there was no real France, no realm governed by one whole law until after the Reformation. If the King of France was the chief man among all these lords and princes, it is only that he was principal war-lord.

By 1328 the kings of France had come to rule the greater part of the lands we now call France. All Lotharingia, that great eastern belt stretching up from Marseilles to Antwerp, belonged to the Germanic Empire ; England held Aquitaine and Gascony in the south-west ; Brittany and the diminished Duchy of Burgundy and the County of Flanders were still free from the French rule. And then the terrible Hundred Years War broke out. The French king must fight his vassal, the English king. In 1453, when the English were driven out, the French kings ruled all France, save Brittany and the Burgundian possessions, Flanders and the Duchy of Burgundy. But Luxemburg and Lorraine lay outside France altogether.

Through all these centuries there had been one continual struggle in France. Until the Hundred Years War the French lords had lived in their castles and ruled their territories very much as they pleased, caring only for their own splendours as knights, triumphs in the fights of chivalry, and their glittering showy festivals. They were very much like the Gallic chieftains at the coming of the Romans, except that they lived in feudal castles, not in wooden halls, and fought in heavy armour on horseback, instead of in chariots. The mass of the people were peasants, serfs, nearly slaves, just as before, trampled down to the greatest misery when the Hundred Years War began. Then in 1358 broke out the fearful peasant rising called the Jacquerie. Nobles and rich people were massacred. The burghers or citizens joined with the peasants, all nobles and knights united against the people. It is said that twenty thousand peasants were slain between the Seine and Marne alone : and in those days the population of Europe was small.

By the close of the Hundred Years War, however, all Europe was changing. France found she must have regular soldiers to defeat the regular soldiers of Edward III. The knights of chivalry, with their feudal armies, were a failure. And to support regular armies there must be regular production at home, there must be supplies raised and money found. Thus industry, agriculture, and commerce became the first interest of man. War merely depended on the great productive activities of a nation. And so gradually the States became occupied with industry and commerce, the force of the new Europe grew quietly strong in France as in Italy. The nobles and princes were all-powerful apparently ; but underneath their martial power merchants, manufacturers, artisans, peasants, a great silent host of producers, were gradually, unnoticeably becoming important.

The Reformation spread from Germany and Switzerland into France. But there it only touched the middle classes. The great nobles would have nothing to do with the teachings of Luther or Calvin, and the mass of the peasants cared not at all for independent religion. They clung to the strange, superstitious Gallic Catholicism. Only the burghers, merchants, lesser nobility, men who were struggling for independence, listened to the new teachings, and were converted. It was not till later that noblemen joined them. These Calvinistic Protestants of France were called Huguenots.

When Protestantism was really established in Northern Europe, the south turned against it in fury. Italy, and particularly Spain, was filled with tremendous hatred of the new religion. The Spanish Inquisition became the terror of Europe, and did cruel work in the Spanish Netherlands. This passion of hatred of the Protestants, which caused the movement called the Counter-Reformation, spread now into France. Some great nobles sided with the Huguenots, some were against them. Such a state was bound to be. France lies mid-way between the north and the south of Europe : she is the centre where the passions of the two halves fuse. So now half the great nobles, headed by the Guise family, were violent Catholics, Spanish in sympathy, whilst the other half were staunch for the Huguenots.

So the religious war in France became a devastating civil war. Nobles fought nobles with intense fury. It was the old battle : the northern Germanic influence fighting the southern Latin influence in the Gallic race. In this last great fight many nobles fell, many ruined themselves, much wealth and power passed into the hands of merchants and smaller gentry. When Henry of Navarre won the Battle of Ivry in 1590 the war was ended. Henry iv. was really Protestant in sympathy. The Huguenots were allowed a fair amount of religious freedom, and they established their headquarters in the great fortress-town of La Rochelle.

Henry iv. was an important king. He ruled whilst Elizabeth and James i. were on the throne of England. He began at last to get France ordered, settled, and prosperous. For this purpose he had to depend a good deal on merchants, rich citizens, and the gentry. For the great nobles still imagined they were the King's equals; they laughed with him and chaffed him and showed him they did not intend him to imagine himself their superior. But Henry was of a generous nature. He cared nothing for their pretensions, but went his own way, straightforward and plain in manner and dress, not caring for show, but getting his own way all the same, doing very much as he liked, and improving the land. In the richness of the middle classes lay the power of the King, and the consequent weakening of the great nobles. Henry iv. did all he could to encourage merchants and manufacturers. He had the land drained and cultivated. He helped on colonisation, assisting Champlain to found Quebec in 1608, extending his dominions. If he was going to be really powerful, he must be more than a mere war-lord, high chieftain of the chieftains, as the Frankish kings had been. He must destroy the chieftains who were more or less his equals, and rule in the name of the people—that is, of the well-to-do merchants and citizens. He must be very much like a Tyrant of an Italian city, ruling his country for the sake of the prosperity of the numerous merchants and smaller gentry and manufacturers, those who supported the body of the nation. Great nobles must go. A king must have no equals. He must have only subjects. But they must be willing subjects. A king was now no longer a war-lord. He was head of a great *productive* community.

Henry IV. was murdered in 1610. His son Louis XIII. was an infant, and therefore Maria de' Medici, mother of the baby King, became regent, assisted by various advisers. There was a good deal of confusion. At last, in 1624, Richelieu, the Cardinal-Duke, became adviser of the boy King and of the Queen Mother.

Richelieu was a wonderful man, with a terribly strong will, and a great, subtle intellect. He saw what he had to do. And he soon had complete influence over the young Louis and the Queen Mother. Richelieu's work was to continue what Henry of Navarre had begun : that is, to make the King supreme in France, and to weaken all the great nobles ; to encourage prosperity in the country ; and to keep in check the great Spanish-German power of the Hapsburgs. His work, really, was to convert France into a land of productive unity, to destroy the old war-spirit.

The first thing, however, was to reduce the Huguenots, who had become almost a little nation in themselves. The Cardinal-Duke himself besieged the great stronghold of La Rochelle. The city yielded to starvation. Richelieu made peace with the Huguenots, and gave them a good deal of liberty. He was not at all their religious enemy. He only wanted to make them submissive to the royal power.

The nobles hated the great Cardinal. They plotted against him continually, and he had many seized and beheaded or kept in the Bastille. He forbade all war between nobles, and even duelling, that last remnant of private warfare between gentlemen, was suppressed. Many of the enormous castles which were scattered over France were blown up by gunpowder at the Cardinal's orders, and the unruly nobles deprived for ever of their strongholds.

Then the government of provinces was taken away from the great lords. Noblemen now became merely courtiers. The land was governed by a little body of men, chosen by the King himself, or the King's ministers, and called the King's Council. The King's Council appointed governors called Intendants. These Intendants were usually rich

citizens or smaller gentry, and these now ruled in the provinces. They bore the titles of Superintendents of Finance
and Superintendents of Police. It was they who, as royal
officers, raised armies and taxes in their provinces, and
superintended the courts of justice.

And so the machinery of monarchy was established. It
was the supreme rule of a king, by means of rich and sub-
missive merchants, burghers, cultivators. The King was
Tyrant, or Absolute Citizen, rather than First Chieftain.
The difference between France and England was that the
French allowed their king to be a real Tyrant, whilst the
English beheaded Charles I. and forced the succeeding
kings to be mere presidents of the rich men.

Richelieu died in 1642, Louis XIII. in 1643. Louis XIV.
at this time was only five years old. The new minister
was Cardinal Mazarin, a subtle Italian, a pupil of Richelieu.

During Mazarin's rule the Parlement of Paris became
insubordinate. The Parlement of Paris was not a parliament in our sense of the word, but a court of justice which
had this further right of registering the edicts or orders of
the King. If the Parlement refused to register the King's
orders, then these orders could not be carried out. At the
very time the English Parliament was becoming so bold,
the Parlement of Paris took bold steps. It refused to
register the edicts of finance for 1648, demanded the reduction of taxes, and the abolition of imprisonment by
royal warrant without trial.

The royal soldiers seized the leaders of the Parlement.
But then came the news of the execution of Charles I. in
England, and the French Court was afraid. Mazarin gave
way for a moment. But only for a moment. He summoned forces under the great Prince Condé, the most
famous general of the day. Paris was blockaded. The
nobles would not stir to help the rich burghers and lawyers
of the Parlement : and thus Parlement was almost wiped
out, defeated completely.

Then the nobles rose against the royal minister. Condé

was arrested in time, but the nobles were in great force. Mazarin had to flee. But he soon returned. With all his skill he gathered the royal forces. The last great struggle between the French Crown and the French nobility took place. The nobles were defeated in 1652, aristocracy was broken for ever. King and merchants ruled France. The Parlement of Paris was forbidden to interfere in public affairs. The system of Richelieu was complete, the monarchic power was perfected. But a monarch was now supreme head of a *civil*, producing people, his realm was no longer martial.

Mazarin died in 1661. France was now already the greatest, most solid power in Europe. The young King Louis xiv. was determined to govern. His Court was astonished when he told them he would be his own first minister. But he kept his word.

Louis xiv. is perhaps the most splendid example of modern monarchy. The French, like the old Gauls, have always loved splendour, magnificence, and showy power : they admired great and resplendent chieftains. Their greatest and most resplendent countryman was the Grand Monarch. Louis was tall and handsome, with those fine manners of his nation, and with a majestic yet graceful, courtly bearing that all men admired. He was patient in his attention, and did not give way to anger. But he was extremely vain ; he loved to be flattered and could not bear to be advised.

Like Charles i. of England, he believed himself king by divine right. He was responsible to God for his kingdom, and to God only. ' I am the State,' is supposed to have been his maxim—' L'État, c'est moi.' He ruled through the King's Council, and the smaller councils chosen from this. Louis selected the men for his Councils from the middle class, his great inferiors, not from the aristocracy, who were most nearly his equals. ' I wanted to let the public know,' he wrote, ' by the rank from which I chose my ministers, that I had no intention of sharing power with them.' He looked down on them all, they all had to flatter him continually. And they all admired him immensely, loved to admire him, in the true Gallic spirit.

The great nobles now became courtiers. Disliking the memories of insurrectionary Paris, Louis established his Court twelve miles out, at the city of Versailles, where he built an enormous and gorgeous palace. This was erected between 1676 and 1688, chiefly by the royal architect Mansart. The Court occupied it in 1682. When completed it could house 10,000 persons.

The naturally barren soil was enriched, an aqueduct brought water which was led into lakes and canals, whilst skilful landscape gardeners transformed the wilderness into a succession of lovely, broad, terraced gardens, in succeeding levels, with wide alleys and paths of geometrical form. Trees were clipped into shape—cubes, balls, peacocks—fountains rose out of marble basins where statues seemed to play with the water, flowers were grouped in masses. Beyond the gardens were cool forest glades and open spaces, with grottoes, caves, small lodges—all artificial.

Here in Versailles Louis XIV. kept his vast and splendid Court, a whole army of people living in extravagance and luxury. The highest men in the land struggled with each other as to who should hold the King's boots, or present him with a napkin. In the royal presence the King's own brother might only sit on a low stool placed behind the King's chair. The rest stood. Then there were dances, banquets, endless shows and pageants of great gorgeousness.

Many brilliant painters, sculptors, architects, were kept busy at Versailles. Louis was very friendly to all artists and works of art. During this time lived the greatest French writers — Corneille, Racine, Molière, the dramatists ; Descartes and Pascal, the philosophers ; Bossuet and Fénelon, the religious writers. The plays of Molière were performed at Court, and the King was a personal friend of the author. This was the greatest day of France. Yet all

the time the King's police superintended all the productions
of literature, there was no freedom of speech.

At the same time, in Louis' reign, two of France's
greatest generals were at the height of their powers : the
impetuous Prince of Condé, and the great strategist, the
Marquis of Turenne. In Europe were no generals like
these, whilst Vauban, the famous military engineer, so
fortified the frontiers of the kingdom that they became
almost impenetrable.

In civil life, Colbert, the minister who had the management of finance, was one of the most capable and remarkable men France has produced. He was of middle-class
origin, and not handsome in appearance, but his energy and
activity were enormous. He relentlessly punished fraud
in the government, and thus greatly reduced the burden
of taxation, while the King's income was greater than
before. He introduced workmen from England, Holland,
and Italy, to start factories for stocking-making, weaving,
lace-making, glass-making, and he protected his new
industries by a high tariff. He established companies to
trade with the Baltic, the Mediterranean, the East, and
with America, in rivalry of England and Holland. He
made splendid roads and famous canals, and he urged on
the building of ships. If Louis ruled in splendour, it was
the burgher Colbert who ruled for prosperity. War became an expensive luxury, not a life-activity.

Thus, at the beginning of Louis xiv.'s reign, France
was the first country in Europe, the richest, most splendid,
and the best governed. For if Louis was absolute he was
just, and no nobleman went unpunished if he broke the
laws, any more than if he were a commoner. At the
same time the King appointed great ministers like Colbert
for the well-being of the land. The people were very proud
of their King and their country ; the government was
immensely popular. France was now a new splendour,
a State such as had not been seen before.

Yet the long reign of Louis xiv. ended in disaster and

unpopularity.   Any proud monarch must make war, and
extend his dominion ; otherwise he feels he has not asserted
himself.   So first Louis claimed the Netherlands from
Spain.   After a hundred and fifty years of power and
richness, Spain was already crumbling to go to pieces.
She could not resist the superb armies of the Grand
Monarch.

But then, fearing the aggressions of Louis, England,
Holland, and Sweden joined in with Spain, and Louis
gave way.   Then came war with Holland.   William of
Orange, who became William iii. of England, was called
in by the Dutch to take charge.   He cut the dykes, made
alliance with Spain, Brandenburg, and then England.
Charles ii. of England had pledged himself to help Louis,
but the English people forced him to change sides.   Yet
France added to her territories.   In 1684 Louis forced the
Diet of Ratisbon to allow him to annex large portions of
Alsace and Lorraine, though Germany was very angry.
But Europe was war-weary, and France was master.

In 1688 came the English Revolution, when James ii.
fled and was received by Louis at the palace of St. Germain,
near Paris.   So great was the fear of France in Europe,
that William of Orange succeeded in allying all the great
powers against her ; first England joined with Holland
and the Emperor, then Brandenburg and Spain came in,
then even Sweden and Denmark.   Yet the war was dull,
like a great siege, the allies trying to break the frontiers
of France, so splendidly fortified by Vauban.   France
won practically every battle she engaged in, and took
every place she besieged, and yet, at the end of nine years
she had spent such vast sums of money and was so hard
pressed financially, that Louis had to sign the Peace of
Ryswick in 1697, yielding some of his advantages, and
allowing William iii. to remain on the throne of England.
This last was much against the will of Louis, who hated
Protestants and was cousin of James ii.

The last great war was the War of the Spanish Succession.

The crown of Spain was left to Louis' grandson, Philip. Louis now considered Spain and France as one great realm. England, Holland, the Empire, and the Electorate of Brandenburg, which last took in 1700 the title of Kingdom of Prussia, at once formed an alliance in opposition. France seemed very strong, with her fine armies and organisation. But Spain had sunk into such a low, confused condition, that she was like a dead body bound to the living body of France.

The war raged in the Netherlands, in Italy, in Milan, and in Spain. Then for a while the French Protestants of the Cevennes rose in fierce insurrection against their Catholic oppressors. In 1704 Marlborough and Prince Eugène inflicted one of the most crushing defeats, at Blenheim, that France has ever suffered. The tide of war flowed wholly against Louis. Gibraltar fell into the hands of the English. When at last peace was made at Utrecht in 1713 France was terribly exhausted, financially almost ruined, and quite cast down from her pre-eminence in Europe. The French people now began to turn against the Crown. Fénelon declared that Louis in his absolutist policy ' had impoverished France, and that he had built his throne on the ruin of all classes in the State.'

Louis was now a very old man. He had come to the throne in 1643, when he was only five years of age. His reign had seen Charles I. executed in England, had seen the end of the Commonwealth, the death of Charles II., the flight of James II., the reign and death of William III., and the death of Queen Anne. And now, disaster overtook him at home. His son died, then his grandson, and then even his great-grandson, who was in direct line of succession. The only heir was now a child of two years. If he were to die, there would be dreadful confusion. Striving to settle the regency for the succession, the old king died, in 1715.

And so we see the old order of mediæval Europe is at last changed. Supreme emperors and popes have fallen, nations have arisen. But the life of a nation no longer consists in war and power. Its real purpose is in its productive work. War becomes a recognised evil instead of a highly esteemed way to glory. The pride and danger of peace takes the place of the pride of war. Money begins to arrogate the privileges of birth.

XVI. The French Revolution

WHEN the Grand Monarch died in 1715 France was already very badly impoverished, far more by wars than by any extravagance of the court of Versailles. Louis spent great sums on his splendid palaces and magnificent way of life. But this would not have ruined France. Reckless war destroyed the prosperity of the country, and after that, careless management.

A strong monarchy has two purposes : first, to increase the prosperity of the nation, to make manufacturers and cultivators richer, so that there is plenty of work and sufficient wages for the poor ; and secondly, to satisfy the pride and stiffen the sinews of the nation by active war. The king is the war-lord, it is he who leads on in pride and glory ; whilst in Louis' time the minister Colbert attended to the productive prosperity of the nation.

It is a difficult matter to balance a kingdom between material prosperity and strenuous war and glory. The pursuit of glory is an expensive business ; but if a people seeks nothing but commercial or material success, then the nation becomes spiritless and fat. Louis XIV. and Louis XV. became too conceited, they forgot that they were enthroned upon the nation's prosperity. This is the secret of the Grand Monarch's failure in his old age. All the glory centred in the King. Louis XV. was so vain that he felt himself to be the very Sun of France. No matter what happened, so long as kingly glory shone out the court and government were satisfied. But to keep this glory shining the country had to sweat out its very blood. The blazing sun of France blazed too brightly. The monarchy was a sunflower which exhausted its own leaves and stem and root, and so fell.

During the reign of Louis xv. the debt of France increased enormously. In 1723 the old Cardinal Fleury became minister, and managed well, keeping good financial understanding with Walpole in England. War broke out, and France gained Lorraine. But it was the last real gain of the monarchy.

The War of the Austrian Succession set Europe in arms. The reign of commerce was at hand. The nations of Europe were like business houses, all in competition. All nations were determined that no one nation should become strong enough to command more than its due share of trade and production. This led to a very shaky balance of power. France and Prussia went against England and Austria.

Prussia was the new state in Europe, and Frederick the Great was Europe's finest war-leader. Both Prussia and France did well in the war. France defeated the English heavily at Fontenoy, in 1745. And yet her government was so weak, that when the Peace of Aix-la-Chapelle came in 1748, France had to let go all she had conquered. The nerve was gone out of the government.

The colonial jealousy of France and England brought on the Seven Years War. This time Prussia went with England, against France and Austria. The mismanagement in France was terrible. Armies were not properly equipped, never ready at the right time; they did not know what to do when they were ready. Unhappy France under her sun-king seemed as if she could find not one good statesman, not one capable general. All was mediocre and muddled, whereas Prussia had the brilliant Frederick in command, and England had her great minister Pitt. Canada was utterly lost to France, and India as good as lost. In Europe the French Army was hopelessly beaten by Frederick at Rossbach, in 1757. When the Peace of Paris was signed in 1763 France was stripped and ashamed.

All this time the gaudy King Louis xv. went on in his foolish splendours and dissipation. He knew what was happening, but he flicked his jewelled fingers, and said with a smile, ' After me, the Deluge.' He knew the flood of ruin was at hand. But he gaily did not care, so long as it did not rise until he was departed.

The French Parlement, or corporation of hereditary lawyers, now began to raise its head. It forced Louis to suppress the intriguing Jesuits in France, in 1764. Then it quarrelled with him about his edicts of taxation. He was vexed. One day the famous Madame du Barry, who was the King's mistress for the time being, determined to move her foolish royal lover. She was sitting with him in one of the gorgeous rooms in Versailles. On the wall hung a fine portrait of Charles i. of England, related to the French through his Queen, Henrietta Maria. ' Do you see him ? ' said Du Barry, pointing to the sad, handsome face of Charles. ' Your Parlement will have your head off too.' So the woman made the King very angry against his interfering lawyers. He arrested the most important members of the court, exiled them, and banished the Parlement for ever.

Louis xv. died at last in 1774, after a long reign during which the court had glittered, chiefly with women, and the nation had sunk into shame and poverty. Louis xvi. was different. Kind, good-natured, moral, and filled with the best intentions, he would have liked to govern the nation for prosperity. But it was too late. The good king must suffer for the extravagant. Moreover, Louis xvi. was a little stupid, and his wife, the Austrian Marie Antoinette, was both clever and proud. If Louis xv. had been managed by his mistresses, Louis xvi. was a good deal under the influence of his wife. And the indirect rule of women was bad for France. The King of France was the most absolute monarch in Europe, to be compared only with the Sultan of Turkey. And in France as in Turkey, women or woman ruled the King more often than not, and the nation went to pieces.

Although the nobles were not much more than brilliant butterflies at court, on their own estates they had a good deal of power. They and the clergy paid no taxes—or very little—and yet they were the rich, great landowners. Towns also, because of merchants, were lightly taxed. It was the peasants, those vast numbers of peasants of Gaul, who, because they could not resist, were forced to pay for everything.

The nobles and great landowners divided their land into small lots, little separate farms. Thus little holdings descended from father to son, in the same family of peasants. The peasant paid a half or a third of his produce, corn, wine, cattle, to the lord of the manor, and did certain forced work, as of old. There were no big farms, except, perhaps, the manor farm itself, attached to the château. The Englishman, Arthur Young, who travelled in France just before the Revolution, said that this dividing the land into so many little farms, little fields, was wasteful, and led to bad farming.

Many little farmers owned their own farms. But even these were not free. They had to do certain service for the overlord; they must give him a certain number of chickens or sheep, or have their corn ground at his mill, or their grapes crushed in his wine-press, and pay his charges. Then the clouds of pigeons and other game could feed on the crops; rabbits, hares, deer might eat the young corn; and the poor peasant was not allowed to shoot one pigeon nor one rabbit, and he could claim no compensation from the nobleman. All this was very irritating.

The chief tax was the *Taille*, a tax on houses and land-property of the unprivileged. As soon as a house was repaired and smartened up, or as soon as the land was in good condition, the commissioner came round and raised the tax. But the grand châteaux and parks belonging to the lord paid no taxes, they were in splendid repair, whilst the villages became squalid, the land was left poverty-stricken on purpose, in order to warrant a low taxation. The people hated the *Taille*. The next was the *Gabelle*, the salt tax. The State sold all salt, the price was fixed, and every individual, man, woman, and child was forced to buy a certain amount of salt each year. The third tax was the *Corvée*. Men were summoned to perform a certain amount of forced labour on government roads, or government buildings, for which they were not paid. It is estimated that in some districts the French peasant paid fifty-five per cent. of all he earned to the government: that is, if he managed to earn thirty shillings a week for himself and his family, he had to pay fifteen and sixpence to the tax collector. Meanwhile the nobles were squandering their thousands at Versailles, and paying nothing.

Therefore the peasants were very angry. The parish priests sympathised with them, though the bishops were with the Crown, just as in the old days. And yet the French peasants were perhaps better off than those of Poland, or Spain, or South Germany, and they had far more liberty. But France was alive and angry, these other States were passive, sluggish. It was not so much the suffering that roused France to her Revolution, though there was much suffering, inevitably. It was rather the angry spirit of men who have had a splendid past, which has collapsed, and who now want a future of their own. It was the anger of men who feel that their lives have been used to support folly and extravagance.

The old ways were coming to an end. In every country men were thinking new thoughts, demanding more freedom. In Germany, England, France, and America great writers began to speak out, giving their new ideas. There was a great reaction against glorious kings, a great dislike of the powers that be. Greatness was out of fashion. The educated men looked back to Greece and Rome, the republics of the past. They detested empire and personal authority, and despised the Middle Ages, the Age of Faith. They began to question religion altogether : they would have no authority, neither divine nor human, imposed on them. They wanted to act just according to their own reason ; they wanted two and two to make four exactly.

In Luther's time, men were passionately interested in religious writings. But never perhaps have new books had such a great influence as they had in the middle and later eighteenth century. It has been called the Age of Reason, the very opposite of the Age of Faith. Voltaire (1694-1778) particularly hated the compulsory belief in religion. He said a man should believe what seemed to him sensible, he should not be forced to swallow extra-ordinary facts just because the Church bade him do so. Montesquieu (1689-1755), in his great book *The Spirit of Laws*, showed how he thought a government should be constituted. He had a great admiration for the English institutions, and when the Americans came to form a government for themselves, they learned much from his book. The man who had most influence, however, was Jean-Jacques Rousseau (1712-1778). He believed in a return to nature, and in an innocent enjoyment of everything in nature. He passionately preached the rights of man. His little book, *The Social Contract*, has been called the Bible of the Revolution. It begins : ' Man is born free, but we find him everywhere in chains.' It then goes on to say that governments should be made by the people, for themselves, that there is no divine right of kings, and that contracts with monarchs are not binding. The people should have a right to overthrow any government they do not agree with ; and then, when they have really set up a government of their own, it should be all-powerful. This book had a tremendous effect. Thousands of people could reel off from it passages which they had got by heart almost unawares.

Louis XVI., the last king of the Ancient Regime, as it is called, really sympathised to some extent with those

new ideas. He wanted to make things better in France.
So he appointed a good minister, Turgot. But the butterfly court intrigued against Turgot, and the King had to
dismiss him.

In 1773 the colonists of North America, after the affair
called the Boston Tea Party, declared a cessation of
commercial intercourse with England. In 1775 the first
blood was shed at Lexington ; and in July 4, 1776, the
American Declaration of Independence was signed, which
was the beginning of a new world.

France watched all this closely. She herself had been
driven from America by the English. So the French
Crown readily gave help to the Americans. Benjamin
Franklin was honourably received at court, and treated
with great consideration and respect for years, whilst he
resided in France negotiating large sums of money which
were paid to him by Louis XVI.'s minister to help the new
states in their young independence. Since this time
America has always felt a great friendliness towards
France, who helped her in her first days against England.

But the French people, though they gloried in their
triumph over the English in the war, were still more excited by the founding of the far-off new republic. It was
an act which struck their imagination and kindled the
desire of their hearts. They thought it marvellous to
have no kings, for men to be their own rulers.

Although the war was successful, it was costly, and
France could not afford it. The minister Necker decided
as the minister Turgot had decided, that the privileged
classes, nobles and clergy and wealthy burghers, must be
taxed. The whole court turned against him, and in 1784
he retired before a storm of opposition.

The King had now to borrow money at a ruinous interest,
to carry on the government. Then he tried to impose
taxes on all classes, by issuing royal edicts. It was what
the other kings had done. But the Parlement of Paris,
which he had revived conscientiously when he came to

the throne, immediately opposed him, and the masses of
the people were with the Parlement. There was now a
weak king and a strong, hostile nation. A general cry
arose, that the Estates General, the genuine old French
parliament, must be summoned, and all classes represented
in that real parliament. But the Estates General had not
met for a hundred and seventy years, and nobody was very
clear as to how it should meet and what it should do if it
did meet. Yet the French nation was bent on having a
parliament which they themselves had chosen.

So Louis agreed to summon the Estates General, and he
restored Necker. The King was now very popular, the
crowds sang his praises. But there was immediate squabbling. The people claimed to have as many representatives
in their Commons as the nobles and clergy had in both
their upper chambers put together : for the Estates General
had three chambers for the three classes. The nobles
opposed this. The King, on Necker's advice, decided for
the people. There was a further rage of controversy, as
to how the votes should be counted. If the chambers
voted separately, and every question was decided by a
majority of chambers, then nobles with clergy could easily
outvote the people all the time : whilst if individual votes
were counted the people, sure of some support from the
clergy, would inevitably carry the day.

The three chambers, or Three Estates, as they were
called, could come to no agreement. Petitions and
clamours came in from all over France, to the Third
Estate, urging the Commons to make a constitution for
France, a set of laws binding on king and people alike.
Many of the clergy declared themselves in favour of this :
they were ready to go over and take their seats with the
Commons in the Third Estate. So in June 1789, the
Commons took upon themselves the name of the National
Assembly, and proceeded to make a constitution for France,
whether the privileged classes agreed or not.

This was one Estate claiming to act for the whole nation,

the populace acting for king and nobles and asking for no consent. The Crown could not allow it. The Court raged and argued. Louis went down to the House of Representatives to make his intentions clear. He wished everything for the best : he promised many reforms : but he said the Estates General must consist of the three chambers. Then Mirabeau, the great orator and statesman, rose against the King. Mirabeau was a nobleman, but he had joined the Commons and sat in the Third Estate. He declared that the three-chamber model gave power to the privileged classes, and that the Commons were determined to resist it. The National Assembly, of one House, must represent the nation, the mass of the people, not just the nobles and clergy.

Now the King must either fight or give way. He was too kind-hearted to call in troops to crush the rebellion in the Lower House. In spite of the bold words he had spoken before the National Assembly, he had to give way. He must have money to carry on the government, and he could not have money unless the people would grant it him ; for he was too weak to force it from them, as his predecessors had done. Therefore at last he asked the nobles and clergy to go over and join the Commons. Many had already done so : many more obeyed. At last, at the end of all the turmoil, all the twelve hundred representatives of France—or at least as many of them as chose to stay in the Assembly—were assembled in one room, and proceeded to draw up a constitution. In the count of votes, the people now had inevitably a fixed majority.

Louis saw that he had ruined the power of the Crown. He did not intend to yield altogether so easily. His courtiers clamoured for him to call up the armies. At last he consented. Necker, whom the people liked, was dismissed. Domineering nobles were gathered round the King. A great movement of troops was ordered, many regiments were to concentrate on Paris.

When the news of this reached Paris, the city went mad

with excitement and wrath. The National Assembly sat at Versailles, twelve miles away. But in Paris were the famous, fiery mob-orators and politicians like Marat and Camille Desmoulins. Meetings were held everywhere, loud cries went up, great crowds gathered and swayed and shouted, the whole city was in the streets. Soldiers quartered in Paris went over to the people.

Suddenly the cry went up, ' To the Bastille.' The Bastille was the famous fortress-prison, a great frowning impregnable place of power belonging to the Crown. It was not any more of any great importance. But the people detested it for what it had been, they hated its very name. The vast masses of the people surged forward.

The Bastille could have resisted for ever, if it had been provisioned. It could have dominated and overawed Paris. But the garrison was half-mutinous. The commander did not know what to do. He was told that the King had surrendered himself to the people. So, in the afternoon, he agreed to yield up the vast fortress if his life and the lives of the garrison should be spared. The promise was given by the leaders of the crowd. But as the commandant and his men were being conducted safely off, the crowd broke through the guard and cruelly murdered them. Then the mob surged delirious through the terrible fortress-prison, liberating the few prisoners and looking with fury and hatred on the dungeons where kings had thrown their victims.

The King and Court were thoroughly frightened. Louis at once dismissed the unpopular nobles from his Council, and recalled Necker. Now the people demanded that the King should come to Paris. He, however, refused to leave the great palace of Versailles. On October 5, a great crowd of fierce and hungry women, who had met to make a demonstration against the shortage of food, surged out on to the Versailles road, and swept like a flood towards the palace. The King heard the strange tumult, and went

to the window. There he saw fierce masses of terrible
women, some bearing arms, mixed with men also bearing
arms. They cried fiercely for bread, and demanded that
the King should come with them back to Paris. He returned a doubtful answer. The mob stayed muttering in
the park and grounds all night. In the morning they swept
up like a sea against the palace, broke in, and surged
through the splendid corridors. The life of the King and
Queen was in danger, when Lafayette arrived with the
National Guard, stalwart Swiss mercenaries, and held
back the mob. Lafayette, however, brought a request
from the town council of Paris, that the King should take
up his residence in the city. Unwillingly, and with fore-
boding, Louis had to give way. On the afternoon of
October 6, the royal party set out, with its guards, towards
the Tuileries. The crowds surged and muttered. But
they did not really hate the King even now. They hated
the Queen more.

The National Assembly, which now called itself the
' Constituent Assembly,' proceeded to form a new constitution, very much on the English model, taking the
power from the Crown and putting it into the hands of
the citizens. ' All sovereignty rests with the people,' they
said. They also reorganised the Church, taking authority
away from both the Pope and the King, and putting it in
the hands of the voters. The Pope issued a Bull of Condemnation against this new order, and excommunicated
all those who had helped in it. The King, however, was
forced to sign the whole order, though he was most unhappy and uneasy, particularly at the religious changes.
He hoped secretly to get a chance soon to undo all this
wicked work, for such it seemed to him.

The people suspected his intentions. Orators and news-
papers charged him with being the enemy of the Revolution. In the wine-shops his name was loudly execrated,
insults against him and the Queen were scrawled large
on the walls. Louis longed to flee. Marie Antoinette

urged him to it. At last, on a night in June 1791, the royal pair escaped in disguise in their coach through the barriers of Paris, and galloped on towards the north-east, to the troops that were stationed near Flanders. Louis thought he would place himself under the protection of his troops. Many miles were travelled, and they approached the frontier. And then, as they drew near to safety, the royal fugitives were detected and escorted back to Paris, real prisoners now.

The Assembly determined to suspend the King from his functions until they had finally drawn up the Constitution. This Constitution he would be asked to sign. If he signed it, well and good. If he refused, he would be considered to have abdicated. But the masses were already raging for the King's deposition, and for the declaration of a republic. A vast crowd met. It was dispersed by the National Guard. But there was great resentment, then resistance, then furious, frenzied fighting and crushing, and many people, men and women, were killed. This put the rest of the citizens of Paris into greater fury.

In September 1791 the Constitution was at last finished. Louis was to be king without any power of making or altering laws : he was to occupy something of the same position in the Government as the English king occupies. Louis formally accepted this Constitution, and promised to rule by it. Many now thought the great aim was achieved, and France would enjoy a free, national government such as Britain enjoyed, a time of prosperity and liberty.

But it did not turn out so. The King did not really abide by the new system. The Queen openly hated it and scorned it all, for she was proud to the backbone. And the people were worked up, their passions were roused, they had not had enough. They wanted to make a clean sweep.

At this time, Austria, Prussia, and Russia were seizing

portions of Poland, dividing the country among themselves. They were too busy to interfere in France. But
when the French declared that feudalism, with the paying
of tithes and taxes to the overlord, was abolished, then the
neighbouring countries began to look round ; for many of
the tithes and taxes of the French frontiers went to German
princes, or to the emperor. All Europe began to think
the French Revolution was going too far, that it would
upset order everywhere.

The French were quite indignant when they were asked
to pay compensation for the tithes and taxes they repudiated. They had a grievance of their own. Many nobles,
the King's brothers among them, had crossed the frontiers
since the Revolution began, and, establishing themselves
in Trèves or by the Rhine, had proceeded to drill troops
and prepare armies, loudly declaring their intention of
marching on the revolutionaries and chastising them
severely.

Therefore the French people, very touchy, were all up
in arms against their old enemy, the Emperor, who was
supposed to be sheltering these runaway, menacing nobles.
On either hand the war fever spread. The French people
clamoured for war against Austria. Louis was quite
willing, for he thought this might be a way out for him.
Only the extreme revolutionaries, those who wanted a
republic at once, were firmly against it. This party was
called the Jacobins, because they belonged to an advanced
revolutionary club which met in a building that once
belonged to the Jacobin friars. The Jacobin leaders,
Marat, Robespierre, Danton, declared that no good could
come of a European war, at the moment where they found
themselves. Yet the people wanted it. War was declared
against the Emperor Leopold in April 1792.

The war began with great enthusiasm on the part of
the French. But the first campaign in Belgium was a
failure. The public now turned on the King. The Queen
was an Austrian. They declared that Louis had been in

sympathy with the enemy, and had betrayed his own nation.

The Jacobins then formed a conspiracy. Danton, a barrister, was the leader. Troops that arrived in Paris from the frontier were secretly won over by the conspirators. Suddenly, on August 10, 1792, the Jacobin force made an attack upon the palace. The King was warned just in time. He fled with his family. But the palace was stormed, the Swiss guards who so faithfully defended it were cut down. The victorious insurgents crowded to the Assembly Room, and demanded that the King should be deposed.

The Assembly could not help itself. Louis was declared deposed : he was no longer king. The people were called to vote for a new Assembly. Each man was to have his vote. The Assembly should be called the Convention, and this should decide the destiny of the new republic of France.

This was the beginning of the end. France was now without a government. Who would lead, what would happen ? People held their breath and trembled. The strong power in Paris was the Municipal Council, called the Commune. The extremist, Marat, was the leader of the Commune. He wanted the revolution to be very thorough, for there was a great, burning bitterness in him against the privileged classes.

The Commune declared that conspiracies were being formed to overthrow the new government. Paris must be searched for arms and traitors. By the end of August, the prisons were crammed with men who had been arrested because they were suspected of being friendly to the King. A tribunal was set up. Ordinary offenders, thieves, or scoundrels were sent back to prison. But men suspected of being friendly to the monarchy were thrust out of the doors and massacred in the street by the bloodthirsty, howling mob. This went on for three, even for five days, and more than a thousand people were butchered. Marat said it was the vengeance of a wrathful people on those who for centuries had ill-treated and trodden them down. But it was in part, at least, a deliberate plan carried out by the Commune.

Meanwhile the revolutionary forces under Dumouriez had inflicted a defeat at Valmy on the Prussians, and the advance of the enemy on Paris had been checked.

The Convention, elected by the men of the nation, met in September. It declared France a republic, and summoned King Louis to trial. He was found a traitor, and guillotined in January 1793.

Now began the Reign of Terror. The Jacobins were certainly a minority, yet they were in power. Civil wars broke out. In La Vendée, a district of Western France, peasants rose in arms because the Republic tried to conscript them into the army, and because they wished to defend the Church. In Lyons and Toulon were dangerous movements. The execution of the King had made enemies of Britain, Holland, and Spain. In 1793 France had to face a coalition of all the great states of Europe, except Russia. The French armies were defeated, and the collapse of the Republic seemed imminent.

Yet the Jacobins were determined to stand against everything. They knew that the majority, even in France, were against them. They were a small body. They must either fall, or deal a great blow at their opponents, that would strike terror into them and cow them for the time being.

They formed the Committee of Public Safety, led first by Danton, then afterwards by Robespierre. This Committee overruled every other authority. It at once set itself to raise troops and organise campaigns on the different fronts of battle.

And then, in Paris, it set up the Revolutionary Tribunal. Men and women were seized, who were suspected of having any connection with the aristocracy or any sympathy with the old system. The Queen was sent to the guillotine, more and more people followed her. It seemed as if the Jacobins got greedier for blood, the more they shed. Victims were condemned in batches. Even good republicans, even the very leaders who had started the Revolution, but who were now not red enough, were seized, condemned, and sent to the guillotine. For the extreme revolutionaries were frightened too. They felt all Europe was against them. They felt that even at home great numbers of the people were ready to betray the Revolution. Unless they struck first, and struck hard, and struck deep, they and all they stood for would be wiped out, the old would come back, all would be again as bad or worse than if they had never existed.

Then the Jacobins divided among themselves. Danton wished to be more merciful, and to limit the foreign wars. Hébert and Chaumette wanted to go further, to utmost extremes, to destroy every trace of the old way. They swept away the calendar, and called the year 1792 the Year One. They christened the months with new names. They made a week of ten days, and introduced the decimal system. They declared Christianity abolished, and the worship of Reason substituted for it.

But the third or middle party, led by Robespierre, ultimately triumphed. He drew the energetic revolutionaries of Paris, men and women, to his side, and obtained control of the fierce armed forces of the streets. He triumphed over his rivals. Danton and the others went to the guillotine. The Terror went on. Robespierre wanted to be supreme dictator, and to bring this about he condemned his victims by batches to death. He knew he could not last. Terror in his own heart urged him to inflict, or to try to inflict more terror on the hearts of the populace. In July 1794 men rose and denounced him in the Convention. He tried to gather his followers together, to fight for his position. But his adherents fell away. He was declared an outlaw, seized at last, and executed without any form of trial. The Terror came to an end.

King, Queen, nobles, gentry, all were gone. Republican leaders were gone too. The bloodstained crowds remained. Louis xv.'s Deluge had indeed come.

While all this was going on in Paris, the rest of France was more or less terrorised. First the provinces had to watch the foreign war, where so many of their men were enrolled and fighting. The enemy were penetrating into France, from the north, from the east, from the south. Every one felt unsafe, everything was in danger. Very bitter insurrections broke out, there was civil war against the hated rule of the Jacobins. The armies sent against the foreign enemies were disheartened and defeated. Things looked very black in 1793.

But the Jacobin leaders were swift and relentless. They crushed the rebels in France and punished them with great cruelty, using the fierce revolutionary troops against them. They appointed new, determined officers to the army, and infused into the men a great passion for the Revolution, a great hatred of foreign emperors and kings who were out to destroy the newly-risen people of France. As the Jacobins were relentless in Paris, against those who might bring back the hated old system of monarchy, the soldiers in the far fields became relentless against the foreigners who would crush the new rule of the people. The tide of war turned. The enemy was rolled back beyond the frontiers, and by the time Robespierre fell, France was almost free.

Men now began to recover their senses. The Terror was over, the hated Jacobins were gone, the people were masters and they seemed secure. What next ? First, there was hostile Europe hemming France in. The French people recovered all their jauntiness. Let France expand, they cried, to her natural boundaries, of the Rhine, the Pyrenees, and the Alps. The Gallic vanity called loudly for the restoration of France to the limits of old Gaul. At the beginning, the Revolution had declared that it did not want to make conquests or acquire territories ; it wanted to live at peace with all men. Now, quite the opposite, it defiantly announced itself at war with its neighbours, and proceeded to extend its dominions at the cost of all.

But at home, people wanted to solidify the country and appease many enemies by making a moderate Constitution. The present governing power was the Convention. It had the armies under its control. Men were now tired of the Convention. They wanted something quite new, an arrangement whereby perhaps there would be more balance of power, where the old Convention would not be so autocratic : for the Convention and the Committee of Public Safety had been far more deadly and overbearing than the old Kings' Councils. But Convention decided that the first assemblies of the new Constitution should consist of two-thirds of its own members. There was an uproar. Convention was not going to be bullied any more by the mob. It called out its soldiers, under their young officer, Napoleon Bonaparte. When the masses attacked the Convention they were driven off with artillery.

Convention now came to an end, in October 1795, and the new assemblies met. People were tired of political troubles at home. They saw, or felt that nothing could be gained by altering the government every year. So they turned round, they looked outwards at the surrounding world. Their hearts fired up. All their enthusiasm they put behind their soldiers in the field. The old regime was smashed in France. Now they were ready to destroy it in all the world.

The victories of the revolutionary armies had caused Prussia to withdraw from the war, yielding to France territories on the left bank of the Rhine, and obtaining promise that Prussia should be regarded as the chief power in North Germany, and should not be attacked. Spain also came out of the war. This left France to face Britain and Austria only.

Austria was the immediate enemy. She was to be attacked by one army in Italy, whilst two others marched towards Vienna. Napoleon had command of the Italian army. The Italians themselves loathed the Austrian rule, so they welcomed his advance against their masters. France watched, electrified. They saw the brilliant way in which Napoleon defeated and broke the Austrians in Italy. Austria made peace in 1797, and this left France with only one enemy, Britain.

The next step was a strange one. The Directors in Paris ordered Napoleon to undertake the invasion of Egypt. He reached Egypt safely, and then his position was endangered by Nelson's victory of the Nile. At the same time Napoleon heard that there was a new coalition of powers in Europe, against the French. He determined to return. Russia had joined Austria in the attack on the Republic. He hastened back. His Italian campaign had made him the hero of France. Everybody believed he could bring peace and order to the land. He was expected with excitement, the coming great man.

Meanwhile the executive government called the Directory, composed of five Directors, were muddling things at home. When Napoleon arrived in Paris many leaders and politicians came to him complaining bitterly of this. He listened to these unsatisfied republicans. They asked him to be the leader, to take control of the government. He was such a hero among the people that they thought this could be done without any more fighting in Paris. But the muddling Directors and assemblies refused to come out of office. Napoleon had command of the troops of Paris. He just marched down to the Assembly Rooms and scattered the obstinate legislators. Then there was nothing to oppose him.

After this, for twenty years the history of France is a history of Napoleon Bonaparte. He was a wonderful military genius, but he was also a brilliant ruler in peace time. He knew that if the government rested with the mass of the people, it would be a disastrous mob rule where everything was pulled down as soon as it was put up. So he most carefully arranged a government which depended upon the richer, more stable, property-owning, privileged classes.   And yet he ruled in the name of the people.

Again we see the Tyrant rising up.   Napoleon became an almost absolute sovereign, much as Louis XIV. had been. But Napoleon ruled in the name of the people, according to the agreement of the people.   Though he was supreme, he was supreme because the people willed it, not because he had been appointed by God.   Louis XIV. claimed to be king by divine right : the people had nothing to do with it. Napoleon was emperor by the will of the people, although, for form's sake, he crowned himself in presence of the Pope.

God-made kings and nobles were destroyed in France for ever.   The new ones would be man-made.   This was the great change.   The actual government rested in the hands of the educated, well-to-do citizen classes, very much as it had done in Louis XIV.'s time.   The poor were not in any very different position.   Money ruled instead of birth, that was all.   A man who had no money found himself pretty much where he was before, though some of the annoyances were removed, and he was free from the insult of God-made inferiority.   In the new system, any man who might become rich might become a ruler.   So a modern commercial or industrial state, be it kingdom or republic, was established.

The difference lies in this, that if a man had ability to make money, he might ultimately govern the republic. Henceforth there was to be no superiority of one man over another : only the superiority of the money-maker. Prosperity was the only clue to life.

XVII. Prussia

THE changes of the Reformation and the difficulty of settling the disputes brought about by the new order led to one of the most disastrous wars that Europe has ever seen, the fatal Thirty Years War. This fearful war between the Protestant princes of the north and the Catholic forces of the imperialists ravished and utterly ruined Germany.

In 1650 Germany was almost a deserted land, the remaining peasants were almost driven to savagery. Hardly any traffic passed along the desolate roads. In the country the people clustered in dilapidated, obscure hovels, rough, brutalised, demoralised. In the towns civilisation was almost at a standstill. By the sword, by famine, by plague, in this horrible war ten million people had perished, leaving only about five millions in the great land of Germany. The population of Berlin fell from 24,000 to 6,000, a mere village. In Hesse, 300 villages, 17 towns, 47 castles were burned out; in Würtemberg, 3,600 dwellings; and these were comparatively small states. Of all countries, only Ireland after the reign of Elizabeth and the wars of Cromwell has ever been reduced to such a ghastly state. It was this destruction of Germany which left France free to become so powerful and dominant under Louis XIV., and which finished the mediæval spirit in Europe.

Germany was left divided into innumerable parts. There were reckoned 343 sovereign states in the country; 158 were under lords and princes, 123 were under bishops,

63 were imperial cities, but all were separate and practically self-governing. The confusion was incredible. The imperial power had almost vanished. The emperors, the Hapsburgs, had to confine their attention to their remaining dominions of Austria-Hungary and North Italy. The rest were gone. Switzerland and the United Netherlands became independent, France had gained Alsace and the three bishoprics of Metz, Toule, and Verdun.

Out of all this chaos the state of Prussia rose. It is Prussia which has led and made Germany. But modern Prussia is a new thing. The core of the state is Brandenburg, the great Mark or frontier-province established in the tenth century to keep off the Slavs to the east. Brandenburg lay between the Elbe and the Oder. Beyond the Oder lay heathen Prussia, Prussia proper, inhabited by pagan Slavs. When the crusades to the Holy Land began to wane, the great Crusading Order of the Teutonic Knights turned to preach to their neighbours, the heathen Prussians beyond the Mark of Brandenburg. Thus the Slavs of Prussia became Christian and Germanised, the Teutonic Knights held the eastern frontier against the wild peoples of Russia.

In 1415 Frederick of Hohenzollern, one of the Emperor's counts, was made Elector of Brandenburg by Sigismund, for Frederick had been a staunch friend to Sigismund all through the stormy times of the Council of Constance, when popes were deposed and Huss was burned. The Hohenzollerns had been minor princes, imperial counts of Nuremberg. Barbarossa long ago had said that he saw the day when the Hohenzollerns would displace the Hohenstaufens, his own imperial house. But the Hohenstaufens were gone before the Hohenzollerns rose to power. Barbarossa overlooked the Hapsburgs, that family which produced so few great men, yet which ruled for so many centuries over such large territories.

When the Hohenzollerns came to Brandenburg they were isolated between Hanover and Bremen on the west, and

the Prussian lands of the Teutonic Knights which lay to
the east. The knights were doing badly. They were
defeated by the Poles, and Poland seized a great strip
of territory, called West Prussia, intervening between
Brandenburg and Prussia proper, and stretching to the sea
at Danzig. So that Brandenburg's new neighbour was
Poland ; Prussia was cut off to the east.

The Teutonic Order needed a new chief. Albert of
Hohenzollern was chosen Grand Master in 1511. He was
a cousin of the Hohenzollerns across in Brandenburg.
He wanted to establish a realm for himself. Wisely, he
calculated that if he became Protestant, then, after the
Reformation was secure his family might really establish
itself as dukes of Prussia. This actually came to pass.
The Albertian Hohenzollerns ruled Prussia.

But this line died out, and the cousin Hohenzollerns of
Brandenburg became heirs to Prussia. John Sigismund
of Hohenzollern, Elector of Brandenburg, became now also
Duke of Prussia in 1618. But his two countries or lands
did not touch : the Polish province of West Prussia lay
between them. After this the Hohenzollerns inherited
Cleves and Berg, away on the Rhine. So now they ruled
three separate territories in North Germany.

During the Thirty Years War George William, Elector
of Brandenburg, played a very poor part. He did not
want to take either side, so the Electorate was ravaged
by both parties, and suffered horribly. But in 1640 the
strong ruler Frederick William came to power. He was
called the Great Elector. At the Peace of Westphalia
he compelled the parties to yield Magdeburg and East
Pomerania to Brandenburg. Pomerania lay just between
Brandenburg and the sea, Magdeburg lay to the south.
So Frederick William stretched his central territory to
the Baltic, and had a sea-board, and advanced his frontier
southwards towards Saxony.

The Great Elector wanted to raise his estate from the
position of shame into which it had fallen in the Thirty

Years War. He made himself master in his own lands, suppressed the estates or parliaments of Brandenburg, East Prussia, and Cleves, and thus obtained clear, single control. This made for unity and success. Then he strengthened his armies and defeated the Poles, making them promise not to attack East Prussia. This was a great step. Next he defeated the French and Swedes when they advanced into Brandenburg, beat them in a fierce battle. For this remarkable victory he received the title of the Great Elector.

He now turned his attention to the commercial prosperity of his realm. He had canals constructed, and encouraged trade along the still waters. His final step for the promotion of industry was taken when, in 1685, he gave houses and many privileges in Berlin and the country round to the Huguenots who were fleeing from the persecutions of the ageing, short-sighted Grand Monarch of France. After the settlement of these Huguenots, Berlin, the central city of Brandenburg, began her course of industrial greatness, while the agriculture in the provinces round was immensely improved by these more civilised new-comers. Thus a new source of riches and strength to the State was established.

Frederick William was succeeded in 1688 by his son, the Elector Frederick III., a pompous and foolish man. At this time kings were being made. The Elector of Hanover was to be King of England, the Elector of Saxony was King of Poland, the Duke of Holstein was King of Denmark. Brandenburg might easily hope for the same title. When the nations began to unite against Louis XIV., after that old monarch claimed Spain for his grandson Philip, the Emperor Leopold thought Brandenburg would make a splendid ally against France. Brandenburg asked for the kingly title. The Emperor agreed, so long as the Elector Frederick should not take his title from any of the territory of the Empire. Now Brandenburg was supposed to be subject to the empire, whilst Prussia was not. So that the Elector Frederick III. of Brandenburg, instead of becoming King of Brandenburg, became King Frederick I. of Prussia. He died shortly after achieving this new dignity. His soldiers had fought well at Blenheim, and kept up the new Prussian reputation.

Frederick I., was succeeded in 1713 by Frederick William I., his son. Frederick William I. of Prussia is one of the strangest men. He utterly despised his father's vanity and pomp of ceremony, and at once dismissed all the showy ministers. Then he turned to his kingdom. ' We remain King and Master,' he wrote, ' and we do what we like.' He appointed royal officials, paid them badly, watched them strictly, and punished them harshly if they were guilty of the least offence. His lands were poor in comparison with those of France or Britain or Bavaria. He was bent on making them produce as much as they could, and in getting out of them all the taxes possible, without damaging the rate of production. His rage against any form of financial dishonesty among his officials was beyond bounds terrible.

His other mania was the production of a perfect army. When he came to the throne in 1713 the army numbered 38,000 men ; by 1739 it had more than 83,000, and this was peace strength. The great France had 160,000 soldiers, and Austria about 100,000. But these were first-rate powers, Prussia was as yet insignificant. And then Frederick William, who was rather a drill-sergeant than a king, clothed, armed and disciplined his forces to a rare pitch of perfection. He made a regiment of giant grenadiers, ransacked the lands for them, and he went almost mad in his admiration of this corps. Yet he was no soldier, and did no fighting. He is the insane royal drill-sergeant.

He had a son Frederick. Frederick William was a coarse, foul-mouthed, uneducated bully, drinking, feeding, smoking, yelling, and domineering. The son was just the opposite, delicate and sensitive, cultured, almost French in his education, loving books and painting and philosophy. The father tormented and tortured his son incredibly, loathed him, calling him a weakling and a ninny and a paltry knave. The young Frederick escaped from court at last, for his father had always taunted him to this. He was caught, brought back, and condemned to death by his father. The violent king raved, and would have shot his son at once. The nobles would not permit it. So, grudgingly, Frederick William spared the life of the young man, whom he almost longed to annihilate. Instead he executed the Crown Prince's dear friend, and brutally punished others of his son's companions.

The young prince yielded, since there was nothing else to do. Like his friend Voltaire, the famous French writer, he was a sceptic in matters of religion : with a bitter heart he professed the religious opinions his father forced on him : he took a wife he neither loved nor wanted, at his father's command : and he obediently began the dreary hack-work of administration to which he was driven.

All the while, the young Frederick was a far finer, more intellectual, and even a much stronger man, in his soul and his will, than the bullying Frederick William his father. But by the time the prince came to the throne, in 1740, the sweetness of his nature was spoiled, his soul embittered. He did not believe in kindness any more. He saw that force, and force alone, triumphed : it was no use a man's being sensitive and wise : he must merely be unbreakably strong.

So the new King Frederick II. came to the throne of Prussia. He became one of the most famous men of the modern world, Frederick the Great, one of the makers of Europe.

At the very beginning of his reign Frederick invaded Silesia, which stretched south of Brandenburg, and belonged to Austria. The War of the Austrian Succession followed, when Prussia and France fought Austria and Britain. When peace was made in 1748 Prussia kept the

large territory of Silesia, though France, who had beaten
Britain at Fontenoy, had to give up everything.

Soon war began again. This time it was Britain and
Prussia against France and Austria, in the Seven Years
War. In this war the great Pitt, Earl of Chatham, arose
in England, and Britain secured Canada and India from
France. But Prussia suffered terribly, almost as badly as
in the Thirty Years War. Frederick had to face the much
improved armies of Austria in the south, and the strength
of France on the west, whilst Elizabeth, Czarina of Russia,
joined Austria and attacked him in the east. Against these
three, the greatest powers in Europe, Frederick had no ally
but Britain, and Britain was a naval power, she could not
at first help him on land.

Frederick showed himself one of the finest soldiers the
world has known, a master of campaign and of battle
attack. In 1757 he won the great victory of Leuthen,
by his quite new methods of attack ; and in the same year
he defeated the French so easily, by his skilful handling
of his troops in the battle of Rossbach, that the enemy
was not only beaten but put to shame. Napoleon afterwards said that the battle of Rossbach was the beginning
of the French Revolution. He meant that an absolute
monarch could only keep firm on his throne by winning
military victories, and that if his armies suffered such
humiliating defeats, as did those of Louis xv. at Rossbach,
then his people were bound to turn against him. Pitt also
proved a great ally to Frederick, unexpectedly sending him
over many troops from England. For Pitt was a great
war-master.

In spite of everything, in spite of all his patient endurance
and skill, Frederick was heavily beaten by the Russians
in 1759. In 1760 Russians and Austrians entered Berlin.
In 1761 the whole of Prussian territory was in the hands
of the enemy. The splendid troops with which Frederick
had set out were for the most part killed or taken prisoners.
His money was exhausted. And then, worst of all,

George III. in England caused Pitt to resign, and the one ally became useless. Prussia now seemed destined to disappear again, divided between the Empire and Russia. Frederick, in his bitter despair, even thought of suicide.

Then suddenly he was saved by the death of the Czarina Elizabeth, who hated him determinedly. Her . weak-minded nephew Peter III. worshipped Frederick, calling him ' my king, my master.' Russia at once made alliance with Prussia, and the whole situation changed. But this only lasted for four months, when poor Peter III. was overthrown and put to death by his own wife, the Czarina Catherine II. She at once withdrew from the alliance with Frederick. But Prussia was saved, Austria ousted. The powers were exhausted by the struggle. In 1763 the Peace of Paris was made, and Frederick still kept Silesia, which Austria so badly wanted back.

Prussia was now the wonder of Europe. A new kingdom of the second rate, she had maintained herself against the three greatest powers. Frederick's system of government, his management of the war, were looked upon with admiration and amazement. Even the neighbours he had beaten began to imitate him.

In the eighteenth century most of the countries of Europe became stronger, more united, more prosperous and developed in every way, through the concentration of the power into the hands of the Crown, which ruled wisely and well. This period is called the age of the Enlightened Despot. Austria, Russia, Denmark, Sweden and Prussia are examples of the great advance made by countries whose monarchs united the scattered powers of their realm into one wise, strong control. But Prussia is the finest example, and she is the very opposite of the Grand Monarchy of France. Frederick's court was simple and natural, there was no show, no pomp. It is said that once, when Frederick the Great walked out in Berlin, he saw on a wall a big placard, or cartoon, abusing him, calling him a bad king and an absurd man. ' Hang it higher,' said Frederick, ' so that the people can see it.'

He built up his State again from the foundations. When he was young he had studied the philosophers of France. When he was older he profited by these studies. He at once abolished torture, and established complete religious freedom in his country. He took great care of education, as most Prussian rulers have done. He was very anxious to repair slowly the terrible ravages of the war, so that his people should not suffer more than was necessary. Supervising in agriculture and commerce, he gradually made the country once more prosperous and happy. All the power was in his hands, and as he used it to the best advantage, nothing could have been better for his land and his people. No popular government could have built up Prussia as her early kings built it up.

Though Frederick fought in no more important wars after 1763, he gained great and valuable territories. The old kingdom of Poland was a large country, stretching from the Baltic straight across what is now Russia, to the Black Sea. But because the kings had so little power in Poland, because the numerous nobles remained independent and vain and quarrelsome, the kingdom inevitably fell to pieces. The people could not unite around one central figure, the monarch. Therefore they were powerless against the neighbouring states. In 1772 Frederick suggested that Russia, Austria and Prussia should divide the helpless, useless state of Poland between them. Russia took a great stretch of land, which is now South Russia ; Austria took Galicia, and Prussia took that section called West Prussia, which ran along the Vistula to the Gulf of Danzig, cutting off Brandenburg from Prussia proper, or East Prussia. When Frederick annexed the Polish territory, the kingdom of Prussia naturally became one united solid state, stretching from Memel in the north of the Gulf of Danzig down to the river Elbe in one unbroken sweep. The people were German or German speaking, naturally near to one another, uniting naturally. When Frederick died in 1786 his kingdom was the envy of all Germany.

Particularly the Hapsburgs envied the growing, solid power of the Hohenzollerns. The Hapsburgs were still emperors of the Holy Roman Empire. But their lands were their own hereditary dominions : and here they were (1) Archdukes of Austria proper, which was Germanic and Catholic ; (2) Kings of Hungary, where the Magyars were constantly claiming independence ; (3) Kings and over-lords of Bohemia and Moravia, where the Czechs and Slavs were chiefly Protestants ; (4) Overlords of North Italy, where the people were utter foreigners to the Austrian Hapsburgs ; (5) Overlords of the Austrian Netherlands (Belgium), where the people were Catholic, but either French-speaking or Flemish. Joseph ii. of Austria, who succeeded Maria Theresa in 1765, hated, admired, and deeply envied Frederick the Great. He wanted to imitate him, and unite his power. But how could the Hapsburgs unite their dominions, scattered as they were across Europe ; still more, how could they hope to unite German Austrians, Magyar Hungarians, Slavonic Czechs, Belgians, Flemings and Italians into one people or one nation ? It was quite impossible.

It was revolution which brought the next great changes in Germany and Austria. Northern Europe was at first busy attending to Poland. That diminished country had made some progress, and King Stanislas ii. really brought in a good constitution in 1790. But the neighbours of Poland, particularly Russia, did not intend the country to revive. They invaded Poland in 1792. Russia seized large territories, Prussia added to her dominions, to make them more compact. Poland was in a state of insurrection. Russia ordered her to disband her armies. The people now rose in rebellion, under the hero Kosciusko. This is called the Polish Revolution, and North Europe watched it even more closely, at first, than the French Revolution. Russia, Prussia and Austria turned against Kosciusko.

He was bound in the end to be defeated. In 1795 the third and last partition of Poland took place. Russia, Prussia and Austria all took their shares, and all promised that the name of Poland should never appear again on the map of Europe.

But by this time the armies of the French Revolution were becoming dangerous. In 1802 Napoleon had himself declared First Consul for life. This was a clear step towards supreme power. On August 4, 1804, the Emperor of the Holy Roman Empire, Francis ii., proclaimed himself Francis i. Hereditary Emperor of Austria. At the same time Napoleon had asked the people of France to vote whether he himself should assume the royal title. They voted that he should, by three million votes against two thousand nine hundred. On December 2, 1804, Napoleon crowned himself Emperor of the French, in the presence of Pope Pius vii. So new titles came into being.

The Treaty of Lunéville in 1801 carried the French frontier to the left bank of the Rhine. Various princes were thus disposed of. It was agreed that they should have compensation elsewhere. The Imperial Diet of the Holy Roman Empire met at Ratisbon to settle the matter. France dictated in the business, and France worked against Austria. One hundred and twelve states were suppressed. Prussia was the chief gainer—she acquired three bishoprics. The political structure of Germany was much simplified from the form in which the Treaty of Westphalia had left it in 1658.

In 1805 a new coalition was formed between Britain, Russia and Austria. Prussia selfishly insisted on remaining neutral. On December 2, 1805, Russians and Austrians were utterly defeated at Austerlitz. Napoleon occupied Vienna. In the peace that followed Prussia gave up Cleves and Anspach, but gained the great possession of Hanover. Napoleon forced the newly created kings of Bavaria and Würtemberg, with thirteen other princes, to form a federation accepting the French Emperor, binding themselves

to support him with their armies, and to separate themselves from all other Germanic bodies.   Later other kingdoms, Saxony and Westphalia, were added, and the Confederation included the region between the Rhine and the
Elbe, and held its Diet at Frankfort.   Then Napoleon
summoned Francis II. to lay down the title of Holy Roman
Emperor.   Francis yielded.   On August 6, 1806, the
abdication was made, and on that day the Holy Roman
Empire ceased to exist.   Francis II. remained Emperor
Francis I. of Austria.   German independence was for the
moment quite under the heel of the little Emperor of the
French.   But Prussia was as yet intact, though Britain
had declared war on her, demanding Hanover, which belonged to the English Crown.

Prussia had not fought with France since 1795.   She
had been handled very carefully by French diplomacy.
Now, however, her turn came.   Her armies were dissatis-
fied, remembering the glories of Frederick the Great, and
counting their neutrality a dishonour.   And although
Prussia had gained Hanover as the price of her peace,
Napoleon was secretly offering this state to Britain
again.

Frederick William therefore declared war on France,
on October 1, 1806.   Within a fortnight, Napoleon was
upon him.   On October 10, the Prussians lost the battle
of Saalfeld, on October 14 they were disastrously
defeated at Jena.   The Prussian fortresses were occupied.
On October 24 Napoleon was at Potsdam.   Two days
after he visited the tomb of Frederick the Great, took
possession of the sword and the Order of the Black Eagle
which had belonged to the heroic king, and sent them as
trophies to Paris.   He remained in Berlin for a month,
and issued against Britain the famous Berlin Decrees on
November 26.

This six weeks' conquest of Prussia staggered Europe.
Napoleon seemed a miracle.   Prussia had collapsed like
a house of cards.   Only in the north-east the King kept

up a fierce resistance, relying on the Russians. But in June 1807 the Prussian and Russian armies were murderously broken by Napoleon at Friedland. Prussia and Russia then accepted the Peace of Tilsit, which marked the summit of Napoleon's career. At this moment he seemed superhuman, almost a god. The Czar Alexander made an alliance with him against Britain. Russia lost nothing, but Prussia was heavily crushed. Large Prussian territories were taken away, and given to the King of Saxony. Napoleon made his brother, Jerome Bonaparte, King of Westphalia. Prussia was compelled to join in the blockade of Britain, to admit French garrisons in all her fortresses, to pay a huge indemnity, and to reduce her army to a very small standing. The kingdom was almost wiped out.

After the Peace of Tilsit, however, Napoleon's fortune declined. He was not successful in his naval conflict with Britain, nor in his Peninsular War, and then he made his utterly disastrous invasion of Russia.

Meanwhile there was a new brave spirit roused in Prussia. Germany was under the heel of Napoleon. Now, with great heroism Prussia began to set her government in order, reorganise her armies, and in a new spirit to prepare for better days. Under the minister Stein serfdom was abolished, the peasants were given a direct interest in the State, whilst conscription, which was already applied to the peasants, was applied just the same to the upper classes. This patient working for improvement and strength, even whilst the French troops were in their garrisons, shows the deep courage of the Prussians.

As the French army, after the catastrophe of the advance to Moscow, began the retreat into Germany, the Prussian armies began to join the Russians. In January 1813 the Prussian king left Berlin for Breslau, and issued the appeal for liberty. The whole German nation rose. English money supplied them with food and clothing, otherwise they could not have stirred. But again Napoleon, gathering a huge army, defeated the Germans at Lützen and occupied Dresden. Crossing the Elbe, he once more defeated Blücher and the Prussians, and then he made an armistice with them.

All the while Britain spent her money freely in helping Prussia and Russia, and in keeping them in the Coalition, into which she persuaded Austria to enter. When, in a few weeks, the armistice ended, Napoleon found himself in Dresden confronted by a world in arms. He won the last great battle of Dresden, driving back the Russians and Prussians after two days' fighting. This was in August 1813.

The end was near. Instead of pursuing the enemy into Bohemia, Napoleon had set his mind on marching to Berlin. It was a mistake. The allies gathered their forces. They were 300,000 men against Napoleon's 180,000 when the two armies met in October. The Battle of Leipsic, or the Battle of the Nations, as it was called, was really a week's campaign, and it resulted in the complete overthrow of the French. Napoleon retired sullenly towards Paris. The allied armies pressed after him. Napoleon was forced to surrender. He abdicated in 1814, and retired to Elba.

The Battle of Leipsic completely destroyed Napoleon's work in Germany. The great Confederation of the Rhine, made of German princes bound to support Napoleon, was dissolved. The princes recovered their territories, the fortresses of the Elbe were regained. Blücher, the Prussian general, marching with the allied armies after Napoleon into France, won victories that led to the sur-render of the Emperor of the French.

After the Hundred Days, Wellington with Blücher's assistance finally defeated the French at Waterloo, and Europe saw the last of Napoleon. Europe now wanted peace. When the allied statesmen met at the Congress of Vienna, they had the whole of Europe to settle. One of the most difficult problems was Germany. France went back to her frontiers of 1792. The old, decrepit Holy Roman Empire was not restored. Thirty-nine sovereign princes and free cities were recognised in Germany—the three hundred and fifty of the Peace of Westphalia thus reduced to about a tenth of the number. These thirty-nine states were joined into a perpetual 'German Confederation,' of which the president was Austria, whilst Prussia was by far the most powerful, and next to Prussia, Bavaria, which was Catholic, and had long been a favoured ally of Napoleon.

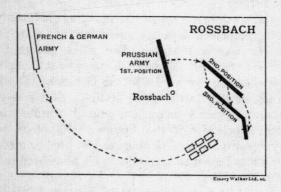

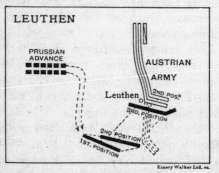

'Frederick, a master of campaign and of battle attack'

See p. 258

XVIII. Italy

AFTER the Renaissance, when the great towns fell from their splendour and independence and came again largely under foreign rule, Italy dropped behind the progress movement of the North. Armies came and went, dukes and emperors appeared and disappeared, kings passed by, German, French, Spanish tongues sounded in authority through the land. And under all this the Italians remained provincial and local, ignorant, apart from the changing world. Catholic in spirit, attached by warm blood-passion to their native place, they kept to that which was sure, the fellowship of their own townsmen, the abiding rock of the Catholic Church. In the towns they governed their own affairs under alien masters, they felt safe and sure in their own piazza, the open square where the church stood, where the priest passed and gave a sense of permanency, where nobles rode gaily through. Their own affairs, their own passions, these alone interested them. And the peasant in the country woke to the clanging of bells : at noon the bells rang sharp across the field to bid him rest awhile and eat : he waited for the bells to call him home at dusk. The church gave him the day and marked it out for him : the priest gave him peace after confession ; and a little wine, a little excited talk with his neighbours, with singing and merrymaking at the church feasts, filled his life well enough. Why should he bother about what was beyond ? He clung sensitively to his own place, his own village fellows, his own priest, the sound of the sacred, sudden bells from the campanile.

So the years passed, while the North, England, Germany, France were struggling with kings and parliaments and commerce. The Italians let those rule who must rule, those think and struggle who must. For their part, they had enough with their own private troubles and passions and intrigues. Out of the bitter Beyond came armies of Germans, French, Spaniards, and into the bitter Beyond they disappeared again. Or else they did not disappear, but remained like a necessary evil.

In the eighteenth century Spanish power practically came to an end in Italy. Austrian possession was confined to the North. The various states of the peninsula were fairly prosperous, poorest in the South ; and on the whole, the people were as free as elsewhere in Europe, save Britain. Those in one state did not bother about those in another state. The subjects of the Pope felt they had no more connection with the subjects of Piedmont in Turin than with the subjects of France in Paris. There was no Italy—only a bunch of states with their peoples and their petty princes or their great princes, the luxurious, refined, profligate courts, the indifferent rule. Feudal conditions still existed, almost mediæval serfdom, and in parts the peasants were bitterly poor. But men were men, and on the whole, rich and poor alike, they were perhaps more human in Italy than in the progressive countries.

Into all this Napoleon Bonaparte burst roughly, in his campaigns of 1796 and 1801. He defeated Austria, he brought the peninsula to his feet, and let in a blast of fresh air from the North which startled the soft Italians. He made Italy a kingdom of his own, took all the power from princes and Pope, set Murat, his general, on the throne of Bourbon Naples, and established a French republican government. Feudalism was abolished, and men were made free to rise in the world, instead of being

tied down to one condition. The land system was
revolutionised, the peasants given their share. Monasteries were suppressed to help to pay the great national
debt. Primary schools were established all over Lombardy and Naples, and priests were put into the background.

So, quite suddenly, Italy came into the grasp of the
modern world. And quite quickly, men began to appre-
ciate the change. They breathed a new air, they felt
more alive, new doors seemed opened. Italian soldiers
brought back a proud name for bravery from Napoleon's
great victories. And Napoleon, who hated Austria and
the Pope, encouraged Italians in all parts to be Italian,
not to think of themselves as Papal or Austrian or
Neapolitan subjects. New ideas spread : ideas of equality
and liberty and free thought. The old monotony was
gone, the old submissiveness interrupted. Doctors,
lawyers, middle-class citizens were given a share in state
government. The power of princes was shaken for ever,
and the ten states into which the peninsula had been
divided suddenly had disappeared. Italy was all suddenly united.

But it was too sudden. There were new grievances.
More than 60,000 Italians fell in Spain and Russia, conscripted by Napoleon for a quarrel that was none of theirs.
Taxation became very heavy. Napoleon insulted the
Pope and angered Italian instincts. After the Russian
campaign French rule became hateful in the peninsula,
particularly in the dark-minded South.

Waterloo made an end of Napoleon's Italy. Down in
the South, the brave Murat was chased away, and finally
killed. With British help, the ignominious Bourbons returned to the kingdom of the Two Sicilies, as Naples
with South Italy and Sicily was called. At the dividing
up of Europe, the Pope added to his papal states the
Romagna and the Marches, the large and valuable province
along the Adriatic, whose towns are Bologna, Ravenna,

Ancona ;   Austria recovered Lombardy, and was given
Venice and the Venetian territory, which before had been
a republic ; in the North, the one strong Italian power
of Piedmont, ruled by the House of Savoy, called Kings
of Sardinia, held its own against Austria and added to
itself the Riviera territory and Genoa, so that the Genoese
republic disappeared, like the Venetian ; Austrian Leopold
returned to the independent Grand-Duchy of Tuscany,
where he ruled, however, with Tuscan ministers ; Duke
Francis, another Austrian prince, ruled in Modena ;
Napoleon's Austrian wife, Maria Louisa, became Duchess
of Parma and ruled kindly enough ; while a princess of
a Spanish house had the little duchy of Lucca.

So there was a great return of princes and rulers back
to their states, whilst republics vanished, after the Congress
of Vienna. In Italy, as in Spain and in Germany, the
people wildly and joyfully welcomed back their old
masters. Even the vile Ferdinand of Naples met with
the same reception as some of the better princes of the
North, and was hailed as if he were a god. Whereas
Murat had been a much finer man.

Safe on their thrones once more, these princes set about
to pull to pieces the work of the hated Bonaparte. The
world must go back, back. But some of Napoleon's
reforms were too obvious to be done away with. Yet the
spirit was killed even when the letter remained. Life
was driven back. And soon Italians were thinking with
wonder and admiration of the great days of Napoleonic
government and Murat's kingdom. Feudal privileges,
monasteries, government by priests, courts of clerical
justice—all the old abuses were restored. Only in Piedmont the people stubbornly but passively resisted the
pushing back of life, and before long certain of the ministers
of Napoleonic days were in office under the King of
Sardinia.

In Lombardy and Venetia the famous Austrian Minister,
Metternich, had promised a rule ' conforming to Italian

character and custom.' Bitter was the chagrin when the people saw Austrian law introduced, conscription enforced, and Austrians and Tyrolese seizing all the higher posts of civil government. The emperor let it be known that he 'wanted not learned men, but loyal subjects.' Austrian soldiers in their white coats were everywhere in the North—Venice, Milan, Verona—brutal and insolent with the populace, despising the Italians as a race.

In Tuscany the Tuscan statesmen held their own, Archduke Leopold was kind and stupid. Florence grudgingly restored some of the monastic possessions, and, following Lombardy, determinedly shut out the sly, retrogressive, intriguing, masterful Jesuits.

Rome and the papal states returned to old clerical rule, depending on spies and police and cunning and cruelty; and the Jesuits, with their determination not to let men escape their clutches, soon had their net over the Romagna, and over brave Bologna and Ravenna, the two fierce cities.

But it was too late to set the tide right back to the old Catholic submissiveness and mindlessness and the feudal rule. The army had become infected with democratic notions, the people were touched by the spirit of liberty, and educated men of the middle classes, longing for their day to come, watched the movements of the British and French Parliaments, of the Greek hetæra, and followed the pamphlets and writings published by leaders of freedom in the foreign countries.

And thus, in the South, the first quick result appeared. In the South the Freemasons had for a long time been a strong secret society, binding men together apart from Church and State. A number of the better-class Freemasons, hating the Bonapartist rule, took to the mountains. There they formed a new society, calling themselves the Carbonari. The Carbonari were a mysterious society, with the same rules, very nearly, and the same ritual as the Freemasons, vowed to purity and a good life like the

Freemason, worshipping the Divine Order in the universe, expressing themselves in profound religious phraseology and occult symbolism, having a Crucifix in every lodge, and calling Jesus the ' first victim of tyrants,' yet amounting in actuality to no more than a political society of republican tendency. What their actual ideas were they kept secret among the higher members of the cult, the initiated. Certainly one of their aims was to have power, unlimited power. But they only taught the rank and file vaguely to worship liberty and resist tyrants.

Great numbers flocked to join the society, and soon anybody was admitted. There was a secrecy, a mystery, a semi-religious, semi-worldly mysticism about it all which fascinated the South. The old dark religious impulse was now grafted on to a political purpose.

And in this way the movement for liberty began in Italy. Now, when so much is accomplished and achieved, we cannot help regretting that ever the deep religious spirit in man tacked itself on to politics. Politics, even liberty from a foreign master, is not a religious affair. Man fights for his liberty as a wolf fights for its liberty, because he wants to go his own way. And politics, at last, works out to nothing more than a mere arranging of the material conditions of life. It is not a religious activity. It is a sort of great commissariat organisation among men : nothing godly. You can't save mankind by politics. Liberty isn't salvation. We must have liberty. But having liberty, we have only got food to eat, clothes to wear, roads to walk on, and language to fill our mouths with. And still we have not even touched the inward satisfaction which the deep spirit demands.

Be that as it may, the liberty movement in Italy started, and ended, as a dual thing : a deep, religious passion, and a clever material scheming. It was both things, and the two things are really contradictory. And so, all the way, we feel a certain dividedness, a breach in our sympathy.

The Carbonari movement, being a secret society,

naturally started in the South. But it spread to the North, where men naturally think and act more openly. The Austrians ruled well enough in Lombardy. Steam-boats and spinning-jennies were being introduced. Milan was to be lighted by gas. Milan was the go-ahead city. The Carbonari were active there. They even started a newspaper of their own. But Austrian governors, smelling powder, snuffed out the flame.

Encouraged by the sudden bloodless revolution in Spain, a revolt broke out all at once in the Neapolitan kingdom in 1820. King Ferdinand was forced to promise a con-stitution, and put Carbonari liberals into power. Then Sicily, which loathed Naples, broke into insurrection, with wild mob atrocities. Europe was scared. Metternich sent an Austrian army southwards. It was met by the new militia and army of the liberals, which was broken. Austrians entered Naples, and Ferdinand sat tighter on his unscrupulous throne.

Three days after the Neapolitan Revolution was de-feated, Piedmont rose. The Piedmontese wanted a con-stitution, and a war with Austria. For they hated the Austrians, ' the white leeches,' as they called the white-coat soldiers. The revolution had effect at first. The King abdicated. A charter was granted. And then it all fizzled out, the old régime seized power again.

In Modena Duke Francis had to crush an incipient revolt. In the ever-stirring Romagna, in the pine forest round Ravenna a brigade of Carbonari called the American Hunters drilled and prepared to rise, while Lord Byron, hand in glove with them at Ravenna, had his house filled with arms in readiness for the rising. It failed to come off, however.

Now the whole country lay prostrate under its tyrants. Metternich indeed tried to prevent persecution and the exasperation of Italy. But Emperor Francis played with his victims cruelly, and we have only to read Silvio Pellico's *My Prisons* to know what the leaders suffered.

Francis of Modena wreaked a savage vengeance. Ferdinand of Naples evaded Metternich's order against persecution, public whippings shocked Naples, liberals were proscribed and fled to the hills, armed bands wandered about, assassinations and reprisals took place. Ferdinand was a superstitious brute, and when he died in 1825 men hated the Bourbon name.

Exiles from Italy were scattered throughout England, France, and Spain. Santa Rosa, one of the heroes, taught languages in Nottingham. Piedmont pursued her liberals with as much vigour as did Austria or Naples.

So, in 1821, the Italian question began to trouble Europe, and the Carbonari made their first great failure. After this, repression was the order in all Italian states. Men were not to think. Above all, they were not to read seditious literature. The censorship on speech and books was more than severe.

Naples had its martyrs and its saints of liberty, men of high birth and understanding who rotted in horrible prisons, yet who would utter no word against their oppressors : pure spirit of love, that is all love, and chooses never to fight. In the South exists the old oriental spirit, all the old abandon to an impulse. The North is more qualified. If the first strange spirit of abandon came from the South, all the fight came from the North.

Piedmont was the one true Italian state, politically. Not that it was Italian by race. The nobles prided themselves on their old Provençal blood, the races at the foot of the Alps claimed to be old Celts, and there was considerable German infusion. The language was not Italian even. But Piedmont had a spirit of independence which finally gathered Italy together.

The Counts of Savoy, lords of a few Burgundian fiefs, had for centuries been wedged in between the power of France and Austria. Fighters, and masters of a mountain people, they had sold their help first to one side then to another, usually coming out with the winners. And so,

bit by bit, they added to their territories, first on one
side, then on the other. Wary and sly, they were always
good at a bargain. And thus they became Kings of
Sardinia, and ruled after Waterloo from Nice to Lake
Maggiore, and southwards to the Apennines. Turin was
the capital, a dull, unintellectual, provincial sort of town,
with a people who spoke a half-comprehensible dialect,
who despised books or art, scorned the Italians to the
South, were cunning at getting their own advantage, and
looked upon the King as a sort of military father. In
some respects, Piedmont resembled Prussia. Trade and
commerce were encouraged after 1821, silk and wine and
oil flourished, Genoa was a busy port. Piedmont knew
how to look after himself.

The people, as in Prussia, were cowed and docile under
their Savoy masters. But, subalpine, they were kept
trained as soldiers, in all the manly fighting virtues so
uncommon in Italy. The hate of Austria in Lombardy,
and the uneasy fear of France in their rear alone made
them Italian by policy.

But in Piedmont were born the four great heroes of
the Risorgimento, as the uprising of Italy is called. In
1805 was born in Genoa a certain Giuseppe Mazzini, a
doctor's son. Two years later, not far away along the
coast, at Nice, was born another Giuseppe, Giuseppe
Garibaldi, son of a small sea captain. Mazzini, a thoughtful, quiet, solitary nature, played among the narrow alleys
of the port of Genoa. Garibaldi, a robust fellow, led his
companions in exploits by the sea.

Both grew up Piedmontese subjects. Mazzini read and
brooded and thought, yearning over Italy, and hard
against autocrats. He saw the failure of Carbonari
revolutions, and his more northern soul resolved itself.
His writings, full of passion on behalf of the oppressed,
had a hard hostility to tyranny which the South could
never show. He was determined that the meek should
inherit the earth—in Italy at least—and he had all the

indomitable persistence of the meek. His words and his spirit flew through the peninsula, as the Carbonari spirit had flown. But Mazzini's was no secret doctrine. Mystery and secret power, dear to southern hearts, were left out. All was plain and open and ideal, purely ideal. Once more politics and liberty became a religion, a self-sacrificing religion of abstract ideals.

Round Mazzini's writings gradually gathered the Young Italy party, vowed to unite Italy into one free republic. The second important Carbonari risings took place in Central Italy in 1831. Young Louis Napoleon, nephew of the great Napoleon, having joined the Carbonari, breathed fire against the Pope in Rome. At the same time Mazzini published his *Young Italy Manifesto*. A real Italy was to be founded on independence, unity, and liberty. Austria must go, autocrats must be deposed, the various small states must be united in one, under a democratic government. Here was a definite programme, no Carbonarist vagueness any more. It seemed like an absurd dream at the time, none the less.

The risings had a brief success, then failed. Rigorous repression followed, for there had been a scare. The brave Menotti was hanged. Mazzini found himself in prison, and then exiled from Piedmont. He took himself to Marseilles, busily continuing his work, issuing pamphlets and addresses which were secretly circulated, at the peril of those who touched them.

Meanwhile Garibaldi, a young sea captain, carrying on his life rather aimlessly, met in the Black Sea in 1833 a certain Cuneo, a patriot. Cuneo told Garibaldi all about Young Italy, and a light seemed to enter the young captain's soul. ' Columbus,' he said, ' was not as happy at discovering America as I was when I found a man actually engaged in the redemption of our country.' Garibaldi's passion was now fixed. The new pseudo-religion had fired his soul. Returning home, he went to Mazzini at Marseilles, and joined the Young Italy Society, under the brotherhood name of Borel. The two young men enhanced the enthusiasm in each other.

Piedmont was harshly anti-liberal at this time, so the Young Italy workers turned their activity against their oppressor. Conspiracies in 1833 were followed by torture and executions. Garibaldi and Mazzini tried to raise an insurrection : failed, and fled. On reaching Marseilles, Garibaldi saw his name for the first time in print—in the newspaper, announcing that the Piedmont Government at Turin had condemned him to death.

For a time Garibaldi went to South America, lived a free life on the pampas, fought for the republics and became famous as a guerrilla chief out there. Mazzini kept his fame alive in Italy, and the national feeling fanned gradually up.

The year 1848 was the meteor year of revolution on the continent of Europe. As before, the fire appeared first in the South—in Sicily. It spread up the mainland. Ferdinand ii. of Naples was forced to grant a constitution. On January 27 he rode through the streets of his capital swearing fidelity to the statute, and being hailed as the darling of the people. On February 8 Charles Albert of Piedmont promised a charter. On February 11 the Grand Duke of Tuscany granted a constitution. The Pope granted a charter to Rome.

In the North the flame flew fiercer. Bohemia and Hungary under Kossuth rose against Austria, demanding independence. The Viennese were even turning upon their adored Hapsburgs. Berlin was barricaded, the Prussian king was yielding.

The French Revolution of 1848 changed the face of European diplomacy. Again France was a republic, the Bourbon power expelled for ever. Again the Napoleonic tradition revived the terror of Europe.

Italy was trembling with rage against her tyrants, Piedmont expelled the Jesuits, the Fathers fled for the time from Naples, the Roman crowd demanded the

expulsion of the order from their city. In vain the
Jesuits hoisted the red-white-and-green tricolour which the
Young Italy had chosen as the flag of Italy United. In
vain the Pope tried to protect these creatures and their
agents. The College of Jesuits had to be closed.

On March 17 the news of the Hungarian revolt and the
Insurrection of Vienna reached Milan, where the Austrians
with their white-coat soldiers swaggered in the Lombard
capital. All at once arose a tremendous insurrection of
almost unarmed citizens. The veteran old tyrant, General
Radetzky, had 20,000 Austrian and Hungarian troops
with him in the city. But such was the passion and
determination of the citizens, that after five days of the
most intense and awful struggle in streets and squares,
Radetzky was forced to evacuate the vast castle, and
retreat from the victorious city. The young hero, Manara,
remained leader of a dazed populace.

The news of the famous Five Days of Milan thrilled
every Italian nerve. Venice rang the tocsin from St.
Mark's, hoisted the red-white-and-green tricolour from the
two immense flag-poles in front of the cathedral, and cut
the cords so that the Austrians could not get the colours
down. Venetian citizens too were beyond themselves.
In an almost inspired hour Manin got rid of the Austrians,
garrison and all, out of Venice. There was a rising everywhere against the hated white-coats, till at last nothing
Austrian remained in Italy but the Quadrilateral, and
Radetzky slowly dragging his way there over the Lombard
roads, with his army.

The feeling against Austria was intense. Austrian rule
in Lombardy-Venetia was probably the best in Italy, the
most free, the most prosperous. But it was foreign, and
it was powerful, and men were beginning to feel they
would die rather than live under foreign domination. And,
moreover, the Austrian white-coats had all the northern
and Hungarian Magyar insolence, all the northern contempt for the southern Italian race.

Charles Albert of Piedmont now declared war on Austria, wrapped himself in the tricolour and offered his help, in the name of God and the Pope, to the peoples of Lombardy and Venetia. But when kings fight against emperors in the name of the people, crowns are bound to tumble. So Charles Albert went very half-heartedly. He was not at all fond of that red-white-and-green tricolour. He knew the Young Italy wanted a republic. They might use him, Charles Albert, King of Sardinia, military lord of Piedmont, as a leader, and then drag his throne from underneath him when he was going to sit down again. Emperors are not such enemies to a king as republican peoples are. So he went half-heartedly, whilst Radetzky had time to reach the famous Quadrilateral, the four massive forts of Verona, Mantua, Peschiera, and Legnano that guard the entrance of the ancient imperial road where it debouches from the Brenner Pass on to the Italian plain. The Quadrilateral formed the four great Austrian gateposts in Italy.

Meanwhile volunteers flocked from Naples, Tuscany, Modena to the Piedmontese standard. The white cross of Savoy waved beside the tricolour. Now it waves in the centre of the tricolour.

Garibaldi arrived from Monte Video and offered his sword to Charles Albert, and was refused. He took service with the provisional government of Milan.

Meanwhile news flew in from outside. The French Republic stood firm. The hated Metternich had fallen. Viennese students were driving the Imperial Court from Vienna (May 17). Hungary and Bohemia had won a short-lived triumph ; the German National Assembly was meeting on May 18. Never had the cause of liberty looked so flourishing in Europe. Yet the unhappy Charles Albert hesitated and floundered, could not gather his resolution.

So Radetzky marched out against him from Verona and defeated the Italian army cruelly at Custozza on

July 25. Blunders of king and generals lost the battle, notwithstanding the magnificent courage of the troops. The royal forces were driven back into Milan. The frantic people, beside themselves, besieged the unhappy Charles Albert in the Greppi Palace. ' Ah, what a day, what a day ! ' he said, wringing his hands. On August 5 he was forced to yield Milan back to the Austrians, for there was no food. He agreed to an armistice.

So Austria recovered all in Lombardy, and prepared to besiege Manin in Venice. Men were beside themselves with anger against Charles Albert. He had saved his crown and betrayed the people, they said. Mazzini and Garibaldi hoisted a republican banner, ' Dio e Popolo,' ' God and the People.'

And thus the defeated Italians hated Austria all the more.

The next events took place in Rome, in this wild year of '48. Garibaldi had moved into the Romagna to gather to himself the fierce spirits that still held out as Carbonarists against the spying priests and the Pope's vicious, secret, police-cruel rule. Bologna and Ravenna were centres of revolt then as they are centres of rebellious Socialism now. So from the Romagnese Garibaldi formed his first legion to fight for free Italy.

Whilst in the Romagna he heard the startling news that Rossi, the Pope's minister, was murdered by the democrat agents in Rome. The people of Rome were enraged because the Pope had refused to have any fighting against Austria, had even issued his censure against Catholics who took part in the struggle. Roused by liberal street orators, inflamed after the murder of Rossi, the angry Romans marched to demonstrate against their Sacred Master before his palace of the Quirinal on November 16, firing on his Swiss guard, and behaving very much as the crowd had behaved outside the Tuileries on June 2, 1792. But Pope Pio Nono, Pius ix., did not stand it out as Louis xvi. had done. On November 24 he fled, dis-

guised as a simple monk, across the Neapolitan border
to his friend King Ferdinand, called *Bomba*, because he
had bombarded his own subjects in Messina.

When the Romans learned that their Pope had gone
they felt as if the sun had fallen out of heaven. They
were all uneasy, and did not know what to do. Republican
feeling gradually became stronger, and in February 1849
the Roman Republic was proclaimed. Mazzini arrived
in March, and was received rather timidly as Rome's last
and greatest citizen.

Meanwhile in the North Charles Albert, a haunted man,
in bitterness ' eating Austria in his bread ' broke off the
armistice, marched over the Lombard border, and was
defeated by Radetzky on March 23 at Novara. Heart-
broken, having in vain sought death in the battle, he
abdicated, rode away in disguise, and died in a few
months' time in a Portuguese convent. Victor Emmanuel,
his son, came to the throne, and confirmed the liberal
charter.

Hearing of Novara, the Roman Republic immediately
formed a Triumvirate or Rule of Three Men—Mazzini,
Saffi, Armellini. Mazzini had much the same powers that
Napoleon had when First Consul. But Mazzini tried to
rule Rome according to the ideal of abstract righteousness,
in purity, forgiveness, gentleness, and complete liberty.
That was his will. Such a rule was successful enough in
many ways, the city was quiet and good. But it is no
use turning the other cheek when men come with cannon.
Rome, the Roman Republic, must fight for its existence.
And there was no money, no military equipment, no
powerful authority.

Garibaldi, with his wild-looking legion, had ridden into
Rome, received with suspicion at first, afterwards with
enthusiasm. Those were wonderful days in Rome, when
men were inspired to be good, freed from real authority,
exalted by the unchangeable idealist simplicity of the
first citizen, Mazzini. Picturesque troops bivouacked in

the convent yards and the squares, everybody talked in excitement.

But it could not continue. Interference was bound to come. It came from the new French Republic. The French had chosen the young Louis Napoleon for their president. And though Louis Napoleon had been an old Carbonaro, he now depended on the strong Catholic party in France to keep him in his conspicuous position. Also he was posing as the saviour of Europe against Socialism. Hence he must rescue the Holy Father, and nip the Roman Republic in the bud. Troops were dispatched under General Oudinot.

Garibaldi was recalled into Rome from keeping his eye on the Pope. In his red shirt he was seen galloping through the city streets, preparing defences. The citizens digged and slaved at the entrenchments, fearless and full of inspiration for the moment. The French were driven off from the first attack on the city, with shame, and Louis Napoleon had a blot to wipe off the French military honour.

More forces were sent from France. Rome, isolated, fell. On July 2 Garibaldi marched out at night, slipped past the French, and escaped into the mountains. Finally he escaped to Piedmont, was moved on, and at last went to America, where he worked as a journeyman candle-maker, then as a sea captain, then a farmer. Mazzini wandered about the streets of Rome for a few days, and the French dared not touch him, for fear of the people. Then he, too, fled, made his way to England, his home by choice. ' Italy is my country, but England is my home, if I have any,' he said. He worked and waited, sending out his threads of conspiracy from London.

The Pope came back, all the old secrecy and spying, police terror, prisons, and galleys. The papal govern-ment was as ruinous to land and people as it well could be.

Meanwhile a new phase was starting. Victor Emmanuel, a plucky little king, was on the throne in Turin. Count

Cavour, his minister, was as clever a statesman as Europe has seen. Profoundly intelligent politically, a man of understanding and of liberal tendency, of great subtlety and of slippery obstinacy, Cavour was determined to have his own way, to make an united Italy by uniting all under the House of Savoy. It was his great scheme, and he carried it out. On the one side we have the political-religious passion of the idealists like Mazzini and Garibaldi, on the other the vigorous, scheming determination to make a big united power out of a small, divided power, the determination which filled the breasts of Victor Emmanuel and of Cavour. Piedmont should become Italy.

Europe at that time was wobbling about in the nervous balance of power. Britain was rather afraid of France : France was jealous of Austria, and was keeping her eye on Prussia : Prussia was looking askance first at Russia, then at Austria, then at France. Everybody was wanting to keep his own end up, and afraid lest anybody else should get his end up too high. So it was a game of beggar-my-neighbour. Piedmont, sharp as usual, made a great win in the South, Prussia in the North. Little Piedmont stroked and soothed the mane of the variable Louis Napoleon, become Napoleon III., Lion of Europe for the moment. Little Piedmont had a big bone to pick with Austria. Cavour looked imploringly to Britain, whose mighty navy patrolled the seas, to throw the shadow of her liberal wing over him.

Now Cavour wanted a war with Austria, and he wanted Napoleon III. to help him, for he was not half strong enough alone. But the big powers did not want war : they were afraid of that shaky balance of power. So it was a great day for Cavour when he had cajoled Napoleon into friendship and taunted unwary Austria into an attack on Piedmont in April 1859. Napoleon marched over the Alps, joined the Piedmontese, won the battle of Magenta in Lombardy, and after this, with Victor

Emmanuel, the bigger battle of Solferino : where the dear emperor wept, seeing the carnage. Now Napoleon felt he had done enough. Half a loaf must be better than no bread for Piedmont. He made peace with the Austrians —who had evacuated Milan and Lombardy—and retired into the Quadrilateral.

During the struggle the smaller states of Italy seized their opportunity. Austrian armies once withdrawn from their cities and borders, Tuscany, Romagna, and Modena suddenly declared themselves free Italian republics, and drove out their rulers. But then came the news of Napoleon's Peace Treaty at Villafranca. Piedmont was to have Lombardy, but Austria was to keep her hold on Venetia, and the old rulers were to go back into the other states. Cavour cried with rage and disappointment, threw up his post and went to sulk in Geneva, when he heard the news. But Victor Emmanuel had nothing to do but sign. Piedmont was only the mountain cat between the two lions.

At this moment came Britain's turn. ' The policy of Her Majesty's Government,' declared Lord John Russell, ' is not to interfere at all, but to let the Italian people settle their own affairs.' Which was as good as saying that the policy of Her Majesty's Government was to oppose any one else's interfering in the affairs of the Italian people. Italian people meant, not Piedmont, but the new republics. And so the old rulers did *not* come back. Tuscany, Modena, and the Romagna united as the free Italian States of Central Italy, soon asking to be united with Piedmont, for safety's sake, since Piedmont was the fighting power and Austria kept Venetia. But Piedmont was not so badly off after all.

The eyes of Europe were also on Naples. Mr. Gladstone had been in the southern city in 1850, for his daughter's health. He had seen the horrors of King Bomba's vile rule, his injustice, and his ghastly prisons for political offenders. All these horrors Mr. Gladstone told to the world in his *Letters to Lord Aberdeen*, in 1851. Naples became the disgraced state in the eyes of Europe, the pariah among the kingdoms.

In January 1860 Cavour came back into office in Turin. Tuscany, Modena, and the Romagna were annexed to Turin, and Savoy, with Nice and the strip of the present French Riviera, was ceded to Napoleon. Piedmont gave an acre and got a mile. But Britain was displeased at France's increase, and Garibaldi enraged at the loss of his home-place, Nice. Victor Emmanuel had forfeited his ancestral territory of Savoy. But it was a sprat compared to the mackerel he was catching.

What was the next step? There remained Venice, the Pope, and Naples—or the Kingdom of the Two Sicilies, to be exact. Venice was too far off for the moment, a second attack on Austria not possible. Quite impossible also to attack the Holy Father in the papal states, because he was still under Napoleon's wing, and the French troops were guarding him safely. What about the Bourbon in Naples?

Cavour dared not send an army to the South, because Napoleon would not have it, Austria would not have it, the Pope would not have it, and Britain would not quite consent. It would look too much like grabbing. Only, if the Southerners would rise in revolt, then the *Italian people* would be deciding their own affairs, according to Lord John, and Piedmont could help them in the decision. At least she could send *volunteers*, who would count as Italian people. Piedmont as a state dared not interfere.

Cavour worked and worked for a Neapolitan revolution: without result. But there was trouble in Sicily. The Sicilians invited Garibaldi: Cavour dared not send Garibaldi openly. He let the lion-faced general know that whatever was done, Piedmont could not have any part in it—for fear of offending the other powers. None the less Garibaldi gathered his famous Thousand from the northern cities, took two steamers from Genoa port, and sailed for Sicily. The troops embarked on the night of May 5, 1860. Cavour knew. But he kept his public eye shut, and pretended he did not know at all.

This was Italy's great year. And perhaps the wonderful adventure of Garibaldi and the Thousand in Sicily is the most moving event of the year. With a thousand untrained volunteers armed with wretched old muskets, and dressed in the civilian clothes in which they had left their offices, their studios, their work-benches, the general captured a great island and expelled a great army of regular troops, complete with arms and ammunition. On the morning of June 7, 1860, the British admiral and his captains watched from their ships two long columns of red-and-blue Neapolitan soldiers file along the esplanade of Palermo, past the ragged red-shirted officers of the remnant of the ragged Thousand; twenty thousand regulars with all their equipment capitulating and evacuating the capital, leaving the island in the hands of the few hundred worn men of Garibaldi. In amusement and contempt the British watched this spectacle from the bay. Bomba had said of his soldiers, ' You may drill them as you like, they will run away just the same.'

And it seemed like it. Yet the troops were not really such cowards. There was room rather for wonder than contempt. Whom the gods wish to destroy they first make mad, said the Romans. And so it was with the Neapolitans—they acted as if they were mad. But in truth they were sensitive Southerners. Somewhere in their souls they felt that life was against them, their position was hopeless, obsolete. Bewildered, therefore, they were huddled about in masses like sheep, their will and their integrity gone.

Europe was amazed, shocked, and delighted as may be, when the news of the fall of Palermo ran through the world. *Now* Cavour was free to act. Now the *Italian people* of Lord John's declaration had started their own

affair in the South, and Piedmont could come in.   Cavour
sent 20,000 volunteers to Garibaldi.

Followed the next great adventure, Garibaldi crossing
the Straits of Messina, dodging the enemy's fleet, defeating
one army after another as by magic, driving the huddled
thousands northwards to Naples.   On the night of September 6 the young King Francis of Naples, son of Bomba,
and his Queen fled by ship from their capital to Gaeta.
Their admiral signalled to his fleet to follow.   The fleet
did not move, but remained lying in Naples bay.   When
next day Garibaldi arrived, and the city received him with
frenzy of joy, the Neapolitan fleet came over to him and
the Italian cause.   Garibaldi handed the fleet to Victor
Emmanuel, to the command of the Piedmontese Admiral
Persano.

Cavour was delighted but uneasy.   Garibaldi was too
wonderful, too successful, too much beloved.   He might
want after all to establish himself as Dictator of a new
Italy, work into the hands of the republican Mazzinians.
This would not suit Cavour and Victor Emmanuel at all.

Meanwhile Garibaldi was in a fever to march on Rome,
the capital, the heart of Italy.   But the Neapolitan troops
would not desert to his side.   They retired northwards
towards their king, and blocked the way effectively at
Capua, at the river Volturno.   The great Vauban had
fortified Capua.   The royal soldiers were determined.
They had their king amongst them, and would stand by
him.   Garibaldi and his red-shirts and his volunteers
from the North could do nothing but face the enemy.   It
was a deadlock.   Out of her half million inhabitants
Naples sent eighty to help Garibaldi.   His dream of a
united Italian people, inspired with one free spirit, was
broken for ever.   The South could never be as the North.

All this was lucky for Cavour.   The Pope was the one
enemy left, and fortunately Garibaldi could not get at
him.   Whom the gods wish to destroy they first make
mad.   It was the Pope's turn.   And so Pio Nono pro-

ceeded in pure madness to offend and insult Napoleon III.
and to cast slights on the French honour. Napoleon was
the one protector of the Papacy, and Pius IX. insisted on
regarding him as a wolf and kingdom-breaker, a vile
Bonapartist. So that when Cavour cajoled Napoleon to
allow an invasion of the papal states, Napoleon consented,
so long as Rome itself was not attacked. ' And be quick,'
said the Emperor of the French.

Cavour was quick. He had Austria to fear. And
Austria had to fear Cavour's plots with Kossuth and the
Hungarians. Flying in the face of all the powers except
Britain, Cavour marched the Piedmontese troops across
the Papal frontier on September 11. They were to take
Ancona, the port on the Adriatic at which Austria usually
entered Central Italy.

On September 16 the Piedmontese met the Pope's army
of Crusaders—Italian, French, Austrian, Swiss, Belgian,
Irish—at Castelfidardo, near Loreto. The papal forces
were scattered. Ten days later the Piedmontese captured
Ancona. Austria could not move. The Pope was confined to Rome and his small province around Rome.

Meanwhile Garibaldi was fixed in the South before
Capua, craving to get to Rome. On October 1 the
Neapolitan Royalist troops marched out against him, over
the Volturno. After twelve hours of tremendous fighting,
Garibaldi beat back the enemy. They retired into Capua,
and the position was unchanged. The Bourbon army still
held up Garibaldi.

Cavour must now be quick. Italy was in his grasp.
The white cross of Savoy was to stand in the centre of
the tricolour. He persuaded Garibaldi, for the sake of
Italy, to invite Victor Emmanuel and the troops of Ancona
to join him in Naples. It meant yielding all to the King;
but the Italian people wanted it. They wanted a king.
' Victor Emmanuel should be our Garibaldi,' they began
to say.

A plebiscite was taken in Naples and Sicily. Should

Naples and Sicily be annexed to Piedmont, or not ? The result was, on the mainland 1,302,064 votes for, 10,312 against annexation : Sicily, 432,053 for, 667 against. That was an end of Dictators or Mazzini republics : even of Garibaldi.

On October 26 Garibaldi advanced to meet the King, across the Volturno. Victor Emmanuel was a little, strutting man with huge moustaches. Garibaldi had a lion face—stupid, Mazzini called it—and a blond beard, his head bound in a silk kerchief, southern fashion, under his hat. He wore his red shirt.

' I greet the first King of Italy,' he cried, saluting Victor Emmanuel, and hinting that he not only greeted but *created* the first King of Italy.

' How are you, dear Garibaldi ? '

' Well, your Majesty. And you ? '

' First class.'

The two shook hands. But they no longer loved each other.

The King treated the Garibaldini shabbily enough, though he was ready to give money and such stuff, which they did not want. ' I am squeezed like an orange and thrown into a corner,' said Garibaldi. The King said he did not want the Garibaldi volunteers in the army ; they were to be disbanded.

So, in pouring rain, Garibaldi and Victor Emmanuel rode into Naples side by side, both in bad tempers. They got on each other's nerves, but the loudest cheering was for Garibaldi, which annoyed Victor Emmanuel.

Next day, rather wistful, Garibaldi left for his little island farm on Caprera, a poor man, choosing to be poor. The King and his party were not sorry he was gone. After all, such a man was a threat to their class privileges, by his very existence, and a thorn in the flesh of royal importance.

Francis of Naples was besieged in Gaeta, and yielded at last on February 13, 1861, to the Piedmontese. The

Citadel of Messina capitulated in March, and Bourbon power was extinct.

Italy was now united, she entered the ranks of the great states of Europe, under her king, Victor Emmanuel. Probably it was best : certainly it was safest so. An Italian republic would hardly have held together, and would certainly never have been safe from the lions of the day.

Cavour died in 1861, a great loss to the young kingdom. His last cry was for a free Church in a free State. His last words : ' Italy is made, all is safe.'

But the Pope was in Rome, a serpent in the heart of the kingdom. Francis of Naples was with him, encouraging brigandage in the South. Austria still held Venetia and the Trentino. It was no rosy task, ruling Italy.

The great craving was to take Rome, without incurring war with the great Catholic powers, particularly France. In 1862 Garibaldi and his volunteers landed again in the extreme South, to march on the Eternal City. But the King's government forbade it. Victor Emmanuel's troops met the Garibaldians on Aspromonte, down in the toe of Italy, and fired on the men. Garibaldi was wounded in the foot. But he had set his face against civil war. He would not fire back, but withdrew.

In 1866 Italy joined Prussia against Austria, and though she failed before the Quadrilateral, she received Venice when Prussia made peace after her great victory of Königgrätz.

Remained now only Rome. Italy needed Rome. Milan, Turin, Florence quarrelled as to which should be capital of the kingdom, there was great jealousy among the old states. Italy must have Rome. But France and the Catholic powers forbade it.

In 1867 Garibaldi again set out, invaded the papal territory with a motley band of volunteers. But he had lost his cunning. He seemed like a shorn Samson since he yielded to Victor Emmanuel ; he could do nothing. He was repulsed. Then new French troops arrived, and at the miserable village of Mentana, twenty miles from

Rome, on the Campagna, the Garibaldians were utterly routed. Many fled, many were mown down mercilessly by the French from behind the walls. It was a bitter event, a cruel blow to Italian prestige, a painful memory for ever—Mentana.

Italy must wait for Rome until 1870, when French troops were withdrawn on the outbreak of the Franco-Prussian War. On September 20, 1870, three weeks after Sedan, Victor Emmanuel's Bersaglieri entered Rome by the breach near the Porta Pia, and the Temporal Power fell. The Royal Court came and occupied the Quirinal, the Pope retired and shut himself up in the Vatican, after pronouncing the Greater Excommunication against those who deposed him.

And so Italy was made—modern Italy. Fretfulness, irritation, and nothing in life except money : this is what the religious fervour of Garibaldians and Mazzinians works out to—in united, free Italy as in other united, free countries. No wonder liberty so often turns to ashes in the mouth, after being so fair a fruit to contemplate. Man needs more than liberty.

XIX. The Unification of Germany

It was after the fall of Napoleon that nations really came to consciousness. In the beginning of Europe, there were many tribes, races, peoples, but no nations owning state property, and no kings as we have them now, representing state interest. Rome was a state of citizens, a republic of free men, when she first began to conquer. In Gaul, in Britain, in Germany, chieftains were chosen as leaders from among the warriors of the tribe. There was no kingship which descended from father to son.

But if men must fight their way forward, they must have a leader whom all obey. And if, after a state or a tribe has made conquests, unity is to be kept, if the people are to be united into one active power, then the leader must not only be absolute, he must be permanent. So we have the great emperors leading Rome, we have hereditary kings at the heads of the tribes.

Still there are no nations, in the modern sense. The whole history of Europe is a history of the breaking down of great institutions to make way for smaller, more numerous, more individual powers. So the greatest of all institutions, the Roman Empire, disappeared utterly. Then arose the Holy Roman Empire, which reached its height in Barbarossa and Frederick ii., and disappeared with Napoleon. The Papacy ran parallel with the Holy Roman Empire; but with Victor Emmanuel the popes were driven inside the narrow bounds of the Vatican.

Under Rome, vast numbers of men were slaves. Under

the popes, men believed darkly what they were bidden, books and free knowledge were hidden away. Kings arose when emperors and popes declined. But kings are really war-lords, war-chieftains. A king was originally the great overlord of the barons : the people were merely serfs, half slaves. Kings and barons existed as proud fighting-powers ; realms consist in the glamour and glory of conflict.

The great change comes when the peoples cease to be unified for fighting purposes, and unite for production. There are two great passions that rule mankind—the passion of pride and power and conquest, and the passion of peace and production. The Renaissance was the time when the desire for peace and production triumphed over the desire for war and conquest.

After the Renaissance, kingdoms were productive in the first place, and in the second place, they were fighting powers. Kings were still war-leaders ; but they must also lead in prosperity. Kings who ignored the national prosperity were beheaded. The passion for peace and production triumphed over the desire for war. Kings must be no longer proud. The greatest man is he who causes the greatest production of necessary substance— the greatest merchant, the greatest owner of industry. The time comes when the leaders of industry, the rich men of the middle class really rule, as they do in Britain to-day, and in the great republics.

Nations, in the modern sense, arise when mankind chooses peace and production rather than war and glory. After the Renaissance and the Reformation, nations like England became conscious of their true purpose. The English people realised that their glory was in a life lived in unison and peaceful freedom, not in triumph over others. They wanted to be free from kingly power. They wanted to sum up to one vast, productive nation, not to a re-splendent monarch.

And so the idea works itself out : it is the producer who

matters, only the producer. Pride is nothing, glory is nothing, only production is important. And the producers in the last instance are the workers themselves. The people now move towards power, as in extreme democracies. Europe is again moving towards a oneness. Nations are once more tending to merge into one vast European state, a vast European rule of the people. Long ago, Europe was one vast realm ruled by a gorgeous emperor in Rome. Now the circle has almost been completed again. Europe seems to move towards unification, towards the institution of one vast state ruled by the infinite numbers of the people—the producers, the proletariat, the workmen.

The national spirit brings us to this, which is ultimately the international or universal spirit. Nations, however, must, in the first instance, be pivoted upon a central power, a king. After the king has served his day, he disappears.

> ' Nation awakens by nation,
> King by king disappears.'

The great Germanic race had never since the Middle Ages had its one king, it had never become a nation. Itself the mother of nations, it was the last to come to national unity. It could only be united under a firm ruler.

The struggle for leadership was between Austria and Prussia. When in 1848 the republicans of France once more drove out their king, Louis Philippe, all Europe was stirred by a revolutionary feeling. France declared a republic, only to elect as president Louis Napoleon, son of Louis Bonaparte, whom the great Napoleon had made King of Holland. In 1852 Louis Napoleon asked the French nation to vote whether he should take the imperial title or not. By 7,800,000 votes to 233,000 they chose that he should. So the Emperor Napoleon III. came to the throne of France, where he sat rather insecurely.

The year 1848 saw the Austrian Empire on the brink

of dissolution. Bohemia, Hungary and North Italy all rose to shake off her foreign sway. Yet chiefly through the activities of the great Austrian minister Metternich, who hated popular governments, Austria kept together.

She had hardly time to notice, at first, what was happening in Germany. There the states loudly demanded independence. The Confederation had been dominated by Austria. With surprising ease they called their own parliament together at Frankfort, in 1848. For a long time they could come to no decision, because they did not want to exclude Austria. Austria proper was German, but the millions of non-German subjects in her empire would swamp the Germans. It was decided to leave Austria out of the new state of Germany, and to face her opposition. A new empire of Germany was to be established, with an emperor entitled Emperor of the Germans. In March 1849, it was decided to offer the new title and office to Frederick William IV. of Prussia.

Prussia herself was struggling with a revolution. In Berlin the people had risen against the power of the Crown. Therefore the King would have nothing to do with offers made by revolutionary parliaments. He refused the imperial crown. And almost at once the whole movement for a united Germany dwindled down and collapsed, and Germany went on as before, with her thirty-nine independent and separate states.

The people's party in Prussia demanded a parliament of their own. The King declared : ' According to the law of God and the country, the Crown must reign according to its free decision and not according to the will of majorities.' Berlin rose in fierce revolution, the King had to escape. The streets were barricaded, hot fighting took place. The King gave way. He declared that Prussia was henceforth to be absorbed in Germany, and he allowed the National Assembly to meet, to form a new constitution.

But when Austria crushed her revolution in Vienna, Frederick William roused again and struck in Berlin.

The Assembly had begun to wrangle. He ordered it to dissolve. It refused. The military marched down and dispersed it. Then, in December 1848, the King gave a constitution framed by himself, and the power of the Crown was safe.

So it was that three months after, he refused the imperial crown of Germany, which the revolutionary parliament of Frankfort offered to him, calling it a crown of mud and wood. But he invited the various German governments to Berlin, with a view to forming a real federal constitution. Austria and Bavaria declined to come, Saxony and Hanover soon retired. In the end a federal constitution was drawn up for North Germany, headed by Prussia, and including about twenty-eight states.

Austria, always afraid and jealous of Prussia, immediately made a southern federation, with headquarters at Frankfort. It was a question whether Prussia or Austria would lead Germany. A quarrel arose. The Prussian king and ministers were timid, Austria was quick, energetic. She demanded the immediate dissolution of the northern federation, under threat of instant war. Prussia cast away all thoughts of resistance, and surrendered at Olmütz. Austria was still triumphant, dominant in Germany. Frederick William's bold words ended in smoke.

In 1861 King William I. came to the throne of Prussia. During the Berlin revolution he had fled to England, for the people hated him as a tyrant. But he did not like English ideas of government. He was a soldier by nature. ' I am the first king,' he said, ' to mount the throne since it has been supported by modern institutions, but I do not forget that the crown has come to me from God alone.' And he prepared to assert the royal power in all its force.

For many years Prussia had been unconsciously leading the way towards union. Every little province and department had its own gate across its own frontier, with customs-officers waiting for every traveller, every wagon either coming or going, to charge a certain percentage on the goods. This very much hampered, and often prevented the selling of commodities from town to town, village to village. So that trade was clogged, industry half strangled, and smuggling was universal. Prussia had gradually done away with all her internal customs barriers. From end to end of Prussian dominions, goods were freely exchanged, there was complete internal free trade. The duty was reduced also on goods which were being brought into the kingdom. But on goods which were being carried across the Prussian territories, say from Denmark to Saxony, a heavy duty was charged. So Prussia stimulated her own trade, and made a profit out of that of others.

The southern states soon saw what an advantage this was. Bavaria and Würtemberg joined and formed a southern union of free trade, another union was formed between central states. But the advantage of free trade within the German lands was too great to be overlooked. South Germany joined the Prussian union of customs-duties in 1834, Central Germany entered in 1854, and soon the whole of the German states were united in one free-trading combine, Austria only being excluded.

Trade, commerce, is really the basis of union between different states which come together. But the Prussians knew that to keep such a union firm, a perfect army was needed. They steadily proceeded to realise the ideas of the reformers who, after the disaster of October 1806, had worked for the overthrow of Napoleon. William I. of Prussia had three remarkably great ministers, Bismarck, Moltke, and Roon. Roon was the war-minister. It was he who established the modern German army. Universal military service for three years was enforced on all classes, with a further obligation to serve in the reserve, the *Landwehr*, for four years. New weapons, especially the needle-gun, were introduced, and new, scientific methods of drill and tactics studied. It was a preparation such as

Frederick William I. had made a hundred and fifty years before.

But in Prussia the same struggle between king and parliament went on, as elsewhere. In 1861 the progressive party had a large majority in the representative house of the Assembly. They demanded that obligatory military service should be reduced to two years ; that the upper house, corresponding to our House of Lords, but much more powerful, should be reformed ; and that the ministers who really governed the country, such as the Chancellor, who may be called the Prime Minister, and the War Minister, and the Foreign Minister, should be responsible to the National Assembly, not to the King. The progressive party demanded reforms according to the British model. The King refused. The Assembly then in 1862 refused to vote the money for the army There was a deadlock. The King could do nothing. In his anger, he even thought of abdicating.

Then appeared the powerful figure of Bismarck. Bismarck was a North German nobleman. He had been a member of the National Assembly during the period of the 1848 revolution. He had strongly opposed the merging of Prussia into Germany. ' Prussians we are, and Prussians we will remain,' he said. In all the diplomatic missions, he had held firm as iron against Austrian demands.

Bismarck was chosen chancellor in 1862. He promised the King he would never yield. He did not believe in votes, in government by the people and their representatives. ' The decision on these principles,' he said, ' will not come by parliamentary debate, and not by majorities of votes. Sooner or later the God who directs the battle will cast his iron dice.'

The old struggle was repeated. Just as Charles I. and Wentworth faced the Long Parliament, just as Louis XVI. and his ministers faced the Estates General, so William I. of Prussia and Bismarck faced the representatives of the people. According to the evidence of history, they were bound to be defeated.

But the defeat was not yet. It was a maxim of those days that an absolute monarchy depended on successful wars—which means, that a nation in its pride of kingship only lives by triumphing over its neighbour. Failure in foreign wars brought down the crown of France, and helped to bring down the crown of England. In the pride of its heart, every nation desires to triumph over its neigh- bours. But pride of heart and the desire for triumph exhaust themselves, it seems. And then in their hearts peoples and nations only wish for ease and prosperity, they have no use for wars. And when they have no use for wars, they have no use for absolute kings with their ministers. Nothing further matters but the dead level of material prosperity.

Bismarck and William I. were successful in war, so they carried Germany with them. First came a great insurrec- tion of the Poles against Russia. The Progressives or Liberals in Germany all wanted to help the Poles. But Bismarck need not ask the people nor the parliament what side he should take. He assisted the Russians in suppress- ing the rising. He next refused even to hear Austria, when she came forward proposing a new union of Germany. Then the duchies of Schleswig and Holstein, which lay between Denmark and Prussia, were left without an heir. Denmark, Prussia and Austria all claimed the provinces. Austria and Prussia soon defeated Denmark, who received no help from the other powers.

Austria had now decided that the Duke of Augusten- berg should receive the duchies, for he had the strongest claim. Bismarck intended no such thing. The King of Prussia would have been glad of a peaceful settlement. Bismarck was determined on war. And now at last the two great Germanic powers were to decide which was to lead.

At this time, Cavour and Garibaldi, helped by the French

under Napoleon III., had freed Italy, all except Venice and Rome. Venetia remained in Austrian hands, the Pope held out in Rome. Victor Emmanuel was the first King of Italy. Bismarck now cleverly made an alliance with the new King of Italy, and promised that Prussia should make no peace with Austria until Venice was surrendered to Italy. So Victor Emmanuel sent the Italian armies against Austria, Garibaldi fighting in the Tyrol. The Italians were badly beaten, and things would have looked very black for them, save for the interference of Prussia.

In Germany things went differently. The war was the first sign to Europe of a new power risen in their midst, using methods hitherto unknown. The whole campaign had been elaborately worked out by the Army Council, before the war began. Moltke, the great general, sat in Berlin and directed the movements of the campaign by telegraph, receiving telegrams all the time. When a decisive blow was to be struck, a swift express-train conveyed him to the front. After the battle he returned to Berlin.

This was something new in warfare : and it was speedily effective. The Hanoverians were overthrown at Langensalza, in June 1866, as they were trying to make their way to join the Austrians. In July the Austrians, after a hard and doubtful struggle, were defeated at Königgrätz in Bohemia. It was one of the shortest wars, but one of the most significant.

Bismarck now showed himself a great statesman. Those states of the north that had opposed Prussia—Schleswig, Holstein, Hanover, Hesse, Cassel—were annexed to Prussia, so that her lands now practically covered North Germany. The southern states, Bavaria, Baden, Würtemberg, were treated very delicately, for Bismarck did not want to make enemies of them. He knew they would immediately join France against him if he did. For Napoleon III. also had the idea that he could only keep his throne in France by winning victories abroad, as his great predecessor had done, and therefore he also was on tenterhooks to declare war somewhere.

Now Bismarck founded the North German Federation, which was the beginning of the German Empire of our day. Bismarck did not follow the British model. He did not like the liberal middle classes of Germany, the tradespeople and manufacturers who were so powerful in Britain. He preferred even the work-people. So he made way for socialism.

The head of the Federation was the Federal Council, composed of envoys, not elected, but chosen from the various governments of the different states. This council brought in all bills, and controlled the administration of the law. Next was the Reichstag, the House of Commons, elected by manhood suffrage, and not by property qualification. Thus it was the people's house. It was not like the British House of Commons, a chamber of rich men. The Reichstag passed or rejected the bills of the Federal Council, and it controlled finance. But it did not govern. The ministers governed. And the ministers were quite independent of the Reichstag. They represented the Crown, and they alone decided what course should be taken. Reichstag and people's representatives could not interfere. They only voted money and accepted or rejected the new bills which the Council offered.

The chief of the ministers was the Chancellor. He was a far more powerful person than the British Prime Minister. The British Prime Minister must answer to Parliament for all he does, and Parliament means the nation. The German Chancellor—and Bismarck was the first German Chancellor—answered only to the King. So his power was immense. It was his success in war which saved him, and made him a popular hero. Prussia was still a fighting state, not a commercial state.

Napoleon III. in France was a despot, but very popular, for he conciliated the people all the time. He was a good deal like an Italian Tyrant in the Renaissance. France flourished under him, and Paris became the beautiful modern city it is now. Trade prospered, France was a commercial nation. But Napoleon III. had a fixed idea that it was necessary ' to gratify the military and domineering instincts of France.' He had very successfully interfered in Italy, and brought France out of her wars with much satisfaction and pride to himself and the people. He had acquired Nice and Savoy, and Europe had become quite alarmed, imagining him a dangerous aggressor like Napoleon I.

But after 1860 the French emperor's foreign policy was a failure, and the people, particularly the commercial and moneyed classes, began to turn against him. They were wearying of their unnecessary war-lord. He attempted to make Maximilian of Austria, Emperor of Mexico. The whole affair was a tragic fiasco, and France lost vast sums of money. Napoleon III. felt very uncertain on his throne.

Yet, on June 30, 1870, when the people of France were asked to vote whether a new, republican constitution should be introduced, or whether they should stand by the Emperor, 9,000,000 votes against 1,500,000 decided for him. Everything seemed most satisfactory. ' On whichever side we look there is an absence of troublesome questions ; never has the maintenance of the peace of Europe been better assured.' Fifteen days later war was declared against Prussia. In two months the second empire of France collapsed and disappeared.

We cannot say exactly why the great Franco-Prussian War of 1870 broke out. Neither France nor Germany desired war : only Bismarck wanted it. There had been a revolution in Spain. The Queen, Isabella, had fled to France. Leopold of Hohenzollern, a Roman Catholic, a distant relative of William I., was proposed for the throne of Spain. Napoleon III. protested. William listened to Napoleon's remonstrance, and Leopold's name was withdrawn. Then Napoleon thought he would show his power a little further. He sent an ambassador to William of Prussia, asking him to promise to oppose Leopold, even should that prince again be suggested for the throne of Spain. William said he could not promise so much, but that he disapproved of Leopold as a candidate for the Spanish throne. All passed quietly and pleasantly.

Bismarck was bitterly disappointed. He had hoped for a quarrel. He wanted war. He even thought of resigning his post. But then, it seems, he so modified the message he had received from the King, and published it in such a form as to make it appear that the Prussian king had been insulted by Napoleon, and had broken off all communications with France. A loud shout for war went up in Germany, and quite as loud a shout in France.

The French were very jaunty and confident of victory. But the German preparations were perfect, while France was in disorder. Half a million German soldiers poured over the French frontier. A marvellously rapid campaign followed. MacMahon was defeated at Wörth with great loss to the French. Then Marshal Bazaine's army was defeated and shut up in Metz. Then the emperor and MacMahon decided to retreat on Paris, to fight under the city fortresses. The Empress Eugenie telegraphed that a retreat would bring about a fall of the dynasty. The army changed its direction and marched against the enemy, hoping to relieve Metz. It was caught by the German army at Sedan, on September 1, 1870, and after losing 17,000 men Napoleon surrendered with 85,000.

At this disastrous news the empire was at once abolished in Paris, and a republic declared. Jules Favre was the Minister of Foreign Affairs, Gambetta was President. The new republic might now have had peace, if she would consent to surrender Strassburg and Metz. She proudly answered that she would not surrender an inch of French soil. So the war went on. The German armies gathered round Paris and the long siege began. No help came. On December 28, the bombardment of the city, which had been deferred so long, commenced. But it was Bismarck's plan to reduce the 2,000,000 inhabitants by speedy starvation. ' Let them stew in their own juice,' he said.

Wildly excited over these triumphs, the people of Germany united and offered the crown of the German Empire to William, whilst he was with the armies besieging Paris. A deputation waited on him on December 18, 1870, asking him to receive the new dignity. He accepted, and the new state was to come into being on January 1. On January 18, while Paris was still holding out, William I. was crowned emperor at Versailles, twelve miles away from the besieged city. In the great hall of mirrors, where the splendours of Louis XIV. had dazzled the world, the German officers and princes met in uniform, a throng of powerful men. With tremendous shouts they hailed the grey-haired King emperor, the German Emperor, Bismarck and Moltke standing by his side, flashing aloft their swords and shouting with fierce joy.

The bombardment of Paris continued till January 28, when an armistice was signed and the city surrendered. The Prussians then occupied the city. And now came another revolution among the French themselves. A National Assembly had been called at Versailles to settle the new republican constitution. Meanwhile Paris was revolution-mad. Socialism, communism, anarchism were preached frantically. Paris proclaimed ' the Commune,' declaring she would go her own way, have her own government, regardless of the rest of France. For the people of Paris were republican, and they feared the monarchist tendency of the Assembly of Versailles. The Assembly decided that the Parisians must be subdued. The French leader Thiers, with the French armies which had returned from the war, now marched on Paris, Frenchmen attacking Frenchmen with utmost ferocity, French armies marching on the capital of France. The German troops, not yet withdrawn, looked on whilst the ghastly fighting between the two French parties took place. At last MacMahon became master of the city. The Communists were destroyed, 17,000 were executed, the Socialists entirely stamped out.

In such a way began the Third French Republic, which is the Republic of to-day. And at such a moment the German Empire began. In 1877 Bismarck wished to resign, worn out by his labours. To this the Emperor would not listen, for the state rested on the shoulders of the Iron Chancellor.

William I. died in 1888. His son Frederick, who was married to the daughter of Queen Victoria, died after a reign of ninety-nine days. The Emperor William II. then succeeded. He was twenty-nine years old. The young emperor was far more positive and dictatorial than William I. He did not agree with Bismarck. The old chancellor resigned in 1890, virtually dismissed.

After this, the German Empire and the Kingdom of Prussia were reckoned the most powerful state organisations in Europe. They did their best to resist the growth of Socialism. And yet labour organisation and socialist influence were perhaps stronger among the German people than anywhere. The state was keenly divided against itself. Germany was the last great military power left in Europe, excepting only Russia. And yet, in Germany as in Russia, the working people were most united, most ready to strike against war-lords and military dominion.

It seems as if North Europe, Germany and Russia, were never to take the course which France and Britain and America have taken. These latter three great states broke the monarchic power and established a rule of rich citizens, merchants, and promoters of industry, the rule of the middle classes. But Germany and Russia step from one extreme to the other from absolute monarchy such as Britain never knew, straight to the other extreme of government, government by the masses of the proletariat, strange, and as it seems, without true purpose : the masses of the working people governing themselves they know not why, except that they wish to destroy all authority, and to enjoy all an equal prosperity.

So the cycle of European history completes itself, phase by phase, from imperial Rome, through the mediæval empire and papacy to the kings of the Renaissance period, on to the great commercial nations, the government by the industrial and commercial middle classes, and so to that last rule, that last oneness of the labouring people. So Europe moves from oneness to oneness, from the imperial unity to the unity of the labouring classes, from the beginning to the end.

But we must never forget that mankind lives by a twofold motive: the motive of peace and increase, and the motive of contest and martial triumph. As soon as the appetite for martial adventure and triumph in conflict is satisfied, the appetite for peace and increase manifests itself, and *vice versa*. It seems a law of life. Therefore a great united Europe of productive working-people, all materially equal, will never be able to continue and remain firm unless it unites also round one great chosen figure, some hero who can lead a great war, as well as administer a wide peace. It all depends on the will of the people. But the will of the people must concentrate in one figure, who is also supreme over the will of the people. He must be chosen, but at the same time responsible to God alone. Here is a problem of which a stormy future will have to evolve the solution.

Epilogue

THE War, called now the Great War, came in 1914, and smashed the growing tip of European civilisation. Mankind is like a huge old tree: there are deep roots that go down to the earth's centre, and there is the massive stem of primitive culture, where all men are very much alike. All men, black, white, yellow, cover their nakedness and build themselves shelters, make fires and cook food, have laws of marriage and of family, care for their wives and their children, and have stores of wisdom and ancient lore, rules of morality and behaviour. All men are alike in these fundamentals: even the crudest black Australian aborigines. We should say, that in its roots and its massive trunk, the tree of mankind is undivided. Mankind is one great race, in its fundamentals always the same. Whereas the gulf that divides man from the animals is so great, that we can see no connection. We can no longer believe that man has descended from monkeys. Man has descended from man.

The difference between the most civilised man and the lowest savage with a black face and a flat nose is as nothing compared to the difference between that same stunted, ugly savage and the highest ape. The pigmy naked Bush-man and the highly educated white man, once they meet and are acquainted, know each other man for man. The savage soon knows if I am a 'good' man: that is, if I am decent and brave and kindly. And if I am foolish, or affected, or even snobbish, the crude savage soon learns to despise me. He may be in awe of my white man's powers:

my gun, my power to write letters, or to send telegrams, or to build railways. But if I am a poor specimen of a man, *inwardly*, even if I have a big strong body, the savage will soon know, and he will despise me, sneer at me, and play tricks on me. To be brave, to keep one's word, to be generous, the savage recognises these as the first qualities in a man quite as quickly, or perhaps more quickly, than we white people do. It is manhood. And manhood is the same in all men, and the chief part of all men. Cleverness, educated skill come far behind.

Man recognises man as his own sort, and manhood is manhood to the pigmy black as to the educated white, the heroic qualities are the same.

But man and monkey look at one another across a great and silent gulf, never to be crossed. The savage shakes hands with me, and each of us knows we are of one ancient blood-stream. But if I attempt to shake hands with a monkey or an ape—it is a gesture only of mockery. We cannot really meet in touch.

In its root and trunk, Mankind is one. But then the differences begin. The great tree of man branches out into different races: huge branches, reaching far out in different directions. And each branch has its own growing tip.

So the races of mankind have grown in their different directions; the Egyptians and the Chinese, the Hindu and the Assyrians, the Aztecs and the Peruvians, the negroes and the Polynesians, the Mediterranean peoples that include Greece and Rome and Carthage, then the Germanic and Slavic races, and the modern Europeans: all huge branches on the one tree of mankind.

Every branch has its own direction and its own growing tip. One branch cannot take the place of any other branch. Each must go its own way, and bear its own flowers and fruits. For each branch is, as it were, differently grafted by a different spirit and idea, which becomes its own spirit and idea. My manhood is the same as the manhood of a Chinaman. But in spirit and idea we two are different and shall be different forever, as apple-blossom will forever be different from irises.

And each branch has its own growing tip. In every race, the growing tip is the living idea, which must never cease to change and develop. Once the living idea, the forward-reaching consciousness of any race dies and goes hard and dry, the vast branch of that race dies upon the tree of mankind, withers, goes dry rotten, and at length falls and disappears. As the great Egyptians and Babylonians have fallen and disappeared.

But as every branch of mankind has its own growing tip, so the whole tree of Man has one supreme travelling apex, one culminating growing tip. If this dies, the whole tree perishes. Or else, from some side socket, a new leading bud appears. Then the whole direction of the tree's growth changes, the movement onward takes a new line.

For a thousand years, surely, we may say that Europe has been the growing tip on the tree of mankind. Man must change. Either he must grow, or he must die. Like a tree. There is no tree in the world which is the same this year as it was last. Either it has grown a bit or died a bit. And the same is true of every man, of every race, and of all mankind itself. Either it has grown a bit or died a bit.

But a man doesn't grow just because he gets fatter. He may be getting fatter, but the spirit inside him may be flagging and dying. The same with a race or a nation. Populations may be increasing rapidly. But the spirit inside the people may at the same time be failing, and then, sooner or later, there will come a crash. Babylon, the great city, once increased by thousands every year. Now there is not a man left.

From time to time the tree of mankind begins to fail, it runs to wood, and its fruit grows more and more paltry. Then it must be pruned, and grafted with a new idea.

For a thousand years Europe has led the world, and grown apace. But our spirit and our manhood begin to weaken. Our idea and our ideal begin to peter out.

So the War came, and blew away forever our leading tip, our growing tip. Now we are directionless.

Our great idea, during the last hundred years, has been the idea of Progress. We must all make progress. Every nation must make its own great strides of progress.

But again, it is like the tree. Each branch starts in its own separate direction. But if any branch spreads too hugely, it will spread above its neighbour, and cut off the light from that neighbour. And any branch that must grow in its neighbour's shadow must slowly and surely die.

And this is progress.

We believed also in free competition, and we said that, as many young trees must grow together in a plantation if they are to grow straight and tall, so must men compete with one another in every way, freely. Every man must be free to compete with every other man, and there must be equality of opportunity.

Since the War these words make us feel sick, they have proved such a swindle. But it is actually true that a plantation of young trees should be thick, the trees growing close upon one another, so that their struggle with one another for the light may send them upwards and keep them straight and erect. All very good for a plantation of young trees, with lots of space. Which is what Europe was, a hundred years ago.

But what of those young trees a hundred years later? They are just choking one another. Some manage to struggle above their neighbours, and there, once having got up into the air, they flourish fast. And the faster they flourish, the more they cut off the light from their neighbours below them. And the more the neighbours lose the light, the more they dwindle and expire.

Nothing is more depressing, in this respect, than a virgin forest. There are giants, and there are great growing youngsters. But at the same time there is a tangle and a misery of dwindling, thin trees which can hardly hold up, and which drop out their thin scratchy branches with dead brown tips; while on the ground a depth of fallen trees lies rotting.

The same applies among the nations. At first, plenty of room for all, and competition is the best thing possible, and equality of opportunity is the ideal. Liberty, Equality, Fraternity. Then some nations forge ahead, and get a stranglehold upon the natural resources around them. Still there must be progress, expansion, progress, expansion, free competition. All very well. But you can't progress upwards if another great tree has risen and sent out branches above you. You can't expand if your neighbour takes up all the room. You can't compete once your 'brother' has got a stranglehold on you.

Then you've either got to give in, and gradually, gradually have the light of day taken from you. Or you have to fight.

Sooner or later war is bound to come. If we continue in our ideal of Liberty, Equality, Fraternity; liberty for every man and every nation to get as much as he can for himself, equality of opportunity for every sharp and unscrupulous man or nation to get the better of the more honest or less shrewd man or nation, then there is bound to come more war, many more wars.

We all know it. We none of us believe in our ideals any more. Our ideal, our leading ideas, our growing tip were shot away in the Great War.

Till the Great War, we believed in Liberty, Equality, Fraternity and in the Voice of the People. The best men and women believed that the poorer classes were simple and honourable, and that when the Voice of the People was heard, it would speak simple, but wise and decent things, free from the falsities of the educated upper classes.

Came the War. And what then? What sort of sound did the Voice of the People make?

Before we answer, let us realise at once that the Voice of the People can never *actually* be heard. If every man got up to say his say in his own voice, there would come a great hoarse hollow bellowing of utter confusion. A number of people is heard, and can only be heard, intelligibly, through a spokesman.

So that if we want to hear the Voice of the People, we must listen to the spokesmen of the People. And by the People we mean the vast majority, people of every class. Each class has its wiser *minority*, with its particular spokesmen. But the vast majority rules in a time of crisis, and puts its spokesmen emphatically forward, as the mass takes fright.

And look at these spokesmen, in every nation. Listen to them. The two great voices in England, during the thick of the War were those of Mr. Lloyd George and Mr. Horatio Bottomley. These two spoke the Voice of the People: in trumpet blasts. They said what the vast majority were choking to say. They said it all enormously, endlessly, and with complete success.

There is hardly an Englishman living who can bear to remember the voices of these two gentlemen when they were uplifted in full blast. Or, if he remembers, can remember without shame.

Why?—Because they said things that were not true, and because they urged us to actions that were meaner, smaller, baser, crueller than our own deep feelings.

And this was the Voice of the People. Let us hope never to hear it again in full blast, the Voice of the Herd.

Every man has two selves among his manifold Self. He has a herd-self, which is vulgar, common, ugly, like the voice of the man in the crowd. And he has a better self, which is quiet, and slow, and which is most of the time puzzled. From his better self, he is almost dumb. From his herd-self, he shouts and yells and rants.

So in the middle of the War, we heard the Voice of the People bullying us. What became of Liberty? No man had any. Every able-bodied man was turned into a mere thing, without a soul of his own. The Voice of the People said the War required it. So every man was turned into an automaton, and the man who has been turned into a mere thing, without a soul of his own, is not going to believe in Liberty again, in a hurry, or to want to listen to the Voice of the People any more.

And Equality? What became of that? When any honest man was spied upon and thrown at the mercy of some ranting 'patriotic' bully to be insulted and maltreated.

And Fraternity, when men were inventing more and more fiendish devices to destroy and cripple one another. Equality of opportunity to throw poison in other men's faces. Free competition in injuring one another, body and soul.

No, the old ideal, the old leading tip was shot to smithereens, and we have got no new one. Nothing really to believe in. Only now, having lost our belief, we know inwardly that it would have been better to lose a war. Men cannot live *long* without a belief.

Comes 'after the War'. The world after the War.

We thought the old times were coming back. They can never come. We know now that each one of us had something shot out of him. So we have to adjust ourselves to a new world.

Came 'after the War'. England, changed inside, did not change outwardly very much. But other countries did. Russia had made one of the greatest changes in history: her Tzar and her nobles gone, her rich people dead or fled, her learned men and professors begging in the streets, only the working classes and the common soldiers left in full possession.

This was the Voice of the People with a vengeance. And Soviets, councils of workmen, ruling the country.

After all, I, who am not a workman, why should I be bullied by workmen? Because bullying is what it amounts to.

The popular philosophy of today, in every country, is the pragmatic philosophy. Which means the philosophy of 'Common sense'. They ask the question: Is it common sense, that a rather foolish Romanov Tzar, with a few unscrupulous nobility, should hold life and death power over millions of poor people? Answer: No! Result: A revolution.

Or another question. Is it common sense that a few men, just because their father or grandfather were clever men or clever rogues, should own huge properties and compel thousands of poor men to work for a miserable wage? Answer: No! Result: more revolution.

So we go on, with the philosophy of common sense.

But what it works out to, in the end, is that every man is just 'rationed' for the rest of his life. Every family is rationed, for food, clothing, and even house-room. That is what common sense works out to.

For rationing is common sense. But do we like it? Did we like it during the War? We didn't. We hated it.

And since we all suffer with our teeth, wouldn't it be common sense to have all our teeth pulled out at the age of sixteen, and false ones supplied? It might be common sense, but we just refuse to do it.

Pragmatism means that a thing is only good if it is common sense, if it works. It says that, just as an engine needs oiling and stoking, so people need food and clothing and housing, etc. Therefore, let everybody be given enough. That is, let everybody be rationed.

It may be lovely common sense, but what's the good, when we detest it? There must be something inside us which plumps for *uncommon* sense. We can't help ourselves. In the long run, we always decide from our uncommon sense, and not from our 'common'. We begin to hate everything 'common', including the so-called common sense.

Man has got to be wise. And to be wise you must have far more than common sense. It *is* bad to have greedy, cruel people called 'nobles' allowed to bully simple men. It *is* bad to have people squandering money and taking on airs, while good men can't find even work to do. It is very bad.

But it is also very bad for everybody to be 'rationed' for life, and spied upon by a 'police of the people'.

What sort of sense are we going to use about it? Common sense says that we are all little engines that must be stoked and watered and housed, so that we can do our share of the work and get our ration of amusement or enjoyment. And this sort of common sense points to communism, sovietism.

At the same time, something inside us hates being rationed, hates being treated as a little engine and made to do our engine's share of work. We would almost rather die.

This is our position after the War.

Immediately after the War, socialism seemed to be the inevitable next step. Russia had taken the step. And Italy, another imaginative country, was on the verge of taking it.

Now socialism, like most things, has various sides to it. But socialism proper is the expression of two great desires in men: the first, the generous desire that all men shall eat well and sleep well and fare well all their lives: but second, the much more dangerous desire, that all existing *masters* shall be overthrown, and that men shall be 'free', which means, there shall be no authority over the people. That is socialism.

1. A desire for the welfare of all people.

2. A hatred of all masters and of all authority, a hatred of all 'superiors'. Some socialists are full of hatred, and some are full of sincere desire for human welfare.

Now take Italy in 1919 and 1920 and 1921. She was rapidly running to socialism. Myself, personally, I believe that a good form of socialism, if it could be brought about, would be the best form of government. But let us come down to experience.

In Italy, in Florence, there was the same lingering ease and goodwill in 1919 as before the War. By 1920 prices had gone up three times, and socialism was rampant. Now we began to be bullied in every way. Servants were rude, cabmen insulted one and demanded treble fare, railway porters demanded large sums for carrying a bag from the train to the street, and threatened to attack one if the money were not paid. The train would suddenly come to a standstill in the heat of the open country: the drivers had gone on, strike for a couple of hours. Trains would arrive two hours, four hours, and going from Rome to Sicily I have been twelve hours late. If in the country you asked at a cottage for a drink of wine, worth a penny, the peasant would demand a shilling, and insult you if he did not get it.

This was all pure bullying. And this was socialism. True it was the bad side of socialism, the hatred of 'superiors' or people with money or education or authority. But socialism it was.

Such socialism made itself enemies. And moreover, it could not trust itself. In an old civilised country like Italy, it was bound to cave in.

In the summer of 1920 I went north, and Florence was in a state of continual socialistic riot: sudden shots, sudden stones smashing into the restaurants where one was drinking coffee, all the shops suddenly barred and closed. When I came back there was a great procession of Fascisti and banners: *Long Live the King*. When I went to Naples, to the big main post office to send a telegram, there were white notices pasted over the doorways: 'We, the mutilated soldiers, have turned out all the young women employed in this office, and have taken their place. No woman clerk or operator shall enter this office etc.'—But the mutilated soldiers did not know how to send telegrams. So I had to look for a little side street office.

This was the beginning of Fascism. It was an anti-socialist movement started by the returned soldiers in the name of Law and Order. And suddenly, it gained possession of Italy. Now the cabs had a fixed charge, a fixed charge for railway porters was placarded in the railway stations, and trains began to run punctually. But also, in Fiesole near Florence the Fascisti suddenly banged at the door of the mayor of the village, in the night when all were in bed.

The mayor was forced to get up and open the door. The Fascisti seized him, stood him against the wall of his house, and shot him under the eyes of his wife and children, who were in their night dresses. Why? Because he was a socialist.

That is Fascism and Law and Order. Only another kind of bullying.

Now one *must* have Law and Order, because lawlessness and disorder in our great communities is hell. We *must* have authority, and there *must* be power. But there must not be bullying, nor the worship of mere Force. A certain group of men in Italy intend to *force* their will on all other men. Earlier, socialists tried to force *their* will. In Russia, the Communists succeed in forcing *their* will.

The forcing of one man's will over another man is bullying. We know what it is, we experienced it during the War. It is a bad, degrading thing. It degrades both the bully and those who are bullied.

Yet there must be *power*. Power there must be. Because, if there is not power there will be force.

What is the difference, among human beings, between power and force. A man invested with power has a profound responsibility. Force is irresponsible, unless controlled by the higher power.

The men in power, in England today, are the Members of Parliament and, chiefly, the Cabinet Ministers. The Force of the country is in the police and the army. But both the police and the army are only tools and instruments in the hands of the higher *power*, invested in Parliament.

In the old days, heaven was supposed to have given the gift of power to some few noble families. The family specially endowed with power from God was royal. A king was not a mere bully and tyrant. His kingship was not a matter of vanity and conceit. He really *felt* that heaven had made him responsible for a whole nation. It was a sacred charge. And many kings really did try to answer to God for their deeds as representatives of the nation, just as fathers answer for their families. But then heaven, or nature, has *really* made a father responsible for his young family. Whereas, once the royal family was established, nature had no more part in making a king. An individual became a king automatically, because he was born of a certain family. And these automatic hereditary kings could at last act as ignobly, towards their nation, as the ex-Kaiser Wilhelm of Germany has now acted.

Therefore in the cry for Liberty, men have refused to recognise any gift of power from heaven. Power, nowadays, is supposed to lie in the hands of the 'majority', the vast mass of the people. And these people by electing a man to be their responsible leader, can confer power on him. It is just the reverse of the old idea. In the royal days, God was a God of Power. He gave some of his power to the King. And the King revealed it to the humble mass of the nation. Today we say that power lies only in the great collective Will of the People, and they hand on this power to a group of men who are thus *placed* in power, but who are responsible to the People all the time.

Which is better? a royal king who is automatically royal by birth, and who is responsible to God alone? Or a vast mass of people electing a group of men to assume responsibility, and by the mere fact of election, automatically investing these men with power?

What is automatic, in human affairs, is bad. And power, true natural power, *does* come from God. That is, it is either born inside a man, or nothing can give it him. The son of a great king and hero may be a poor weakling: that we well know. But also, the man elected by fifty million people to be their leader may just as well be a poor weakling. The fact that fifty million people say he is great, will not make him great. You will never get great men by election, unless people are seeking after greatness. If the majority are, as today, seeking some special material advantage, like the raising of wages or the reduction of taxes, then they will elect some *tool* for their own purposes, and a mere tool he will be, without a spark of true power.

So that we see, democracy, government by popular election of representatives, becomes even more dismal than government by kings. Kings are at least supposed to be descendants of heroes, and they at least keep up a bluff of royalty and nobleness: as the late Kaiser did so successfully. But our Prime Ministers are forced, obviously, to be the *servants* of a huge discontented mob, who all want more money and less work. Till democracy becomes a thing of shame.

And meanwhile, there is one mysterious Force which is under no control. A mysterious force, like a great Secret Society spreading through all nations and controlled by no nation. This is the Force of Finance. A few hundred men on the face of the earth, with huge sums of money behind them, exert their wills and minds in order that money shall and must go on producing money, no matter what lives or loss of honour it may cost. Here is a great irresponsible Force which has escaped from the control of true human power, and which is likely to work enormous evil.

Now we begin to understand the old motto, *Noblesse Oblige. Noblesse* means, having the gift of power, the natural or sacred power. And having such power obliges a man to act with fearlessness and generosity, responsible for his acts to God. A noble is one who may be known before all men.

And even the automatic, hereditary nobility were born with *this* advantage: because of their birth they were expected to be brave, generous, and according to their station, wise. What a man is expected to be he will more or less try to be. So that in hereditary nobility there were great advantages. But even there all is decayed. A nobleman by birth is no longer expected to be braver than other men, an example to men. He is only expected to be conceited or snobbish.

Then aristocracy becomes *so* hollow, mere snobbish conceit and bluff, as in the ex-Kaiser's case, then it *has* to be swept away.

This does not automatically sweep away *all* aristocracy. There is an aristocracy inside the souls of some men, and that you can never sweep away. And *Noblesse Oblige* will ring out as a challenge for ever.

Which brings us back to common sense. Hereditary nobility is not common sense, and it is a fiasco. Democracy and government by Parliament is, in a way, good common sense: letting the mass of the people indicate what they want, and providing the chance to get it. But when what they want is never anything but more wages and less taxes, then common sense begins to stink in our nostrils.

Some men must be noble, or life is an ash-heap. There *is* natural nobility, given by God or the Unknown, and far beyond common sense. And towards this natural nobility we must live.

The simple man, whose best self, his noble self, is nearly all the time puzzled, dumb, and helpless, has still the power to recognise the man in whom the noble self is powerful and articulate. To this man he must pledge himself. That is the only way. To act according to the spark of nobility we have in us, not according to our greediness and our cowardice, our hard selves.

The hereditary aristocratic class has fallen into disuse. And democracy means the electing of tools to serve the fears and the material desires of the masses. *Noblesse n'oblige plus*.

This is really the worst that can happen to mankind, when *Noblesse n'oblige plus*. Goodness and badness there is bound to be. But a spark of nobility redeems everything.

For this reason we cannot help preferring Tzarist Russia to Soviet Russia. The tsar's Russia, with all the crimes laid at its door, and with all its ignoble nobles, had at least some lingering *appearance* of the old inspiration of *noblesse oblige*. Russia's was always a wild strange *noblesse*. But it had its splendours and its consolations.

Whereas about Soviet Russia we can only feel that *Malice Oblige* or *Misère Oblige*. And one cannot live all the time towards poorness or common sense. It wastes the spirit out of a man. We *must* live with some natural, pulsing nobleness.

And again, one feels that Soviet Russia is probably only the temporary grave of the old, not-quite-real Tsarist Russia. In this grave the great nation must stay, for the three days. Then there will be a resurrection towards a new nobility, the true or natural nobility of the people.

This is our job, then, our uncommon sense: to recognise the spark of nobleness inside us, and let it make us. To recognise the spark of *noblesse* in one another, and add our sparks together, to a flame. And to recognise the men who have stars, not mere sparks of nobility in their souls, and to choose these for leaders. We can choose for *noblesse* and we can choose for *bassesse*. We chose Mr. Bottomley for *bassesse*, lowness, commonness. Nations are slowly strangling one another in 'competition'. The cancer of finance spreads through the body of mankind. Individuals are diseased with the same disease. To get money, and to spend money, nothing else remains. And with it goes all the strangling, and the bullying, and the degradation, the sense of humiliation and worthlessness of life, which is bitterest of all.

There is nothing to be done, *en masse*. But every youth, every girl can make the great historical change inside himself and herself, to care supremely for nothing but the spark of *noblesse* that is in him and in her, and to follow only the leader who is a star of the new, *natural Noblesse*.

Index

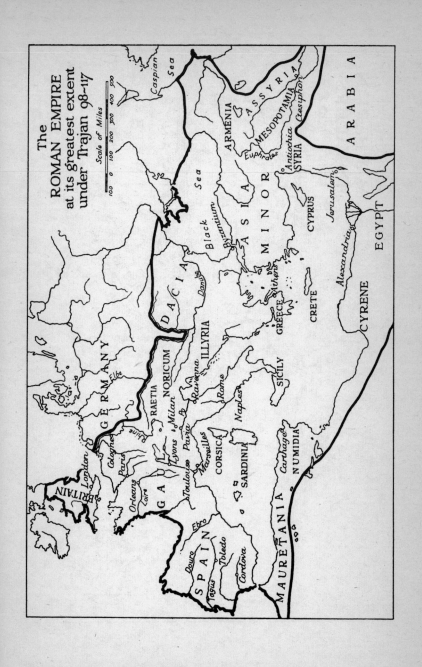

The
ROMAN EMPIRE
at its greatest extent
under Trajan 98-117

Scale of Miles
100   0   100   200   300   400   500

BRITAIN

London

Cologne

GERMANY

Elbe

Rhine

Paris

Orleans

Loire

GAUL

Tours

Toulouse

Marseilles

Lyons

Pavia

Milan

RAETIA

NORICUM

Ravenna

Po

Rome

Naples

ILLYRIA

Danube

DACIA

Black Sea

Byzantium

ASIA MINOR

Caspian Sea

ARMENIA

ASSYRIA

MESOPOTAMIA

Ctesiphon

Euphrates

Antiochia

SYRIA

CYPRUS

Jerusalem

ARABIA

Athens

GREECE

CRETE

SICILY

Carthage

NUMIDIA

CORSICA

SARDINIA

MAURETANIA

Ebro

SPAIN

Douro

Tagus

Toledo

Cordova

Alexandria

EGYPT

CYRENE

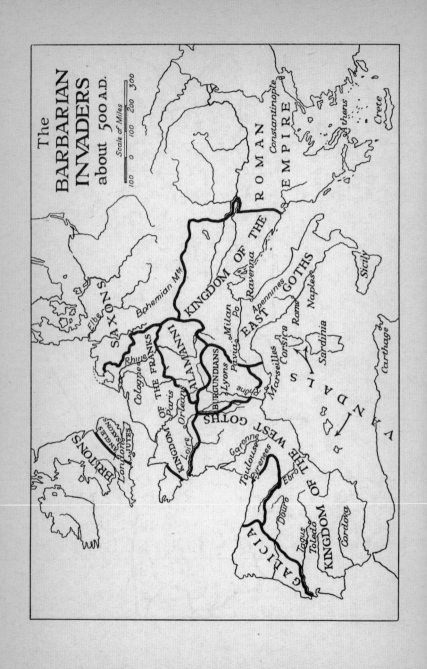

The
BARBARIAN
INVADERS
about 500 A.D.

Scale of Miles
100 0 100 200 300

BRITONS

ANGLES
JUTES
LONG
SAXONS

SAXONS

Elbe

Bohemian Mts.

KINGDOM OF THE

ROMAN

EMPIRE

Constantinople

Athens

Crete

Cologne
Rhine

KINGDOM OF THE FRANKS

Paris

Orleans

Loire

ALAMANNI

BURGUNDIANS

Lyons

Rhône

Pavia Milan
Po

Ravenna

Apennines

EAST GOTHS

Rome

Naples

Corsica

Sardinia

Sicily

Carthage

Marseilles

V A N D A L S

KINGDOM OF THE WEST GOTHS

Garonne

Toulouse

Pyrenees

Ebro

GALICIA

Douro

Tagus

Toledo

Cordova

KINGDOM OF

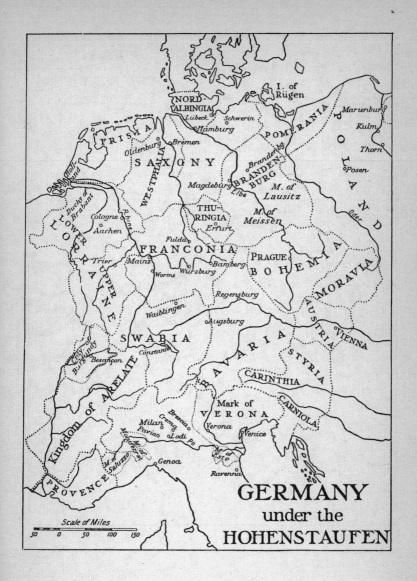

I. of Rügen

NORD-ALBINGIA

Lübeck
Schwerin
Hamburg

Marienburg
Kulm
Thorn

POMERANIA
P O L A N D

FRISIA

Oldenburg
Bremen

Holland

SAXONY

WESTPHALIA

Brandenbg.
BRANDEN-BURG

Magdeburg
Elbe

M. of Lausitz

Posen
Oder

Duchy of Brabant

Cologne
Aachen

Rhine

LOWER

UPPER

Trier

THU-RINGIA
Erfurt

M. of Meissen

LORRAINE

Mainz

Fulda

FRANCONIA

Worms
Wurzburg
Bamberg

PRAGUE
B O H E M I A

MORAVIA

Regensburg

AUSTRIA

Waiblingen

Augsburg

VIENNA

SWABIA

Cty. of Burgundy

Besançon

Constance

BAVARIA

STYRIA

CARINTHIA

Kingdom of ARELATE

CARNIOLA

Mark of VERONA

Milan
Cremona
Pavia
Lodi
Po
Verona
Venice

Monferrat

M. of Saluzzo

Genoa

M. of Este

Ravenna

PROVENCE

GERMANY
under the
HOHENSTAUFEN

Scale of Miles

50   0   50   100   150

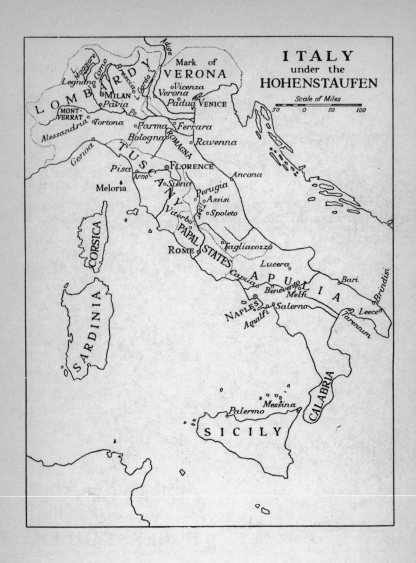

ITALY
under the
HOHENSTAUFEN

Scale of Miles
50   0   50   100

LOMBARDY

Mark of
VERONA

Maggiore
Como
Bresciano
Garda

Legnano
MILAN
Pavia

Vicenza
Verona
Padua
VENICE

MONT-
FERRAT

Alessandria
Tortona

Po
Adige

Parma
Ferrara
Bologna
ROMAGNA
Ravenna

Genoa

TUSCANY

Pisa
Arno
FLORENCE
Ancona

Meloria
Siena

Perugia
Assisi
Tiber
Spoleto

Viterbo

CORSICA

PAPAL STATES

Tagliacozzo

ROME

Lucera

Capua
APULIA
Bari
Brundisi

Benevento
Melfi

NAPLES
Salerno
Leece
Tarentum

Amalfi

SARDINIA

CALABRIA

Messina

Palermo

SICILY

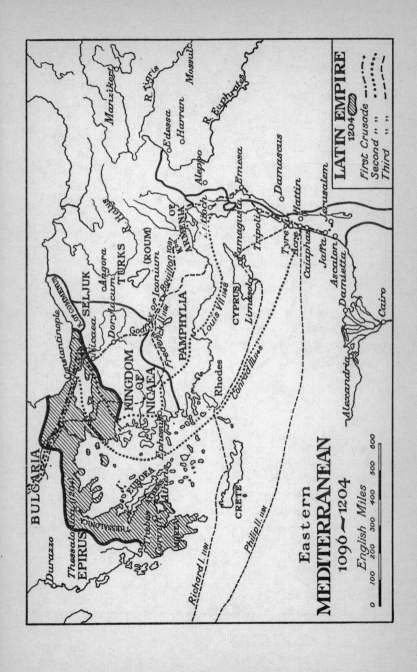

Eastern
MEDITERRANEAN
1096~1204

LATIN EMPIRE
1204

First Crusade ..-..-..
Second ,,   ,, ...
Third   ,,   ,, -------

English Miles

0   100   200   300   400   500   600

BULGARIA

EPIRUS

Durazzo

Thessalonica (lost 1204)

THESSALONICA

THESSALY

Euboea

Thebes
Athens
Corinth
MOREA

CRETE

Constantinople

K. OF COMNENUS

SELJUK

Nicaea

Angora

Dorylaeum

TURKS

(ROUM)

KINGDOM
OF
NICAEA

Ephesus

Rhodes

Richard I. 1191

Philip II. 1191

Conrad III. 1148

Louis VII. 1148

PAMPHYLIA

Godfrey or Iconium

Frederick 1190

Bohemond 1097

KING OF
ARMENIA

Antioch

Aleppo

Emesa

Damascus

Hattin

Tripoli

Tyre

Acre

Caiaphas

Jaffa
Ascalon
Jerusalem

Damietta

Alexandria

Cairo

CYPRIUS

Famagusta

Limasol

Manzikert

R. Tigris

Edessa

Harran

Mossul

R. Euphrates

R. Halys

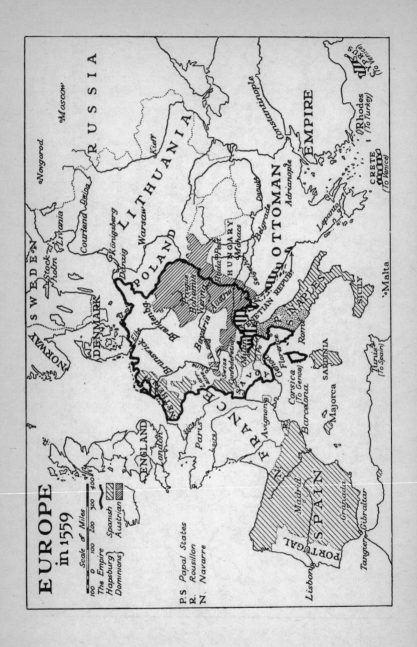

EUROPE
in 1559

Scale of Miles

100 0 100 200 300 400

The Empire

Hapsburg
Dominions

Spanish

Austrian

P.S Papal States
R. Rousillon
N. Navarre

NORWAY

SWEDEN

Stockholm

DENMARK

ENGLAND

London

Brunswick

NETHERLANDS

Paris

Seine

Loire

FRANCE

Avignon

N

Rousillon

Barcelona

SPAIN

Madrid

Granada

Tangier

Gibraltar

PORTUGAL

Lisbon

Majorca

SARDINIA

Corsica
(To Genoa)

SAVOY

Genoa
Florence

Rome
P.S

NAPLES

SICILY

Malta

Tunis
(To Spain)

RUSSIA

Moscow

Novgorod

Courland

Livonia

Dwina

Königsberg

Danzig

LITHUANIA

Warsaw

Kieff

POLAND

Brandenburg

Elbe

Bavaria

Swiss
Confederation

Milan

VENETIAN
REPUB.

Prague

Bohemia

Vienna

Austria

Buda-Pest

HUNGARY

Mohacs

Save

Danube

Belgrade

Adrianople

Constantinople

OTTOMAN
EMPIRE

Lepanto

CRETE
(To Venice)

Rhodes
(To Turkey)

CYPRUS
(To Venice)

FRANCE
1610 – 1715

English Miles

0   50   100   150

R. Rhine
Calais Dunkirk
Boulogne
FLANDERS Antwerp Cologne
Brussels Bonn
Lille Tournay Liège Coblenz
ARTOIS Charleroi
Namur
MANAULT Phillippeville
Cherbourg Dieppe PICARDY Luxemburg Duchy of Zweibrücken
Havre Amiens Vervins Luxemburg Trier
Rouen Thionville Saarlouis
Caen NORMANDY Verdun Strassburg
St Malo Seine ISLE OF FRANCE Reims Bar LORZ Breisach
BRITANNY Chartres PARIS CHAMPAGNE FRANCHE Friburg
Fontainebleau Rheinfelden
MAINE Troyes DUCHY COMTÉ Basel Bern
Blavet Orleans OF Rheinfelden
Nantes ANJOU Blois BURGUNDY SWITZERLAND
R. Loire Tours Bourges NIVERNOIS
Belle Isle Chinon TOURAINE Nevers Geneva
Richelieu Poitiers BERRY R. Loire Bresse Valromey
POITOU Bourges SAVOY
Isle of Ré La Rochelle BOURBONNOIS Lyon
LA MARCHE LYONNOIS
SAINTONGE Limoges R. Saône Ressy
LIMOUSIN DAUPHINÉ PIEDMONT
Bordeaux R. Dordogne AUVERGNE R. Rhone Barcelonnette Pinerolo
GUIENNE C. de Orange COUNTY
Bayonne AND Montpellier Nîmes Avignon OF NICE
S. Sebastian GASCONY R. Tarn LANGUEDOC PROVENCE Nice
Toulouse R. Garonne Arles
LOWER Narbonne Toulon
NAVARRE FOIX Perpignan Marseilles
NAVARRE ROUSSILLON
R. Ebro

French boundary in 1610 ——————
Acquisitions under Henry IV 1589–1610
"   "   Louis XIII 1610–1643
"   "   Louis XIV 1643–1715

GERMANY
at the
PEACE of WESTPHALIA
1648

Scale of Miles

50   0   50   100   150

Route of Gustavus Adolphus, 1630-32 �

Schleswig

Holstein
Lübeck

HAMBURG   MEC.

Bremen   Neu...

Bremen   Verden   BRUNS-
WICK   B

LÜNEBURG   Magdeb...

UNITED

AMSTERDAM
PROVINCES

Hague   Utrecht   Osnabrück
Osnabrück   Wolfenbüttel
Münster   Lutter

Breda   Cleves   Lutter
Bergen op Zoom   Rheinberg   Hesse
Bruges   Antwerp   Rheinberg   Cassel   S.
Dunkirk   Duchy   Erfurt   Saxe-
Spanish   of Julich   Cologne   Weim...
BRUSSELS   Maastricht
Lens   Netherlands   Coblenz

Amiens   Bpric of Liege   Frankfort   Bpric
of Schweinfurt

Luxemburg   EL. OR...   Bpric
MAINZ   Würzburg   of
Sedan   Trier   LOWER   Bamberg
Luxemburg   Worms   Mannheim   Fürtha   Nurem...
Verdun   Thionville   PALATINATE   Heidelberg
Metz   Speyer   Wimpfen
Nancy   Philippsburg   Heilbronn   Pal...
Toul   Hagenau   Duchy   Nördlingen   BAV
of   Donauwörth
STRASBURG   Wurtemburg   Int...
Ulm   Augsburg   Munic...
Breisach   Danube   Zusmarshausen

Besançon   Constance   Lech   Inn
Basel   Rheinfelden
Franche   SWISS
Comté   CONFEDERATION   Tyrol
Besançon
Saône   Grisons   Bre...
Valtelline   Inn

DUCHY OF   Duchy
of Milan   VEN...
SAVOY   Milan

Paris   Seine   Loire   Rhône   Turin   Po

Memel

Königsberg

Pillau

Danzig

Elbing

DUCHY OF PRUSSIA (To Brand.)

Rügen
Ruden
Usedom
Wollin

Cammin

East Pomerania

West Pomerania

Stettin
Gar~
Greifenhagen

BURG
~denburg

Bärwalde

DEN

NDENBURG

Spandau
BERLIN

Brandenburg

Küstrin
Frankfort

Oder

P O L A N D

Vistula

Warsaw

~sen

~au

BURG

Lower Lusatia

Upper Lusatia

Breitenfeld
Leipzic
Dresden

~XONY

Klostergrab

B O H E M I A

White Hill
Eger
PRAGUE
Elbe

Pilsen

Jankan

~him

~on

~t

~hut

Budweis

S I L E S I A

Breslau

Braunau

Cracow

M o r a v i a

Passau

A U S T R I A

VIENNA

Pressbury

Danube

Budu~Pest

H U N G A R Y

T U R K I S H   H U N G A R Y

Salzburg
~pric
of
Salzburg
~ass

Styria

~IA

Carinthia

~E

Carniola

VENICE

Drave

Save

Acquisitions of

Sweden

France

Brandenburg

Saxony

Bavaria

Extent of the Empire

The Partitions of
POLAND & the
RUSSO~TURKISH WARS

NORWAY & SWEDEN

FINLAND

The Dales

STOCKHOLM

St. Petersburg

Gothenburg

Moscow

DENMARK

Copenhagen

Baltic Sea

COURL 1772
1795

S.W.Pom Pomerania 1793
Königsberg
Danzig

PRUSSIA

Grodno

BERLIN
Branden-burg
1772
Thorn 1795
1793

P R U S S I A

Dresden
Pilnitz
Reichenbach
Teschen

BOHEMIA

WARSAW
POLAND
1795
Breslau

Cracow
GALICIA

Bar

1793

BAVARIA
Tyrol
Carinthia
Styria
Carniola

AUSTRIA
VIENNA
Pressburg

H U N G A R Y

Jassy
Bessarabia
Oczakoff
Kherson

Russian
in 1784

Moldavia
Foksany

Crimea

Belgrade

Rymnik
Bucharest

ITALY

SERVIA WALLACHIA

Sistova

Kutchuk Kainardji

Black Sea

T U R K E Y

CONSTANTINOPLE

Dardanelles

To Prussia
To Russia
To Austria
Scale of Miles

0 50 100   200   300   400

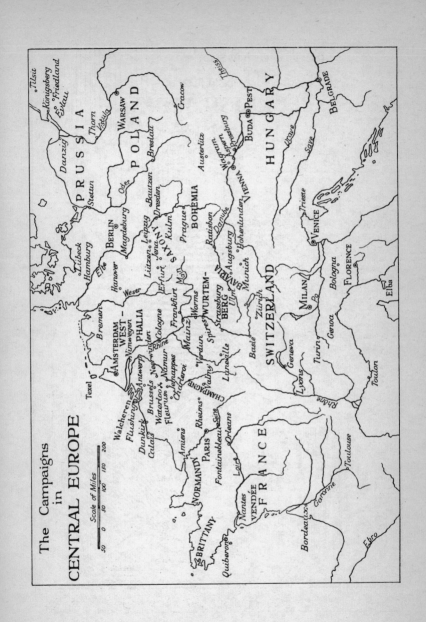

The Campaigns in
CENTRAL EUROPE

Scale of Miles
50 0 50 100 150 200

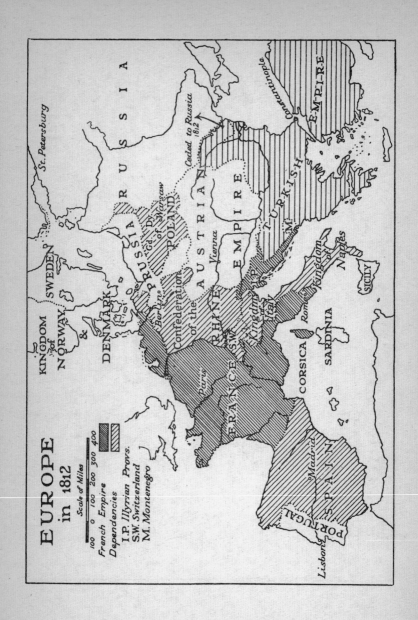

EUROPE
in 1812

Scale of Miles
100 0 100 200 300 400

French Empire
Dependencies

I.P. Illyrian Prors.
S.W. Switzerland
M. Montenegro

St. Petersburg

KINGDOM
of
NORWAY

SWEDEN

&

DENMARK

RUSSIA

PRUSSIA

Berlin

Gd. D.
of Warsaw

POLAND

Ceded to Russia
1812

AUSTRIAN

EMPIRE

Vienna

Confederation

of the

RHINE

Kingdom
of
Italy

Paris

FRANCE

S.W.

Rome

Kingdom

of

Naples

TURKISH

EMPIRE

Constantinople

M.

CORSICA

SARDINIA

SICILY

SPAIN

Madrid

PORTUGAL

Lisbon

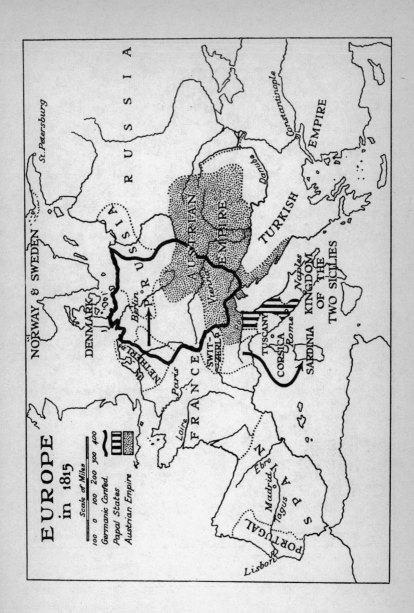

EUROPE
in 1815

Scale of Miles
100 0 100 200 300 400

Germanic Confed.
Papal States
Austrian Empire

St. Petersburg

NORWAY & SWEDEN

RUSSIA

DENMARK

P R U S S I A

Berlin

NETHERL

Paris

FRANCE

Loire

SWIT-
ZERLD

AUSTRIAN EMPIRE

Vienna

Danube

TURKISH EMPIRE

Constantinople

TUSCANY

CORSICA

Rome

Naples

SARDINIA

KINGDOM OF THE
TWO SICILIES

S P A I N

Madrid

Ebro

Tagus

PORTUGAL

Lisbon

The
UNION of ITALY
1859~70

Scale of Miles
50   0   50   100   150

Piedmont Sardinia in April 1859
Added in November 1859
  "   "   March 1860
  "   "   October & November 1860
  "   "   October 1866
  "   "   October 1870
Lost in March 1860
Districts claimed by Italy in 1914

SAVOY
Magenta
LOMBARDY
Solferino
PIEDMONT
VENETIA
Trieste
PARMA
MODENA
ROMAGNA
Bologna
Luccao
Nice
TUSCANY
MARCHES
Ancona
STATES
UMBRIA
OF THE
CHURCH
Mentana
ROME
CORSICA
Caprera I
NAPLES
Naples
SARDINIA
Messina
Aspromonte
Marsala
SICILY
Reggio

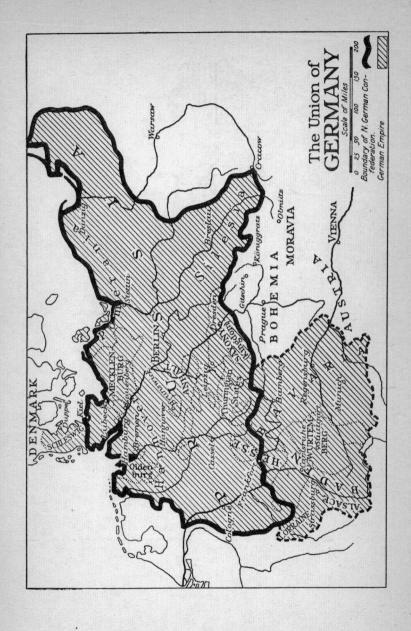

The Union of
GERMANY

Scale of Miles
0 25 50   100   150   200

Boundary of N. German Confederation.
German Empire.

DENMARK

SCHLESWIG Düppel
Kiel

Lübeck
MECKLEN-
BURG

Hamburg
Bremen

Oldenburg

Cologne

ALSACE
LORRAINE
Strassburg

Carlsruhe
WURTEM-
BERG
Stuttgart

Cassel
HESSEN

Frankfort

BADEN
Murten

BAVARIA

Bamberg
Regensburg

Munich

AUSTRIA

VIENNA

MORAVIA
Olmütz
Königgrätz

BOHEMIA
Prague
Gitschin

Dresden

SAXONY

Leipzig
Thuringian
States

HANOVER

Brunswick

PRUSSIA

BERLIN

Stettin

Pomerania

Danzig

Warsaw

Cracow

Breslau
SILESIA

More Oxford Paperbacks

*

THE COLLECTED POEMS OF
EDWARD THOMAS

Edited by R. George Thomas

'Thomas's bleak, heart-catching verses have won him a steadily rising reputation and challenge comparison with Hardy, both for their observations of nature and their inner desolation. Killed in France at Easter 1917, Thomas wrote all his 144 poems in the last two years of his life: this pocket-size edition, chronologically arranged and well annotated and introduced by R. George Thomas, also includes his last war diary.'

The Sunday Times

A. E. Housman: The Scholar Poet

Richard Perceval Graves

A. E. Housman (1859–1936), romantic poet and classical scholar, is best known as the author of *A Shropshire Lad*, and the meticulous editor of the Latin poet of astronomy, Manilius. In this first full biography, based on detailed research, and incorporating a wealth of previously unpublished material from both public and private sources, Richard Perceval Graves convincingly reconciles the two apparently conflicting sides of Housman's personality, and reassesses the reputation of a man who was something of a mystery even to his closest friends.

'This is bound to become the standard life.'

John Carey, *The Sunday Times*

'throws a vivid light on the life of an extraordinary man'

Rachel Billington, *Financial Times*

THE SHORTER STRACHEY

*Selected and Introduced
by Michael Holroyd and Paul Levy*

Eminent Victorians, *Queen Victoria*, and *Elizabeth* and *Essex* are justly celebrated as biographical master-pieces, combining wit, perception, and a vivid read-ability; yet, as Michael Holroyd and Paul Levy point out, 'the essay was the form most congenial to Stra-chey's talents. His literary virtues were those of the miniaturist: close observation of detail, and exquisite care in its selection and presentation. The limits of the smaller canvas brought out his strengths – concision and precision.' Published in 1980 to coincide with the centenary of Strachey's birth, *The Shorter Strachey* is a provocative and consistently entertaining selection of thirty of his best short pieces.

'Strachey is undoubtedly on the up again: he is recog-nised once more as the modern pioneer in treating his-tory as an art. The selection of his shorter essays which Michael Holroyd, his frank and sympathetic biogra-pher, and Paul Levy have made in *The Shorter Strachey* shows the range of his erudition and his skills.'

The Sunday Telegraph

A complete list of Oxford Paperbacks, including books in The World's Classics, Past Masters, and OPUS series, can be obtained from the General Publicity Department, Oxford University Press, Walton Street, Oxford OX2 6DP